Christian Evidence Society

Popular Objections to Revealed Truth

Christian Evidence Society
Popular Objections to Revealed Truth
ISBN/EAN: 9783744727976
Printed in Europe, USA, Canada, Australia, Japan
Cover: Foto ©Lupo / pixelio.de

More available books at **www.hansebooks.com**

POPULAR OBJECTIONS

TO

REVEALED TRUTH.

CONSIDERED IN A

Series of Lectures

DELIVERED IN THE NEW HALL OF SCIENCE, OLD STREET, CITY ROAD, UNDER THE AUSPICES OF THE CHRISTIAN EVIDENCE SOCIETY.

New York:
A. D. F. RANDOLPH & Co.
770, BROADWAY.

MDCCCLXXIII.

PREFACE.

THE Lectures contained in this volume were delivered to audiences consisting almost exclusively of working men, and are intended to deal with some of the objections to revealed religion that are current amongst them. This will explain the allusions that are made in some of the Lectures, and will supply the reason for dwelling more emphatically upon some of the points which are introduced, as being points which, it is known, are felt or regarded as special difficulties by those to whom the Lectures were addressed.

At the close of each Lecture, discussion was invited, and three speeches followed on either side, of ten minutes in duration. It will be seen that reference is made in several places to the subsequent discussion.

The Lecture on the " Historical Evidence of the

Resurrection" was not actually delivered as part of the series, but it was written by the Rev. C. A. Row, at the request of the Committee, and has been embodied in the volume as a supplemental Lecture.

A considerable number of the single Lectures have already been circulated: the Committee hope that additional interest will be taken in them now that they are collected into one volume.

A tolerably full "Table of Contents" has been drawn up and prefixed to the volume. The outline of the argument in each lecture may thus be readily seen; and it is hoped that the usefulness of the volume will be hereby increased.

The Committee perhaps ought to add that no censorship has been exercised over the Lectures. Each author is responsible for his own Lecture, and for that alone.

OFFICES, 2, DUKE STREET,
ADELPHI, W.C.,
June, 1873.

TABLE OF CONTENTS.

LECTURE I.

SECULARISM AND ATHEISM.

BY REV. A. J. HARRISON.

PAGE

I. Examination of certain terms, phrases, etc., commonly associated with non-Christian Secularism : Infidelity, Scepticism, free-thought.—Non-responsibility for belief.—Sinlessness of sincerity.—" Wide spread " of Scepticism (Atheism).

II. (1.) Secularism, in its strict sense, and as popularly employed.—(2.) Mr. Holyoake's scheme of Secularism.—Implicit acknowledgment of possible existence of God, and of need of revelation.—(3.) Value of Christian Secularism.—(4.) Mr. Bradlaugh's Secularism ; confessedly leads to Atheism ; otherwise nothing distinctive in its principles.—(5.) Atheism is simply a negation : cannot supply any positive scheme of morality.—(6.) Is it necessary to give up belief in God in order to learn Science ?—(7). Inconsistent conduct of Atheists in arguing as to nature of Deity.—(8.) Examination of the principle

that "Secular reason is sufficient for guidance in human duties."
III. Conclusion. Belief in God an instinct of mankind.—Appeal to examine and weigh thoughtfully the claims of Christianity. 1

LECTURE II.

ON HUMAN RESPONSIBILITY.

By Rev. C. A. Row, M.A.

I. Belief in responsibility universal.—Proved by the structure of language.—The instinctive feeling of.—Responsibility implies freedom.—Nature and limitations of freedom.—Freedom implied in assigning virtuousness or viciousness to any action.

II. Atheism teaches that all the laws of the universe are necessary and unalterable.—Whence then came the power of choice, and the phenomena of moral action? Proof of freedom derived from the testimony of consciousness.

III. Objections considered. (1.) That the testimony of consciousness to a fact, does not make that fact certain; (2) that our actions are simply regulated by the strongest motives; (3) that our tendencies, whether to good or evil, are very greatly hereditary; (4) that we are the creatures of birth and education, etc.; (5) that the law of averages shows that we are not free.

Belief in freedom remains, notwithstanding all these objections. If then man be responsible, *to whom* is he responsible? to himself? or to society?

Contents. ix

PAGE

or to One who is altogether higher than, and external to himself, *i.e.*, God? The facts of consciousness prove finally that man is responsible to God, and that, so far as his actions are voluntary, he is accountable for them. . . 29

LECTURE III.

CHRISTIANITY IS NOT THE INVENTION OF IMPOSTORS OR OF CREDULOUS ENTHUSIASTS.

BY REV. JOHN GRITTON.

I. Impossibility of denying the *existence* of Christianity; still there are various views as to its *origin:* (1) The mythic view; (2) that it is the invention of enthusiasts; (3) of impostors; (4) that its origin is really such as described in the Gospels.

II. Examination of the view that it is the invention of credulous enthusiasts.—(1.) General description of the character of an *enthusiast.*—(2.) Incompatibility of this assumption (i.) with our Lord's character; (ii.) with the minute, historical, geographical notes, etc., contained in the Gospels; (iii.) with the moral teaching contained both in the Gospels and Epistles.

III. Examination of the view that Christianity is the invention of impostors. Objections urged.—(1.) Manifold probability of an imposition being detected on the ground of inaccuracies in history, geography, etc.— (2.) The great improbability that a pure morality should be invented by impostors; (3) or a perfect ideal, such as we find in the character of Christ.—

(4.) How, on this view, can we account for the actual results of Christianity on the consciences and lives of men?

IV. Brief survey of the external evidences to the truth of the Bible 61

LECTURE IV.

THE FACTS OF CHRISTIANITY HISTORICALLY TRUE.

By B. Harris Cowper, Esq.

I. Christianity open to criticism equally with any other history. Its supernatural facts must be examined in the same manner as its ordinary facts.

II. (1.) The form of the New Testament is real and historical.—(2.) the facts recorded belong to a known historical age.—(3.) The accuracy of its geography. —(4.) Absence of imaginary characters.—(5.) Incidental confirmation of its historical trustworthiness. —(6.) Absence of rhetorical phraseology.—Simple and natural style of writing.—(7.) High character of its moral teaching.

III. External testimony to the truth of the New Testament. (1.) It was accepted from the earliest times by men of learning and philosophers; (2) acknowledged even by heretics.—Objections considered: (i.) The existence of the Apocryphal Gospels.—(ii.) The alleged silence of contemporary historians.

IV. Testimony to the truth of Christianity borne by the lives of the early believers 89

Contents.

LECTURE V.

SCIENCE AND SCRIPTURE NOT ANTAGONISTIC.

BY REV. G. HENSLOW, M.A., F.L.S., F.G.S.

Part I. Introductory—The objects of Science.—Notice of objections that are sometimes made to various branches of Science, especially to Geology and the doctrine of Evolution.
Part II. The Scripture, or the Bible: its moral characteristics.—The object of the Bible distinct from that of Science.—Mode of stating scientific facts in the Bible.
Part III. Genesis compared with Geology.—Use of the word "Yom" (day) in Gen. i.—Suggested explanation.—Comparison of the order of Creation, as recorded in Gen. i., with the teachings of Geology.
Part IV. The Doctrine of Evolution.—No real opposition in Genesis, rightly understood, to this doctrine;—man, in his intellectual and moral nature, being exempted from its scope.—General support given by scientific examination of Nature to the truthfulness of Scripture 115

LECTURE VI.

MORAL TEACHING OF THE OLD TESTAMENT VINDICATED.

BY REV. J. H. TITCOMB, M.A.

1. Position of primæval man.—Objections to the History of the Fall considered.—2. Early deterioration of

morals.—3. The Flood : "God repented that He had made man."—4. The Flood, no objection to the Divine benevolence.—5. The early History of the Old Testament shows the development of moral progress to have been slow and gradual, just as we should have anticipated.—6. Manner of God's moral government : tolerance of evil in order to progressive amelioration.—7. Consideration of the destruction of the Canaanites and Amalekites:—(i.) Has God a moral right to annihilate nations which are incurably corrupt ? (ii.) or to make their fellow-creatures their executioners ?—8. Difficulty considered respecting Noah's curse upon Ham.—9. Respecting Abraham's intended sacrifice of Isaac.—10. Some canons of criticism:—(i.) Every sentiment in a book written by inspiration is not itself necessarily inspired. (ii.) Every action of inspired men not necessarily performed under the guidance of God. (iii.) Jewish writers frequently attribute to God Himself the evils which He permitted in His Providence.

Summing up of the principles applied in the lecture to the solution of Old Testament difficulties . . 143

LECTURE VII.

THE METAPHORICAL LANGUAGE APPLIED TO GOD IN THE OLD TESTAMENT.

By Rev. R. B. Girdlestone, M.A.

I. Teachers must adapt themselves to the capabilities of their scholars: and so God, in His revelation of

Contents. xiii

Himself to man, uses terms intelligible to him, and reveals Himself under human metaphors.
II. Objections made to the manner in which God is described in the Old Testament.—Collection of some of the human attributes assigned to God in the Bible.—Cautions requisite in interpreting them.
III. These anthropomorphic expressions are not intended to describe the *essential* nature of God, but only to reveal to us God *in His relations to man.*
V. Important to notice that, man having being created in God's likeness, we should expect to find in man the characteristics of God : hence another justification of anthropomorphic language.
V. The Old Testament itself contains sufficient safeguards against the possibility of a literal interpretation of its figurative language 175

LECTURE VIII.

MIRACLES AS CREDENTIALS OF A REVELATION.

By J. H. Gladstone, Ph.D., F.R.S.

I. Manner of regarding miracles is different now from what it has been in any previous age.—Advance of Natural Science the principal cause of this change of view, not so much in demonstrating that nature is regulated by order, as in showing that its arrangements are independent of men's interests.
II. A miracle implies that the course of nature sometimes is altered for the benefit of man.—Chief difficulty in believing this lies in our conception of

God, as One with whom is "no variableness," etc. As man may alter the course of nature for his own good by a new direction of force, etc., so may the Supreme Will effect such a new distribution of force as is necessary for working a miracle,—something beyond man's power to effect, this distribution, however, being part of the fore-determined order of the universe.

III. A miracle is not an effect without a cause, and is always wrought with a definite purpose.—Man's need of a revelation: how are we to decide whether a messenger professing to bear a revelation be true or false?—Advantages attending a miraculous confirmation of his claims.

IV. Examination of the Bible History—Miracles group themselves mainly round Moses, Elijah, and Christ, and are appealed to in each case as credentials of the preacher's mission—Some objections considered.—Each separate miracle must be regarded, not merely by itself, but as *part of a system.*—The testimony of miracles must be taken in connection with the other evidences of Christianity . . . 201

LECTURE IX.

THE HISTORICAL EVIDENCE OF THE RESURRECTION OF JESUS CHRIST.

By Rev. C. A. Row, M.A.

I. The truth of Christianity dependent on the fact of the resurrection.

The subject treated on grounds purely historical.

Contents. XV

PAGE

Nothing assumed as fact, but what is admitted to be so by all eminent modern unbelievers.
First point of proof.—The historical existence of the Christian Church.—Its nature and importance.—The Church a community.—The resurrection of Christ a rational account of its origin.—Nothing else is.—As the Church was based on the belief of the Messiahship of Jesus, His crucifixion would have destroyed its cohesion, unless its members could have been induced to believe in His resurrection.—A living Messiah essential to its existence.—It is the most certain of facts that the Church attained a new life after the crucifixion.

II.—Answer to the charge of want of contemporaneous evidence.—Four epistles of St. Paul admitted by the most eminent unbelievers to be genuine.—The importance of contemporaneous letters as historical evidences.—These letters written within the most distinct period of historical recollection.—Illustrated by modern examples.—The impossibility of the growth of myths or legends under the circumstances.

III. (1.) That St. Paul himself believed in the fact of the resurrection within less than ten years from its alleged date. (2.) That the Churches to whom he wrote assumed its truth as the only ground of their existence within twenty-eight years of the crucifixion.—(3.) That these Churches accepted it as a fact at a still earlier period.—(4.) That they all accepted it as the ground of their existence, notwithstanding the presence of a strong spirit of party.—(5.) That all the parties in the Church accepted it. —(6.) That it was equally accepted by Churches not planted by St. Paul, as by those founded by him.—(7.) That the belief was spread over a wide geographical area.—(8.) That it was the belief of

PAGE

the great Gentile Church at Antioch, and of the mother Church of Jerusalem.—(9.) That the testimony of these epistles carries with it that of Peter, James, and John, that they had seen Jesus Christ risen from the dead.—(10.) The belief in the resurrection no late fiction, but can be traced up to within less than ten years of the crucifixion, as the universal belief of the Church.—(11.) The impossibility of its having been either a myth, legend, or lying invention.

The only satisfactory and rational account of the character and acts of the early Church is, that Jesus did really rise, and appear to those who are asserted in the Gospels to have seen Him.—Difficulties as to details in the Gospel narrative no sufficient objection to the credibility of that which they profess to relate.—The character of the Gospels as histories . 225

APPENDIX.

Collection and brief examination of several passages in St. Paul's Epistles to the Romans, Corinthians, and Galatians, in which reference, either direct, incidental, or inferential, is made to the fact of the Resurrection 255

LECTURE X.

THE MORAL TEACHING OF THE NEW TESTAMENT.

By Rev. Henry Allon, D.D.

Christianity distinct from philosophy, morality, or social economy; yet includes all these, and professes to exhibit them in their highest form.

Examination of the moral system of Christianity.—I. The general principles of Christian Ethics.—1. The moral sentiment of human nature has two necessary relations to Christianity : (i) To this moral sentiment every religious system must ultimately appeal. (ii.) The final cause of every true religious system must be *righteousness*.—2. The root of all morality is the consciousness of right and wrong.—3. Comparison of Christian morality with the Ethics of some other systems.—4. Progressive growth in the perception and realization by Christian men of Christ's teaching.— 5. Christianity a *system* embracing principles applicable to all men everywhere. —6. Enthusiasm for righteousness created by our personal relation to Christ.

II. The moral value of the separate elements of the Christian system briefly considered.— 1. The nature and importance of dogma in general. Value of the dogmas, (i.) of the Incarnation ; (ii.) of Christ's human sinlessness ; (iii.) of His sacrificial Atonement (vindication of its morality) ; (iv.) of spiritual regeneration ; (v.) of election ; (vi.) of the final destiny of the wicked.—2. Excellence of the principles and precepts enunciated by Christ.—3. The moral teaching of St. Paul's Epistles.—The ideal of Christianity to be realized hereafter . . . 263

LECTURE XI.

THE GRADUAL UNFOLDING OF REVELATION.

BY REV. GORDON CALTHROP, M.A.

I. The teachings of the Bible constantly exemplified in the history of society and the world.—Assuming xviii · *Contents.*

PAGE

the existence of God, it follows (i.) that it must be very important for man to know his relations towards God; and (ii.) that any knowledge of Himself which the infinite God may give to finite man, would be in the way of a gradual unfolding.

II. Geology teaches that the world was being gradually fitted through long ages for being the abode of man; analogously we may believe that God is preparing mankind by progressive stages for some great end still future.—It is difficult for us to understand the character of a building, whilst still surrounded by scaffolding, etc., or to criticize a piece of music, until we have heard the combined harmony of its several parts : a similar difficulty hinders us from perfectly understanding Revelation, until we can survey it as a completed whole.

III. Gradual growth in moral sense of children; similar growth in that of the human race: illustrated in the Bible History.—Comparison of Adam with David. Value of the Levitical system.—Gradual education of the Jews until they were in a position to understand Christ's doctrine of the Fatherhood of God.—Gradual growth of Christianity itself, analogous to God's ordinary mode of dealing with men . 299

LECTURE XII.

PERFECTION OF THE HUMAN CHARACTER OF JESUS CHRIST.

BY REV. CANON BARRY, D.D.

Influence of a man's *character.*—Interest attaching to the character of Jesus Christ.—In considering a man's life, two classes of facts—visible and invisible

—must be taken into account. The perfection of Christ's character bears upon both these classes of facts.—Meaning of the term "perfection."

Three ways of estimating character.—1. In relation to its general tone and impress. The character of Jesus Christ bears both the mark of strong deep individuality, and of true universal humanity;—the two sides of perfection.

2. In relation to its component parts, and their harmony with one another. A character is perfect which fulfils all the relations of humanity, viz., to self, to men, and to something above mankind, *God.*—(i.) Three qualities belonging to man, as an individual, viz., the love of truth, the spirit of purity, and the spirit of manliness: Christ perfect in respect of all these.—(ii.) Two ruling principles in our relations to one another, viz., the spirit of righteousness and the spirit of love: Christ's character considered in respect of both.—(iii.) In our relation to God, perfection consists in the spirit of Sonship, fully illustrated in the life of Jesus Christ.

3. In relation to the great aim of life, and its devotion to it. Christ's aim,—both the regeneration of the individual, and the renewal of the social life of humanity.

Conclusion.—Christ's character consists in something else than mere human perfection.—Nature of His self-assertion.—Reasonableness of believing in Christ's teaching, even though it passes our full comprehension 319

THE PRINCIPLES OF SECULARISM AND ATHEISM INADEQUATE TO SATISFY THE WANTS OF MAN.

BY THE

REV. A. J. HARRISON,
CURATE OF SHUTTLEWORTH.

Secularism and Atheism.

I PROPOSE, in the first part of my lecture, to examine certain phrases, arguments, and assertions which are commonly associated with non-Christian secularism or atheism; in the second part to deal with the claims of the systems of which Mr. Holyoake and Mr. Bradlaugh are, respectively, the chief representatives, and with the pretensions of atheism itself.

I. (1). The words "infidel" and "infidelity" have in common speech almost lost their first meaning, and are now chiefly used as terms of reproach or abuse. If we call Secularists or Atheists infidels, Mr. Holyoake or Mr. Bradlaugh has a perfect right to retort that though the name applies truly enough to them in one respect, it applies with no less truth to ourselves in another respect. If they are infidels in relation to our teaching, we are as certainly infidels in relation to their teaching. If they are unbelievers in Christian or even Natural Religion, we are unbelievers in Secular or Atheistic Irreligion. And if we resume its original meaning, we shall never use the word "infidel," unless when we intend to convey the reproach of unfaithfulness to moral obligation.

(2.) Sceptic and scepticism are another pair of words whose use requires peculiar care. A sceptic is properly a thinker who is determined, with physical, intellectual, or spiritual eyes, to *see into* physical, intellectual, or spiritual *facts*, before forming, and especially before teaching, any doctrine concerning those facts. And scepticism denotes the mental attitude of the enquirer towards any doctrine whose truth he is examining, but concerning which he has not yet decided. But, as commonly used, scepticism simply denotes unbelief; and in this sense has received on the one side most unreasoning blame, on the other most extravagant praise. Some unwise theologians have denounced it as a vice; some equally unwise antitheologians have commended it as a virtue; whereas both ought to have known that the worth or worthlessness of unbelief wholly depends upon the truth or untruth of the teaching in relation to which it is exercised. But even in its proper sense, to glory in scepticism, as such, is certainly no sign of sober thought; seeing that the highest function of doubt is to make way for a wise faith.

(3.) Free thought is another word very frequently misapplied. Atheists claim it as peculiar or almost peculiar to themselves; they glory in it as almost their highest intellectual good. And yet their use of the word is unfair and unwise. Unfair, because it conveniently assumes what needs to be proved, that only atheists are free thinkers; unwise, because they who deny to the mind *all* self-determining power cannot reasonably claim to be *free* thinkers. If by free thought is meant thought wholly uninfluenced by past or present, no such thing as free thought exists. But if the phrase simply mean honest thought, then the use of the word as if it were peculiar to atheists would simply stop all argument; for who would engage in a discussion, the first condition of which implied that the disputant did not honestly hold the views for which he contended? He who would do so would receive little respect from others, because he had none for himself. If, however, the phrase is simply employed as a loose expression of opposition to creeds, then it is certainly a very inaccurate term, inasmuch as it does not contain even a hint of the meaning intended. In any case, it ought not to be difficult to convince the extremest unbeliever that free thought which is not also true thought is scarcely a thing to boast about. The man who, in the sphere of understanding, would choose to ignore the laws of intellect, who, in the sphere of conscience, would choose to be blind to moral law, and this in order that he might boast of being a free thinker, would only deserve unrelenting and utter contempt. Hear the words of one of your own leaders, who, though he is not always true to his own logic, has earned the regard to be heard with respect. "If men are silent," says Mr. Holyoake, "concerning objects and principles, it is said they have none; and it is impatiently asked where is their bond of union? and no sooner is it explained, than they are told it is very unphilosophical to think of setting up a creed. Where the alternatives are thus put against them, they should take their own course. Creeds are the necessary exponents of conviction. The creedless philosopher is out on the sea of opinion without compass or chart. To bind yourself for the future to present opinions is doubtless unwise; but he who has enquired to any purpose, has come to some conclusion, affirmative, negative, or neutral, and it is the province of a creed to avow the actual result and the consequent conduct intended to be followed. It is the vice of free-thinking that it spreads universal uncertainty, and assumes right and wrong to be so protean that no man can tell one hour what opinion he shall hold the next."* After this, we ought to hear no more about the glory of free thought.

(4.) Non-responsibility for belief is another phrase in reference to which it is necessary to come to a distinct understanding. Many writers on the Christian side have seen the consequences of belief or unbelief rising in such vastness before them as to be unable to see that this special subject was but a part of the larger one of responsibility for conduct. Writers on the other side have made a similar mistake. They urge with evident earnestness and feeling that it is unfair to assert responsibility for belief, inasmuch as whether they believe or believe not is dependent on evidence, and not on their wills. But is it true that the will has nothing to do with belief? Let us take as an example the evidence of Christianity. Let us assume that a man's belief or unbelief must depend on the strength or weakness of that evidence. What then? Does it follow that his will has nothing to do with his belief? Whether and how he shall study the evidence, how little or how much attention he shall give to the subject, with what calmness and fairness he shall inquire, with what impartiality and honour he shall draw his conclusions, depends largely upon his will, and merits praise or blame accordingly. Now no one can doubt that belief or unbelief is dependent, not only on evidence, but on how the evidence is studied. To this extent then a man is clearly responsible, to the extent in which his belief is affected by the way he studies. It is manifest, therefore, that a man who has not taken and will not take the trouble to examine the evidence, or who does not examine fairly, has no right to plead that

* Logic of Facts, p. 82.

belief is dependent on evidence as a reason for unbelief. For in his case the evidence has not produced the unbelief, but his unbelief has produced his unwillingness to examine the evidence. If, however, a man does not admit responsibility in any sense, not to himself, or to his fellow-man, or to God, it is necessary to meet him on another ground, if indeed such a man could be worthy to be met at all. For a man cannot deny responsibility in every sense, without becoming practically an outlaw, with whom society in self-defence can hold no terms. But they who say that a man is not responsible for belief do tacitly admit that he is responsible for something; otherwise they would deny responsibility altogether, and not simply for belief. Now we have seen that if a man is responsible at all, he is responsible for the way in which he treats the evidence. And until he not only examines the evidence, but examines it honestly and with due care, it is useless to say he is not responsible for his unbelief.

(5.) There is a similar plea sometimes put in the phrase "It does not matter what a man believes if he is only sincere." This plea does at least admit the possibility of the unbeliever not being sincere in his arguments against religion; and implies that his insincerity will matter a great deal to him. But is it true, as a matter of fact, that in the case of a man who *is* sincere, his beliefs are of no consequence? Certainly beliefs are of immense importance in the political life of a nation. Whether Englishmen believe in this or that form of Government, or in any Government at all, makes considerable difference to our national and individual safety and progress. We often hear complaints made, and justly made, against persecution and persecutors. But persecutions have often been the result of certain beliefs of sincere men. If then, in such cases, men suffer from persecution, they ought not, on this principle, to complain, seeing that it does not matter what a man believes if he is only sincere. But you will say that the principle does not apply to this life, only to the future. Yet if it work badly here, why should it be supposed to work well there? And sincerity no more saves a man from the effects on himself of wrong-doing, than it saves others from those effects; nor is it less blamable, as a principle, when he himself suffers, than when he makes others suffer. A sincere man may be ignorant, or infatuated, or prejudiced. Where it was within a man's power to know, to be sober-minded, to look fairly at a question, does not ignorance, infatuation, prejudice, deserve blame? Will sincerity keep a man well who breaks the laws of health? Will sincerity make the man wise who ignores the laws of understanding? Will sincerity make the man good who trusts to instinct without learning the simple laws that ought to govern moral effort? And yet the sinlessness of the sincere man is a doctrine popular with many atheists, though Mr. Holyoake has seen it morally necessary to abandon the dogma. He now holds that sincerity, as such, is not sufficient. It must be well-informed sincerity. He says: "If a man is to justify his sincerity to his conscience, if his sincerity is to be without sin, then he must make up his mind; he must know all about the subject he can know when he professes to be sinless upon it. I use the term to put an end to that common-place sincerity which so many people have, which is ignorant sincerity, which is cruel and blind, notwithstanding it is sincere, because it is ignorant. A man has no right to say, My sincerity shall be respected, until he has taken care not to have an ignorant and narrow and prejudiced sincerity; he is bound to have as enlarged a sincerity as he possibly can compass."* I am very glad that Mr. Holyoake has come to see and to say this truth so clearly; but it is a manifest abandonment of the old plea, that if a man is only sincere he can have nothing to dread in another world. If sincerity may be cruel, blind, ignorant, sinful, clearly it cannot save a man from the natural consequences of cruelty, blindness, ignorance, sin, either in this world or in the world to come.

(6.) The wide spread of scepticism is another phrase we often hear. But the question is, what scepticism? If positive unbelief is intended, I for one do not believe that it is widely spread. But if by scepticism is meant uncertainty which waits to become certainty, on one side or another, in relation to several theological subjects, then I have no doubt that ours is a very sceptical age indeed. It is not my province to-night to plead for this or that special theology, but I know that the Christian Faith, as distinguished from the additions or mutilations of men, is able to bear the strongest light which this age can turn upon it. But as to whether atheism is increasing in the country there can be few better witnesses than Mr. Holyoake. And I am sure his testimony ought to convince you. He says: "Mr. Bradlaugh wanders through his land, proclaiming the principles of secularism as though they were atheism, and arguing with the clergy. Why, when I go now to Glasgow, to Huddersfield, to Liverpool, to Manchester, I find the secularists there unadvanced in position. Even in Northampton, which Mr. Bradlaugh knows, I found them lately meeting on the second floor of a public-house where I found them

* Debate with Mr. Bradlaugh, p. 22.

twenty or twenty-five years ago. In Glasgow they are in the same second-rate position they were in twenty-five or thirty years ago. What have we been doing? Does not this show an obsolete policy? Ranters, Muggletonians, Mormons, and men of their stamp are superior to acting so. Any party in the present state of opinion in the world could with thought have done more. The most ordinary sects build or hire temples and other places where their people decently meet. Mr. Bradlaugh, with all his zeal and appeals, finds to-day that all London can do is to put up this kind of place in which we now meet opposite a lunatic asylum, where people, so the enemy says, naturally expect to find us."*

II. I now proceed to speak of Secularism in the non-Christian sense in which the word is employed by Mr. Holyoake and Mr. Bradlaugh, and of atheism itself.

(1.) Secularism, in its proper meaning, as indicating the just principles, laws, and objects of the present life, is an appropriate and even noble word; but as used by those who claim it as their distinctive title, as a convenient intimation of unbelief in God and in a future life, it is one of the vaguest terms in our language. It is true that he who thoughtfully studies and obeys the laws of the present life, even though he think not that those laws extend further, is a secularist. But in a profounder sense, he also is a secularist who regards those laws which govern him now as being essentially the same as those which will govern him hereafter, as laws of a life which never ceases to be life. Indeed, while a true atheist *may* be a secularist, a true theist must be a secularist; that is to say, it is in the very essence of his theism to live as nobly, as rightly, as wisely as he can in this present

* Debate with Mr. Bradlaugh, p. 72.

life. Secularism is not necessarily involved in atheism, but it is necessarily involved in theism. A genuine atheist, as an atheist, may not choose to trouble himself about the present any more than about the future life; a genuine theist, as a theist, must study to live well now, if he would not lose both present and future life. We shall now be able to examine the system associated with the name of Mr. Holyoake, and ascertain whether it possesses anything, as peculiar to its author, deserving the name of secularism.

(2.) The following are the five articles of Mr. Holyoake's creed. 1. "Secularism maintains the sufficiency of secular reason for guidance in human duties." This principle, as being the most important, and as being held by all classes of atheistic secularists, I purpose to examine towards the close of my lecture. 2. "The adequacy of the utilitarian rule which makes the good of others the rule of duty." On this I shall make some remarks presently. 3. "That the duty nearest at hand, and most reliable in results, is the use of material means tempered by human sympathy for the attainment of social improvement." On this also I have some remarks to make. 4. "The sinlessness of well-informed sincerity." On this I have already commented at some length.* 5. "That the sign and condition of such sincerity are free-thought, expository speech, the practice of personal conviction within the limits of neither outraging nor harming others."† Of this I have also spoken. ‡ Now, dealing for the present with these principles as a whole, they seem at first glance to contain very little objectionable matter; very

* I. (4), (5), p. 6, etc.
† Debate with Mr. Bradlaugh, p. 4.
‡ I. (2), (3), (4), (5), p. 4, etc.

little which might not harmonize with the convictions of a theist. But examine them closely, and you with find that so far as they are not atheistic they are in no wise peculiar to Mr. Holyoake and his followers; and that so far as they are atheistic they are in no true sense secular. Besides, I notice that even atheists might be tempted to doubt their value on some points, and to question whether they did not admit too much. The third principle speaks of material means. If what we call mind be material, if love, thought, faith, conscience, be functions or qualities of a material organization, then no doubt material means are not simply the best, but they are the only means we can employ. Mr. Holyoake would include all available science in the means to be employed for social improvement; and so also would Christian secularism, without implying that there are no means not material. But this principle also speaks of a duty *nearest* at hand and *most* reliable in its result. What does this mean? Are there other duties not so near at hand? other results not so reliable? Is this an implicit acknowledgment that there may be a God, whose will may be known and ought to be done? But if so, it is preposterous to speak of duties not so near at hand. All duties, just in so far as they are duties, are close at hand. Why, too, is the duty of employing material means *most* reliable in results, unless it is admitted that there are also spiritual means whose results are not so reliable? But if so, the spiritual means should, in their own province, be as much employed as material means in theirs. Yet if this be true, to exalt material means at the expense of spiritual, is to treat the thought of God in a way far more offensive than actual atheism. And this would render it impossible for any conscientious theistic secularist to be a member of a society having such an article in its creed. But if it is *intended* to express indifference to or unbelief in God, then for this reason also no theist could have anything to do with such a society. It appears then that this principle has nothing peculiar to Mr. Holyoake's position but a doubtful atheism. Then the second principle would make the good of others the law of duty. Now one would expect a fair rule of duty to include the right treatment of ourselves as of others; and therefore this rule is *not* adequate. Again, it is a question whether the utilitarian rule does make the *good* of others the law of duty; whether at the best the "good" it would supply ought not rather to be rendered "goods," whether therefore it is not simply a commercial rule, and not a moral law. But even granting that it is moral, this rule of utility is not sufficient; for before you begin to do good you must find out what *good is*. But then it is said this can only be known by experience, so that you must act for some time without morality in order to learn what morality is. Again, you ought to do good to all men, or at least to the greatest number. But you cannot do this until you find out what the greatest number needs. Now as the greatest number consists of some hundreds of millions of human beings, you would probably be a considerable age before you began to be moral. So far is this rule, considered in itself, from being adequate. It has, however, this use. It points out most clearly the need of revelation as a moral guide. For, assuming that the good of others is to be the law of duty, then who so well as God can know what that good is? And if the "others" whose good we are to study means *all* others, then who but God can tell us what all need? So then utilitarianism, which Mr. Holyoake calls secular, and Mr. Bradlaugh atheistic, is itself a witness for the need of revelation.

(3.) Mr. Holyoake has striven hard to establish a non-Christian secularism, that should assert nothing about God. With consummate tact, with great earnestness, he has endeavoured to persuade all who would listen that there might be a secularism which was neither theistic nor atheistic. Had Mr. Holyoake contented himself with saying that any two men ought to be able to work together without asking each other any questions about their theological views, he would have asserted a principle of humanity which appears to me a very important and very Christian one. But when he virtually says to the theist, In your secularism ignore your theism, he asks him to do what no theist could do without becoming unworthy of the name of man. No true theist dare, nor if he dare would he choose, to ignore the idea of God. And though Mr. Holyoake dreamed a noble dream which he called secularism, yet its interpretation has always been atheism. Of positive teaching his system gives us nothing that is not the common inheritance of man; extract this, and atheism only is left. And it is so far true that man needs no atheism to work for human good, that Christian secularism is the only genuine secularism this country has known. We have been accused justly of the guilt of slavery, but it was the quickened Christian conscience of England that abolished slavery. We have been accused justly of intolerance, bigotry, and cruel wrong in days of persecution; but it is just because Christianity has stronger hold on our passions that we are better now. We have been accused justly of indifference to the state of the poor; but it was the Christian spirit in the heart of the nation that abolished the corn monopoly, that built and now supports our hospitals; that poured the wealth of England into Lancashire in the cotton famine, as it did years before, when food failed, into Ireland. I know there is yet a tremendous work to be done. The agricultural labourer is ill-paid, ill-fed, ill-clothed, ill-housed; let us with all heartiness help him to improve his condition. The poor in our great towns are suffering fearfully from drunkenness and improvidence, we ought to help them to be sober and prudent. The great corporations are dull, and sluggish, and careless about the sanitary condition of the masses; we can rouse them to activity by a ceaseless and fearless criticism. Parliament does not always understand working men's questions; it is but fair to educate public opinion until members shall be returned who do understand such questions. The people are liable to suffer from combinations that bring evil only; it is right to teach them the secret of co-operation. Bad passions have flamed up between employer and employed; we ought to create a wise public opinion that will rule both. These are only broken hints of the manifold work that still needs to be done, which our Christianity will rouse us to do. Our faults are of ourselves; our virtues are of our faith; and our faith will yet conquer our faults.

4. I now examine the creed of Mr. Bradlaugh and of those who hold with him. 1. This association declares that the promotion of human improvement and happiness is the highest duty. 2. That the theological teachings of the world have been most powerfully obstructive of human improvement and happiness; human activity being guided and increased by the

consciousness of the facts of existence, while it is misguided and impeded in the most mischievous manner, when the intellect is warped or prostrated by childish and absurd superstition. 3. That in order to promote effectually the improvement and happiness of mankind, every individual of the human family ought to be well placed and well instructed; and all who are of a suitable age ought to be usefully employed for their own and the general good. 4. That human employment and happiness cannot be effectually promoted without civil and religious liberty, and that therefore it is the duty of every individual,—the duty to be practically recognised by every member of this association,—to actively attack all barriers to equal freedom of thought and utterance for all upon political and theological subjects.* Now, before examining these four points in detail, I have some remarks to make upon them as a whole. They are the manifesto of a certain number of persons calling themselves the National Secular Society. They assume the name (National), not because they are, but because they wish to be. These principles are intended to take the place of theology as soon as Mr. Bradlaugh and his associates, with the immense broom of which Mr. Holyoake speaks, shall have succeeded in sweeping the world clean of all religious conviction. Now, it is very important to know how Mr. Bradlaugh understands his own principles. I therefore give you his own words. "Although at present it may be perfectly true that all men who are secularists are not yet atheists, I put it to you as also perfectly true that, in my opinion, the logical consequence of the acceptance of Secularism must be that the man gets to atheism if he has brains

* Newcastle Debate, p. 14.

enough to comprehend." * From this passage alone it would appear as if Mr. Bradlaugh held that though secularism itself was not necessarily atheism, yet it was a sort of inclined plane, conveniently smooth, upon which, if a man once set himself, he must slide down into atheism, unless through some perversion of intellect he were induced to make a violent effort, and stop himself half-way. But six months later Mr. Bradlaugh expressed his views in much stronger language, from which it appears that he does not simply think that secularism *leads* to atheism, but that it *is* atheism itself. His exact words are: " Then there is another point that I do not know that I need trouble to discuss, whether secularism is atheism or not, because I think it is. I have always said so, I believe, for the last thirteen years of my life, whenever I have had an opportunity of doing so; and it is hardly likely, therefore, that I should come here tonight, without any reason for doing so, to recant all my previous convictions, and to make an allegation utterly inconsistent with all my previous arguments."† It is clear then that Mr. Bradlaugh does not dream with Mr. Holyoake of a Secular Society, which should include both theists and atheists, and yet exclude both theism and atheism. Mr. Holyoake failed because his principles did, when fairly examined, involve atheism; Mr. Bradlaugh avoids that difficulty by making atheism itself the basis of co-operation in a secular society. And yet, when Mr. Bradlaugh talks of the secular work he has done, it is only fair to let him know that if he has not hindered more work than he has helped, it is only because the people refuse to believe that there is any

* Debate with Mr. Holyoake, p. 16.
† Newcastle Debate, p. 13.

opposition between Christianity and secular work. You may more easily persuade the people to abandon secular work than to abandon their belief in God; so that when Mr. Bradlaugh tells ignorant people that they must become atheists before they can do secular work, he has small right to complain if the work should not be done. Happily, they have a nobler creed, and are little likely to be moved from it; and therefore go on with their Christian secular work, notwithstanding that Mr. Bradlaugh says they cannot do it. He says it cannot be done; they answer by doing it. But it is very curious that though Mr. Bradlaugh's secularism is atheism, yet in those four principles it is not visible at the first glance. It is concealed in a corner, and only comes out when dragged out. It is not to be found in the fourth principle; it is not visible in the third; you search in vain for it in the first, it is only hidden behind one phrase in the second. And yet it is confessed that *this* secularism is atheism. How then is it that we have here four principles of which only one contains it? Is it not because atheists themselves feel that they must add something to their atheism, before they can have any useful principles at all? Is it not a tacit confession that atheism, as such, has no positive teaching to give? One little phrase belongs to atheists; all the rest are common property. We may differ in judgment as to the mode in which they are to be carried out, not as to the substance of the principles themselves. We hold that the promotion of human improvement and happiness is an imperative duty; and if we do not call it the highest, it is because we do not believe in setting one duty against another, each being in its own place and in its own time of infinite authority. We desire every individual of the human family to be well placed and well instructed, and all who are of suitable age to be usefully employed for their own and the general good. We desire civil and religious liberty; our fathers bled for it, and who amongst us would not do the same, did the same necessity arise? There *are* barriers to be attacked, barriers of pride and passion and prejudice, remnants of barbarism to be removed; evils still in our constitution; blots still in statute books; sorrows innumerable among our people. In the noblest Christian secularism, it is our duty—a duty pressing upon every Christian—to take our place and do our share of the work, do it honestly, earnestly, constantly, adding to the strong tide of influence that flows through successive generations, until there be no evil left in the land. It appears then that these four principles, except the phrase about the theological teachings of the world, are involved in the very heart of theism, and are in no sense peculiar to the so-called secular society. Atheism alone is its distinctive mark.

(5.) But what *is* atheism? and what is its practical value? I need hardly tell you very often the real meaning of the word has been forgotten on both sides. Just as in the early days of Christianity those who did not believe in the heathen gods were called *atheists* by those who did; so too many Christians have given the name atheists to those who do not agree with them in their conceptions of God. It ought to be unnecessary to explain that they only ought to be called atheists who do not believe in God at all. An infidel, in the *usual* sense of the word, is one who does not believe in Christianity, a theist or deist is one who believes in a personal God, without necessarily accepting the common conceptions of deity. A pantheist is one who believes that all is God; an atheist who believes that nothing is God, or believes not that anything is God. So also on the other side there is a curious misuse of the word. One would imagine that in the proper meaning of the word atheism, for which any dictionary may be consulted, no one could find anything but negative force. A man who is an atheist may be more than an atheist; for he may be a workman, a student of science, a politician, and so on. But in his character as an atheist all that he is may be put into the little negative, no. When he becomes a positive teacher, he emerges from his atheism, and leaves it behind; though when he has finished his teaching for the time, he may go back into it. In atheism, as atheism, there is not only no science; there is nothing, except two or three words that represent merely certain states of mind. The atheist's vocabulary is confined to the words "I doubt,' "I do not know," or "I deny." Mr. Holyoake admits that atheism, as such, gives you no system of truth, no scheme of morality. But Mr. Bradlaugh's vigorous imagination scorns such narrow bounds. Never mind the proper meaning of the word; it *shall* mean whatever I please. This is what Mr. Bradlaugh's method implies. "Atheism properly understood"—that is, understood, not according to the Greek language, nor according to the English language, nor according to the language of common sense, but according as Mr. Bradlaugh is determined it shall mean—"is in no sense a cold barren negative; it is, on the contrary, a hearty, truthful affirmation of all truth." What a modest, what a remarkably unassuming claim! Atheism identical with all science! Here is a royal road to learning with a vengeance! Here is a new solution of the educational question! Away with school boards! Away with school rates! Only let the people cease to believe in God, and they have at one bound the "affirmation of all truth !" After this you will not be surprised to learn that Mr. Bradlaugh says, "You cannot get your scheme of morality without atheism." To which it is enough to reply with Mr. Holyoake, "There is no scheme of morality in it." But these modest claims of Mr. Bradlaugh are simply idle talk. Of all the "isms" of the day, atheism is simply that which doubts (though a simple doubter is not necessarily an atheist), denies, or professes ignorance of the existence of God. Whatever its negative value, it has no pretensions to be considered as either an intellectual or a moral guide. Having nothing to give, it gives nothing.

(6.) But it is sometimes urged, that though atheism is not science, yet it is necessary to give up belief in God in order to learn science. Certainly science helps us to get rid of false and unworthy views of God; but I have yet to learn that there is anything in the nature of man which requires the paralysis of his faith, before he can exercise his faculty of knowledge. As I have said in substance elsewhere, science, to the theist, does not lose its practical value because it has also a spiritual meaning. Chemistry, anatomy, physiology, mechanics, dynamics, pneumatics, optics, and the sciences of electricity and heat, are not the less practically serviceable to the theist because he also deems them a proof of the varied power and wisdom of God. Botany, ranging over the globe, describing all vegetation of all climes, is no less useful because it breathes upward to heaven, from depths of leafy shade, from deepening vales, from open verdant plains, the fragrance of His name who has crowned the hills with waving forests, gemmed the valleys with incense-breathing flowers, and filled the fields with the gracious harvest whose grain is the "gold of God." Zoology, displaying every form of animal life, from the zoophyte up to man, is no less practically serviceable because it acknowledges Him from whom the life of both is. Geography, describing the whole surface of the globe, is no less valuable to the merchant, the traveller, the sailor, because it testifies how excellent is the name of the Lord in all the earth. Geology is surely not less instructive because it writes on the rocks its testimony for God. And astronomy, recording the movements of the heavens, with star differing from star in glory, is no less beneficial to man because it is also to the theist almost a revelation of infinite spiritual intelligence and power. The truth is, the wise theist cannot but rejoice in true science; for to him true science is of God. But it by no means follows that he is to content himself with science alone. He would be glad and rejoice in *all* truth. And so science, philosophy, and theology, derived from nature, man, and revelation, are to him a trinity of thought, in which none is opposed to the other, but in fact constitute one manifestation of the Infinite Personal Spirit in whom "we live, and move, and have our being." A true theism welcomes all knowledge; but atheism, throwing off all disguises, must stand forth in its own nakedness as either confessed ignorance of the subject, or as the simple negative of the proposition, There is a God.

(7.) And yet, curiously enough, almost all atheists shrink from the logic of their own position. Instead of being told there is no God, we are informed that the popular conceptions of Deity are contradictory and absurd. If this were true, it were yet nothing to the purpose. So wide spread theological views are more likely to have some basis in fact than none. But whether popular theories be true or no, is not the question. The atheist, while he keeps to the logic of his position, is necessarily opposed to every idea of God. We are sometimes told, as by Mr. Bradlaugh, that every child is born an atheist. If that were true, it would prove nothing in favour of atheism. For on this assumption atheism must have existed before theism. How powerful then must be the evidence which has changed the convictions of the human race! If all children are atheists, very few men are. Is not atheism then childish? "When I was a child, I thought as a child, I spake as a child, I understood as a child; but when I became a man, I put away childish things." Possibly you may listen to Professor Newman, who says, "The sole question between us and the atheist is whether there are or are not marks in the universe of superior mind. What are the qualities, the power, the purposes of the spirit whom we discern, and whether there are many such spirits, are questions for theists among themselves, with which the atheist, while he keeps to his argument, has nothing to do."*

(8.) I have now examined in some detail the claims of atheistic secularism, and given my reasons for saying that except its hostility to theism it has nothing to give which we do not already possess. But at the same time let it not be supposed that I am casting any reflections upon the capacity or character of men who have become atheists. Our judgments of their capacity must be determined by the powers they manifest; our opinions of their character by the uprightness of their conduct. All that I urge is urged against atheistic secularism itself. But there is one principle, *the sufficiency of secular reason*, with which I have yet to deal, and which, on account of its importance, I reserved to the last. "Secularism maintains the sufficiency of secular reason for

---

* Causes of Atheism, p. 21.

guidance in human duties." But the question is, *what* secularism? Some hold the sufficiency of the reason who are not atheistic, though they do not believe in revelation. But then they speak simply of reason, without the distinctive word secular. Mr. Holyoake will hardly grant that there is any reason not secular; for then it would be natural to suppose that the non-secular reason had a non-secular sphere of its own; and this would be giving up his position. Neither, I suppose, will it be admitted that there are duties not human; though I am not sure that Mr. Holyoake does not imply a possibility of duties relating to God rather than man. But certainly these phrases, secular reason and human duties, seem to admit that there may be a God in reference to whom faith becomes a Divine reason, and towards whom Divine duties may be performed. If, on the other hand, it were true that there is no God, no immortality, then all our thoughts, passions, purposes, life, can only have reference to this present world; they cannot have reference to God, if God exist not; they cannot have reference to future life, if no such life can be. Not only on this shewing is secular reason the only reason we have, but our imagination, conscience, and faith are also secular, and secular only. But if so, what is meant by duties? Is there in man a sense of obligation to do certain things, to leave certain other things undone? Is this sense of obligation natural and constitutional? If so, does it not point in the direction of a moral Creator? But is conscience simply an impression which circumstances make on the mind? In that case would it not be reasonable to say that there are no duties, or that what we call such mean only that there are actions which society compels us to perform? But then why talk of morality at all? I might urge these and other questions of a similar kind. But I only wish, at present, to bring before you the truth that if the atheist's position be right—that there is no God, no immortality—then it is absurd to make any distinction between secular and non-secular, since in that case we have nothing but the secular. Let it then be granted, for the sake of argument, that the atheistic secularist is right; that there is no God; that there will be for us no future life; let this be granted: let it equally be granted that there never has been a God; that man never has found any life after death; then it must follow that men have not now, that men never had, anything but secularism. But this secularism excludes the supernatural; it is therefore atheistic; and so there never has been anything in the world but atheistic secularism. Now, during the long period man has existed on the globe, there have come into being a great many theologies. On the assumption that there is no God, no immortality, these theologies must have been invented by atheistic secularists. But you say that they are the offspring of the imagination and faith. But if there be no God, no immortality, are not the imagination and faith as truly atheistic and secular as the reason itself? And thus the atheistic-secular imagination and faith war with the atheistic-secular reason. But even the reason itself cannot escape. No system could exist without some help from the reason. The imagination may be the chief power at work; but if there be a system at all, reason must have been at work to produce the arrangement indispensable to a system. So then the atheistic-secular reason must itself have contributed to the very theologies it now condemns. But you say it is impossible that atheism should have invented theism. Granted. But then you must admit that man is *not* a secular being only; that there are capacities in his nature to which theology is adapted; that there are powers in his nature which find their exercise in theology. In other words, you must admit that man has a natural tendency towards, a natural capacity for, what is called the supernatural. But then is it not reasonable to regard the capacity for, and tendency towards, the supernatural as a very strong presumption that there is a God? But whether this last point be admitted or not, the capacity and tendency do exist, and cannot be governed by atheistic-secular reason. In this respect, therefore, what is called secular reason is *not* sufficient. But if during so many thousands of years the atheistic-secular reason has failed to control imagination and faith, it is too late to tell us now that it is sufficient for guidance in human duties. Once more. It is inconceivable that theology could have existed so long, in every part of the world, and should have such powerful hold upon the world now, if it did not meet some wants in human nature which secularism, even in its noblest sense, cannot wholly supply; and which in its atheistic sense it cannot supply at all. Take which horn of the dilemma you will. Either man is, on the assumption that there is no God, no immortality, an atheistic-secular being only, in which case atheistic secularism is responsible for all the theologies that exist, or else there are capacities, powers, and wants in human nature for which ath.istic secularism provides no exercise, and can find no supply.

The truth is, belief in God has proved itself in all history to be an instinct of the race. When it becomes a question of argument, it is sufficient to prove that there is as much evidence of the existence of superior mind in the universe as there is of the existence of mind in man. We have no need to resort for proof to metaphysical subtleties. The evidence rests, as Professor Newman remarks, on the common perceptions of common men; and metaphysical argumentation is chiefly useful, not so much for the imparting the idea to those who say they have it not, as for the refutation of objections, and the confirmation of faith already existing upon the ground of such palpable evidence as common men may see. It is remarkable, that though men commonly rebound to the utmost extreme when they rebound at all, very few atheists are prepared to say plainly, "There is no God." Mr. Holyoake simply says, as Thomas Cooper, who is now a Christian, once said, "I do not say there is no God, but this I say, I know not." Even Mr. Bradlaugh, who is, I think, the most reckless* speaker I ever heard, does not often, if ever, go so far as that. And so, when atheists urge that God, if there be a God, ought to have made the evidence so clear as to be beyond the possibility of doubt, I answer that it is so far clear, that they do not venture to say there is no God. And for the rest it is not unfair to reply, that if doubt were impossible there could be no trial or discipline of faith. In conclusion, let me point out that, as a matter of fact, we need more than reason, more even than theistic reason. Reason alone has never governed, and, unless man's nature be radically changed, never will govern the world. The chief difficulty of self-government is the passions; and you might as well try to control a wild beast with a silken thread as attempt to govern the passions by reason alone. The passions can be governed, but only by means of the

* I use the word, not insultingly, but in its strict sense, as of one who "reckons" not consequences.

passions. A man cannot become good by the simple suppression of all passion. If the evil passion be strong, the good passion must become stronger to control it. Tell men that a given action is unwise; if their hearts are in it, they will do it still: tell them it is wrong; they will do it still: win their hearts from it; they will do it no more. It is this power to win that is the secret of Christ's influence in the world. You do not confess any religious need; but at least consider. Had there been, in the human heart, no sense of perplexity, there had been no supplication for guidance. Had there been no longing for communion with the unseen, there had been no prayer for the manifestation of God. Had there been no consciousness of guilt, there had been no sacrifice offered. Had there been no feeling of moral weakness, there had been no entreaty for help. Christians say their hearts' deepest and purest longings are satisfied to the full in Christ. You alone can decide whether *you* also can rest there. At least, give fair play to the evidence that would waken your belief in God from its long slumber. At least, consider thoughtfully the claims of Christianity. I pray you to *examine* its evidences; giving no more weight to the authority of writers of integrity and learning on that subject than their integrity and learning deserve; just as you would with scientific men when they write on science. And I think it is not unreasonable to say you ought not to call yourselves atheists, or secularists, or sceptics, or freethinkers, or infidels, until you are sure that those evidences are *false*. And for the sake of others, in the name of what is honourable and fair and kind, in the name of our common humanity itself, I venture to ask you not to scatter, among the ignorant, infidel dogmas, until you are sure that those dogmas are *true*.

ON HUMAN RESPONSIBILITY.

BY THE

Rev. A. C. ROW, M.A.,

AUTHOR OF "THE NATURE AND EXTENT OF DIVINE INSPIRATION," "THE JESUS OF THE EVANGELISTS," "THE MORAL TEACHING OF THE NEW TESTAMENT," ETC.

On Human Responsibility.

THE questions, Are we responsible for our actions, and if responsible, to whom are we responsible? or are our actions the inevitable results of certain laws, over which we can exert no more control than we can over the law of gravitation? are of the most surpassing interest. The whole course of human conduct must be profoundly influenced, in proportion as we view ourselves responsible to a Being external to ourselves, who has the right to enforce obligation on us; or as we consider ourselves entitled to regulate our actions, in conformity with our idea of what best subserves our own interests, irrespective of every other consideration.

If the universal testimony of mankind possesses any value as a witness to truth, it proves that we are responsible for our actions. It has been asserted that there are barbarous tribes, who possess no idea of religion. Whether it be so or not, is not my present business to inquire. But it is a fact that even the most savage members of our race admit a responsibility of some sort. Men nowhere exist but in a state of society; but the man who acted on the principle, I will do whatever I choose, without regard to any other person, would be incapable of being a member of either family, clan, or tribe. It follows therefore that a feeling of responsibility of some sort is a necessary part of our mental constitution.

To the truth of human responsibility, the whole structure of language bears a clear and decisive testimony. It is impossible to write perspicuously without using words which contain the ideas of ought, duty, and obligation. The first principles of grammar prove that mankind have ever viewed themselves within certain limits to have been voluntary agents. The various moods of the verbs expressed by such terms as "I might," "I could," "I would," "I should," "I ought," and "let me," imply that we feel that we have a power over our actions, and a duty in the performance of them. The most strenuous deniers of human freedom are compelled to use language which is a real concession of the point of issue.

I rest the proof of our responsibility on the instinctive feelings of man. From them we cannot divert ourselves. It is easy in this, as well as in many other questions, to urge intellectual difficulties. It is even quite possible to produce plausible arguments in favour of necessity. But after a man may have persuaded his intellect that his actions are the results of necessary laws, his instinctive feelings are too strong for his logic. Every believer in necessity or fate is compelled to act on the principle that freedom is true, and necessity is false. If a thief were to urge that he could not help picking our pockets, we should at once treat his plea as unworthy of consideration. All of us *know* that no overwhelming necessity constrained him to do so.

My next point is, that if we are responsible, we must be free agents. On this subject a number of fallacies have been scattered widely. Before I can advance a step, I must clear them away.

First then, let us inquire what we mean when we assert that men are free agents; or as the same thing is expressed in books, when we affirm the doctrine of the freedom of the will.

When we assert that we are free agents, we by no means intend what our opponents charge us with affirming, that the human will is unfettered by conditions, or that a man can call up any feeling he pleases, by merely willing to do so. Still less do we assert that freedom is the same thing as caprice. On the contrary, I readily admit that our freedom is limited by a variety of conditions. We are only able to love a thing which our moral nature feels to be lovely. What it pronounces to be right, holy, and good, no bare act of our wills can enable us to think wrong. Also, within certain limits, the acts of our intellects are necessary. We have no freedom to choose whether we will believe that two and two make four. Yet, notwithstanding this, ignorance is sometimes wilful, and therefore voluntary. Education, mental constitution, and various other things, exercise a modifying influence on our responsibility.

Nor is it true that the assertion of the freedom of the will is equivalent to the affirmation that we are capable of acting independently of reasons or motives. A being who acts without reason, renounces his rationality.

What then do we mean when we affirm that we are free agents? We assert that we possess a power of choosing between the various reasons which present themselves to our minds; that these do not exert a necessary influence on us in compelling us to action; and that motives differ from each other, not only in degree, but in kind. We mean therefore, when we assert that we are the free causes of our own actions, that we are capable of exerting a rational choice on the various motives presented to us, that we can select those which our judgment approves, and banish the rest from our consideration.

Secondly: the next point of my proof is, that where there is no freedom to act or to forbear, there can be no responsibility. The proof of this rests on our instinctive feeling that we cannot be responsible for an action or an event over which we can exert no choice. We measure responsibility by the praise or blame which we attach to actions. We are incapable of praising or blaming what we cannot help. Who ever blamed a stone for falling, or a fire for burning? It is true that when a stone unexpectedly hurts us, under the influence of passion we may give it a kick; but the moment we recover our rational self-possession we free it from all responsibility. In one word, we bestow praise or blame in exact proportion to the voluntariness of the action.

Let us take another illustration. If some one were to hit either of us a blow on the face, we should feel indignation at the person who inflicted it. But if another were to take hold of his hand, and use it as an instrument for striking us, our indignation would be aroused, not at the person whose arm struck us, but at the person who used it. It follows, therefore, that voluntary actions only are the subjects of praise or blame, and involuntary ones of neither; and that responsibility attaches only to voluntary actions, and that for those which we cannot help doing we are not responsible.

From this a further conclusion follows, that for an act to be either virtuous or vicious it must be voluntary. An action which we cannot help doing may be our sad misfortune—it may be even the subject of our regret—but it cannot be our crime. It is necessary, before we can feel an action to be a crime, that we should feel the consciousness that we might have avoided doing it, if we had so chosen. For actions of this kind only are we capable of feeling repentance. In the same manner its voluntariness is essential to the virtuousness of an action. No amount of mere utility will make it such. Many things may be highly beneficial, but this can make them neither moral nor virtuous. Thus the Thames is highly beneficial to the inhabitants of London, but no one would think of praising it for its good qualities. But when Captain Knowles stood at his post of duty at the sacrifice of his life, we at once recognize the grandeur of the act, although it seems to have been attended with no beneficial result. Why this difference between the cases? The Thames cannot help bestowing the benefits which it confers. Captain Knowles, by playing the coward, or, as some might say, by a wise self-love, might have saved his life. But he voluntarily chose to sacrifice it at the post of duty. Shall we affirm the position of the atheist, and say that the Thames will continue for centuries to be the unconscious benefactor of the inhabitants of London, and that all which was great and noble in Captain Knowles was in the space of five minutes reduced to nothing in the ocean waves? Yet such must be the result, if there be no God, and for man no hereafter.

It follows, therefore, that if man is impelled by a set of impulses, over which he can exert no choice, his actions can possess no moral quality. The highest act of self-sacrifice, the most unselfish promptings of benevolence, the most disinterested pursuit of truth, would have no more value than the falling of a stone. The instinctive promptings of our moral nature refuse to assign to the fall of a stone in any particular way the idea of virtue. Why is this? Because the stone cannot help falling as it does. It might have fallen within half an inch of our heads, and by this we may have escaped the fracture of our skulls. The atheist would say, How lucky it was that it fell thus; or the Christian, By what a merciful providence have I escaped; but neither would assign praise or virtue to the stone. When, however, we contemplate an act of self-sacrifice, like that of Captain Knowles, we at once assign to it the highest praise, as pre-eminently great and noble. Why the difference? Because what Captain Knowles did was a pure act of his free choice. He had before him the alternative of following the dictates of his lower nature, and thereby saving his life; but he chose to obey the higher law of duty, and to sacrifice life in obedience to its demands. He has thus realized the language of Jesus Christ, " He that loveth his life shall lose it, but he that hateth his life for my sake shall save it to life eternal."

My argument therefore stands as follows: Mankind have asserted with unanimous voice that certain actions are virtuous and vicious. But they can be neither, unless men are voluntary agents. All voluntary agency involves responsibility. Men therefore feel themselves to be responsible. Its modifications I will consider presently.

Thirdly: it is an essential principle in the teaching of Atheism, that there existed nothing in the original state of the universe but matter, force, and law, and that neither mind nor rational volition had in it any existence, or have exerted any influence in its formation. Its laws are necessary, and never have been and never could have been otherwise than they are. How then have these been able to evolve the phenomena of moral action? How can necessary laws evolve the power of choice, the essential idea of which is an ability to act independently of their control? It follows, therefore, if man is the necessary outcome of matter, force, and law, and nothing more, that he must be incapable of virtue or vice, praise or blame. But we know as a fact that he is capable of these. Therefore we infer that the theory that man has originated out of these, and nothing more, must be untrue; and that there must be a fallacy either in the premises with which we have started, or in the inferences which we have drawn from them.

But it has been objected, Our powers of willing and of choice are only the results of particular arrangements of particles of matter, and that the brain secretes volition like a gland does saliva. I own that I am incapable of comprehending what those who make this suggestion really mean, or whether they mean anything at all. What! laws which cannot be otherwise than they are, matter devoid of sensation and of thought, and force devoid of reason and of will, produce by their self-evolution, that which is capable of the highest acts of self-sacrifice and all the phenomena of rational will! Gentlemen, I cannot really bring myself to believe that any one in this room seriously thinks that the timbers which compose this platform, by any varied arrangement of their particles, by any application of motional forces, or by the blind action of dead laws, could generate a being who would be capable of sacrificing his life to save our own. Intelligence must originate in intelligence, and not in non-intelligence; rational acts cannot flow from unreason, voluntary actions from necessary law, or self-sacrifice from self-love.

But it will be objected, How do we know that we are voluntary agents? I will answer this question, for it is a reasonable one.

The evidence is not far to seek. To prove it requires no long course of logical inferences. Our free agency is a matter of our direct knowledge. There is no truth of which we have greater certainty. Our consciousness directly testifies to the fact. Whenever we act, we know that it is in our power either to do it or to forbear. Nine hundred and ninety-nine out of every thousand of mankind habitually assert this in the language which they use. If there is an odd one in a thousand who does not (which I greatly doubt), he may full well be ranked with those who are born either blind or deaf. Even the man who by the aid of a number of intellectual puzzles has persuaded himself into a belief in necessity, acts on the principle that he and all other men are free.

Let me illustrate the argument by an example. We are each of us certain that it is by a simple act of our choice that we have come here this evening. We are certain that after each step on the road it was in our power to have turned back. By a mere exertion of my will it is in my power not to deliver another line of this lecture, or to make any substitution I please in the words and sentences. Each of you feels certain that it entirely depends on yourselves, whether you will sit here and listen another minute. There are no facts of which we are more certain than these. The table here before me cannot help being what it is, and doing what it does. We can. In this power a man differs from a machine. A machine exerts no control over its own actions; we, within certain clear and definite limits, can. Certain functions of our being are placed, for wise purposes, by the great Creator, entirely beyond our control, as, for instance, those on which our lives depend, as the motion of our hearts, etc. Had these been made dependent on our wills, the functions of life would have been impossible. For these we have no responsibility. Not so with our moral actions.

It is impossible that we can have stronger evidence of anything than the testimony of our consciousness. When I see a thing before me, I am as certain that I see it, as I am that two and two make four. How do I know that I see this or that particular thing? I have the testimony of my consciousness. I am therefore certain of it. I have a similar testimony that I am able to do or to forbear doing a particular action. I am therefore certain that I am a free agent.

I am aware that a number of objections are all ready at hand to be adduced against the fact of our free agency, and the consequent doctrine of our accountability for our actions, in the same way as they can be adduced against any other class of facts. They are all sets of metaphysical puzzles. But all reasonings which contradict palpable facts must be fallacious somewhere. We accept the facts, and reject the reasonings. I will attempt to deal with some of these difficulties.

First: it has been urged that the testimony of consciousness to a fact does not make that fact certain. Thus some persons would tell us that we have no certain evidence of the existence of this material table before us, because we think that we see it. You do not, say they, see the table. All that you perceive by the senses is a certain colour, form, hardness, etc. Nay, more; this form is nothing more than a painting on the retina of your eyes; and even this painting undergoes a further modification by the percipient power of the mind. It is a mere delusion, therefore, that you see a material table. All that you are really conscious of is a mental perception, and it is quite uncertain whether there is any outward reality corresponding thereto.

I reply that after all this reasoning, some portions of which may be difficult to answer, we instinctively return to the conviction that this table is a materially existing thing, quite independent of our preceptions of it; and as such, the kicking of our bare toes against it will be attended with discomfort. The objector will say the sensation is only an idea. Still I return to the instinctive belief in the reality of the existence of the material table, although I cannot answer all the difficulties with which the fact of its existence is attended. But this difficulty is powerless against the fact that our consciousness is a true witness to our freedom. The objector fully admits that our minds really perceive certain qualities which we suppose to exist in the table. The only doubt raised is as to whether the external table corresponds to these mental perceptions. It is not attempted to be denied that we actually perceive them, and so far they are true facts. In the same manner it is an equally true fact that we are conscious that we are free agents. We therefore must be free.

This objection may be made to assume a more specious form. It is urged that our consciousness is frequently mistaken as to the reality of facts. Thus it by no means follows because men think that they have seen a ghost, that they have really seen one. Again, one man says that his consciousness tells him that a particular object is red; another says that it bears witness to the fact that it is yellow. The truth is, that in this latter case a man has the jaundice. The inference which is drawn is, that our consciousness is not reliable.

I answer first, that the testimony of 999 out of every thousand of mankind must be taken as representing the truth; and that of the one thousandth, if in opposition to it, as false. If this is not so, we may as well give up the inquiry into truth altogether.

But secondly : the objection is founded on a palpable fallacy. It confounds between our consciousness and the fact external to it. While our consciouness may not be an adequate witness of the truth of an external fact, it must be so as to the truth of its own perceptions. The man who affirms that he is conscious of seeing a ghost states a true fact, that his mind perceives one, although he may be under a delusion as to its external reality. The man who mistakes a red object for a yellow one, actually perceives it yellow. In a similar manner, when the mind testifies to the fact of its own freedom, it testifies to the truth of an internal perception which in this case has nothing external corresponding to it, respecting which deception is possible. As therefore we are conscious that we are free, and this consciousness testifies to a fact, we must be free.

The next objection which I have to answer is that men are actuated by motives; that these vary in power; that in the struggle between them, the most powerful must prevail; and therefore the assertion that we are masters of our own actions is an absurdity.

First : the objection involves the following fallacy. It presupposes that our motives are separate things from ourselves, and can exert in us a power of compulsion.

But they are not separate from, but a portion of ourselves. A motive means a reason which acts on the mind, and nothing else.

Secondly: the assertion that motives vary in power, and that the most powerful must invariably prevail, contains a multitude òf fallacies.

I fully concede that whenever we act, we have some reasons or motives which urge us to action; but these cannot be put into a pair of scales, and weighed one against the other. A mass of iron of a certain weight we cannot lift; but it by no means follows that an impulse of a certain character we cannot resist.

The fallacy arises from confounding together our motives and the pleasures with which particular kinds of actions are attended. But even here it is impossible to weigh the force of different kinds of pleasure by a common measure. Pleasures differ in quality as well as in quantity. The pleasure which attends a great intellectual exertion, and that of drinking oneself drunk, differ wholly in kind. If estimated by its intensity, the pleasure which a man can attain by a combination of gluttony and drunkenness in a single day may greatly exceed what he would derive from any mental occupation. Still there exists a power within us of choosing the higher pursuit, and despising the lower.

The assertion that we are necessarily impelled by the amount of pleasure with which our actions are accompanied contradicts the most palpable facts. It is absurd to say that the martyr is impelled to his acts of self-sacrifice by considerations of pleasure. I appeal to your common sense. A man gives his body to the burning flame, sooner than deny the dictates of his conscience. Another drinks himself drunk, to gratify the lowest appetites of his nature. In what scales will you weigh the motives of these? Who will presume to say that the pleasure of the martyr exceeds that of the drunkard? It is obviously impossible to measure the motives which impel them by any common standard of quantity; or to say that the martyr is impelled to his martyrdom by a self-love over which he could exert no control. The truth is, that the philosophy which teaches that we are the mere creatures of physical law, and that virtue is only a modification of selfishness, leaves little room for martyrdom.

It will be objected that the martyr is animated by the hope of being compensated for his sufferings in the world to come; and that he suffers to obtain a greater good or to avoid a greater pain. I shall not dispute that hope helps to support him in his agony. But mightier support than distant hope—every motive which can be summoned to bear on the mind—is necessary to support him in this deadly struggle. It is certain that the numbers of those who have died in torture to testify their belief or atheism have been few.

Let us take a case nearer home. An artisan wishes to elevate his condition, and to see his wife and family happy and comfortable. To effect this he submits to various acts of self-sacrifice. Another, intent on self-indulgence, expends everything on his own bodily gratification. Will any one tell me that the former of these is the necessary prey of a set of motives which he cannot resist? Could not the prudent man be imprudent, if he so willed, or the reverse? It is clear that if a man is the slave of his strongest impulse, to talk of resisting a temptation is an absurdity. How can I resist it, if I do not possess the power of self-control? The power which we unquestionably possess of resisting and struggling against temptation, although in many men it may be weak, proves that we are in possession of freedom, and that therefore we are responsible.

I by no means wish to deny that many men have become the slaves of habits, which in a certain sense are irresistible. There is a state of degradation into which human nature is capable of sinking under the influence of habits of long and confirmed vice. To take a very telling instance : Of all vices, perhaps none is more difficult to cure than confirmed drunkenness. In a very advanced stage of it, the power of moral self-restraint seems to be almost, if not entirely gone. The sight of the bottle, nay, even the thought of it, acting on a state of miserable restlessness and *ennui*, inflames his whole being to madness. Something similar takes place in all stages of advanced vice. Will it be pretended from this that man has no responsibility? I admit that, in the case before us, the power of self-command has become almost destroyed. But how came this state of things about? Has it not been the result of the drunkard's own voluntary agency? Has he not made himself what he is by the gradual formation of evil habits? Is he not therefore responsible for their formation?

An old heathen moralist could tell us that no man became sunk into a state of utter baseness on a sudden. I by no means deny that it is possible for a man to sink into a state in which he almost says, " Evil, be thou my good." Certain it is that habitual vice can so lower the moral principles, that degraded man fails to see the evil of wickedness and crime. The power of habit is mighty in man, in its influence both for good and for evil. It elevates him high; it causes him to sink low. But the question is, how does he get thus? Is it by any inevitable necessity which man is powerless to avert?

I fully admit that a state of confirmed evil is a thing terrible in its consequences, and that the force of habit exerts a modifying influence on responsibility, though it cannot supersede it. Human nature is mysteriously and wonderfully made. Men, by an indefinite progress in goodness, can become elevated to a height which can almost set the power of temptation at defiance. By progress in evil they can sink to a state of degradation, in which their powers of resistance are reduced almost to nothing. Under the influence of acquired habit, an action which was once very difficult, can be performed, not only easily, but almost instinctively. You who are engaged in any kind of mechanical occupation are well acquainted with the nature of this power, in the dexterity which it confers on you in the use of your instruments. Under its influence complicated actions are performed instinctively, with almost the rapidity of thought, and with an ease to which an unskilled workman is a stranger. I do not think that any of you suppose that the possession of this power is at all inconsistent with your free agency.

It does not, however, lie within the scope of the present lecture to consider whether the power of habits is or is not a desirable one. I accept it as a fact, and readily admit that when a man has formed habits of evil, his powers of resistance have become greatly impaired: *e.g.*, when a man has yielded himself to the dominion of rage, he is frequently hardly responsible for his actions. But the real question at issue is, what has brought him into this state? Is he not himself the cause of his own degradation? If so, he is still responsible.

But it will be objected that a great number of men

are born with bad qualities, perhaps with hereditary tendencies to particular vices as, for example, some are born with naturally bad tempers : others are born with, or at least very early develop, opposite tendencies, whereby the pursuit of what is good and noble is comparatively easy. I think it indisputable that there is a great variety in the mental constitutions of different men ; or at least, that it displays itself from the earliest dawn of their reason. So far this modifies, but does not destroy responsibility. These evil qualities, as they first display themselves in human nature, are within our power to restrain, and it is the duty of each of us to do so. When passion becomes ungovernable, it is always the result of a formed habit. I never saw a boy whose temper was so naturally bad as to be ungovernable. Nay, in cases where the habit has acquired considerable strength through indulgence, it can be restrained by a strong exercise of the will. I have known a man, whose bursts of passion in his own family were excessive, who was as smooth as oil before the world.

Another objection has been urged, that we are so completely the creatures of our birth and our education, that we can be responsible neither for our characters nor our actions. I will put the case as strong against responsibility as I can, and perhaps I shall do so more clearly if I adduce a particular case, rather than put it in an abstract form. We will suppose that a child is born a native of Bengal. I take this particular instance, because Lord Macaulay tells us in one of his Essays, that the Bengalese, as a race, are the greatest liars on earth. What, says he, the Greek is to the European, the Asiatic is to the Greek, and the Bengalese to the Asiatic. We will suppose that a child is born and educated in the moral and intellectual life of this race; can he be responsible for his character?

Or take another instance. A child is born in a family of thieves. The family associate only with persons of the same description, and he lives in the moral atmosphere of plunder, and ultimately becomes a thief; can we hold such a one responsible?

I answer that, in both cases, responsibility, though greatly modified, is not destroyed. The effects of habitually breathing an impure moral atmosphere, and of an evil education, are frightful to contemplate. Still it is not a fact that every one who is born and brought up under vicious influences inevitably becomes a bad man. It sometimes happens that the sense of the evil conduct of parents, and of the society in which one has lived, turns a man strongly in the opposite direction. In not a few cases, men have seen their fathers' sins, and have turned from them, and have not done after their abominations. If this were not so, the reform of society, after it has attained a certain stage of corruption, would be hopeless, and the only means of staying its progress would be to cut it off from the earth.

What effect have these considerations on individual responsibility? They modify, but do not destroy it. The Judge of all the earth will hold a man accountable for what he has, and not for what he has not. Nothing but His all-penetrating eye can thoroughly disentangle the complicated web of human actions, and estimate the exact good or evil in human conduct. I think this is one of the strongest arguments for the being of a God; for if there be none, and if there be no hereafter, neither the individual nor society can estimate at their right value the various circumstances which modify our responsibility. It follows that difficulties such as I have considered cannot over-balance the primary consciousness of freedom, which is inherent in human thought. Even in the most demoralized states of society man has some power—it may be a small one—of discriminating between right and wrong. Until he has attained a most advanced stage of moral recklessness he is not wholly insensible to the evil which surrounds him. The man who has been educated a thief may have a very imperfect sense that it is wrong to rob another. But how does he feel when an attempt is made to rob him? The lowest amount of moral perception affords room for responsibility.

It has been urged that the effects of food, climate, peculiarities of the country in which men live, and, in general, their outward surroundings, bring them under the law of physical necessity. Among the writers of eminence who have urged this difficulty, the late Mr. Buckle holds an important place. Many of the points taken by him afford the strongest proof that men of high reputation can be guilty of pre-eminent rashness of assertion. I will adduce a single example, selected from a great number of others. He is endeavouring to account for the difference of mental constitution between the Greeks and Hindoos, and he does so by means of the local characteristics of their respective countries. Among other things, he assigns an important influence to the gigantic character of the mountains of India, compared with those of Greece. We all know that the Himalayas are the highest in the globe; but Mr. Buckle forgot to take into account the most important fact, that before mountainous scenery can influence the character of a people, it is necessary that they should be able to catch sight of it. Now it so happens that an overwhelming majority of the inhabitants of India have, in all ages, inhabited the valleys of the Ganges and the Indus, and thus have never had the opportunity of seeing the mighty mountains of India. What should we say of a writer who would ascribe the character of the inhabitants of Cornwall to the scenery around Ben Nevis? Until facts are correctly stated I need not occupy your time in refuting theories founded on them. The influences of climate, etc., exert a modifying influence on man; but to assert that they make him what he is, or that they nullify his responsibility, is absurd.

A great number of writers in the present day call on us to believe that our freedom is crushed beneath the pressure of a number of hard invariable laws, which we are powerless alike to modify or control. These invite us to renounce our belief in the freedom of our actions, at the bidding of what you may have heard called the science of statistics. Staticians tell us that numerous classes of actions recur in nearly the same numbers year by year, in proportion to the total number of the population. Thus the numbers of murders committed year by year are said to vary in this proportion. The same is asserted of suicide and various other crimes. Nay, we are told that the great principle of marriage is subject to the same law. In the name of such facts we are invited to believe that human actions are governed by as necessary a law as that of gravitation.

This objection presents at first sight so great an amount of plausibility, that I must give it a careful consideration.

1. I observe that the word "Law," as used in the objection, is ambiguous. The Duke of Argyle, in his work entitled "The Reign of Law," tells us that this term is used by philosophers in five different senses,

e.g., we say that a weight falls in accordance with the law of gravitation, which is impressed on all matter. A statician tells us that a murder took place in accordance with the law of averages. It is quite evident that there is nothing in common between these two expressions, but the word "law." To infer that an action that occurs in conformity with a law of averages is necessary, because one which takes place in conformity with that of gravitation is, requires only common sense to see that the reasoning is fallacious.

2. The objection that we can predict an action by the aid of statistical tables, and therefore that such actions must obey a necessary law, involves a gross fallacy. What is meant is, that if we take large numbers of men, we may be tolerably sure that a certain number of them will do a particular act. But if we were to apply this principle to any particular man, and say that he would do a particular act, it would only turn out true by a lucky guess. Thus, it is tolerably certain that twenty-five out of every thousand men will die in any given year. But it is in the highest degree uncertain whether this or that particular person will. I ask you to observe that no such uncertainty prevails in the results of the laws of nature. We are not tolerably certain as to these results, but absolutely so. We do not conclude that nine hundred and seventy-five stones out of a thousand will drop to the ground, if we let them fall, but that each one will. There is therefore no parallel whatever between the two cases.

3. The so-called laws of averages are not invariable. Strictly speaking, therefore, they are not laws at all. It is not true that the same number of murders are committed year by year in proportion to the population in

this country. All which can be asserted is, that they are nearly the same. I ask your attention to this word *nearly*, for on it the whole force of the argument depends. If they were the result of any necessary law, they must always be the same under similar circumstances.

4. The statistics do not count actions separately from the results produced by our wills, but include these, and those of every impulse which can be exerted on the mind. It is quite possible to reduce a number of the most fortuitous events to a statistical table. If any one were to throw up a penny piece 5,000 times, and ask me to guess heads or tails, there is no doubt that I should be right in my guessings about 2,500 times, even though I might invariably say heads. Nothing, however, could be more absolutely fortuitous; and to say that my right guesses were the result of any necessary law, which controls human actions in any proper sense of that term, is absurd.

5. Let us look into this matter with the eyes of common sense. Mr. Buckle tells us "that murder is committed with as much regularity, and bears as uniform a relation to certain known circumstances, as the movements of the tides, and the rotation of the seasons." What are the facts? Taking a large number of years, the number of known murders perpetrated in England amount to a certain average, or to express the same fact in other words, they will amount to one out of so many thousand of the population. Now observe what this means. Not that the number of murders which will be committed next year, or any other year, will be exactly the same as this average number; but will be not very far off from it. Where then is the invariable law which proves that the actions of men are governed by influences as

necessary as the ebbing and flowing of the tides, and the regular succession of spring, summer, autumn, and winter?

6. But what about the alleged uniformity of the law of suicides? Does not this prove that when we talk about the freedom of human actions it is all nonsense. Here again I might apply precisely the same argument, but it is needless to repeat it. But the case of suicide is particularly ill chosen by our opponents. It only avails on the supposition that we mean by freedom a power to act capriciously. On the contrary, we connect it with the highest acts of our rational judgment. Now the verdict of juries tells us, that in nearly every case where a suicide takes place, the person who kills himself is under the influence of unsoundness of mind. In one word the rational will, which ought to hold the sovereignty in man, is dethroned, and mere passion and caprice has taken its place.

7. I must now draw your attention to a position far more startling than any which we have considered. We are told that everything connected with one of the most delicate affairs of human life, courtship and marriage, is necessary, and that neither our wills, our whims, nor our caprices have anything whatever to do with this important matter, but the average price of corn and wages. Lest you should think I misrepresent him, I will quote Mr. Buckle's own words; he says :—

"Even the number of marriages annually contracted is determined, not by the temper and wishes of individuals, but by large general facts over which individuals can exercise no authority. It is now known that marriages bear a fixed and definite relation to the price of corn; and in England the experience of a century has proved that, instead of having any connection with personal feelings, they are simply regulated by the average earnings of the great mass of the people; so that this great religious and social institution is not only swayed, but is completely controlled, by the price of food and the rate of wages."

Ladies and gentlemen who are contemplating marriage, I am a bearer to you of a piece of unexpected news. You need not take any pains whatever about this matter; it is simply waste of time to make any efforts to be mutually pleasing—it is all determined for you by a power over which you can exert no control. As to us married people, we have been under a fond delusion in thinking that personal influences, attractions, or even caprices have exerted any influence in bringing this matter about. To think that love has exerted any influence over it is all delusion. We have been the hopeless prey of corn averages and rates of wages.

I am quite ready to allow that every prudent person, before he thinks of marriage, ought to consider whether his horse will carry double, and to look forward to the possible contingency of its having to carry five or six. Still, many people are not prudent. Ireland has been a remarkable instance, which proves that prudential considerations have far from exerted a potent force on marriage in that country. In the days of its greatest misery, marriages were contracted with the greatest recklessness. But when, in the name of the fact that marriages ought to be contracted with an eye to prudential considerations, and that many are so, we are asked to believe that we ourselves, our rational wills, our affections, nay, our sentimentalities, and even our caprices, have exerted, and can exert, no influence over this matter, but that all has resulted from the iron law of necessity, we are asked to believe what exceeds the powers of even the most credulous of mankind. I will not assert that there are not certain hard-headed men who consult the tables of averages during every month of their courtship. Whether this was the case with the writer whose opinions I am combatting, I cannot tell, but he ought not to have assumed that it was so with ordinary men and women. I am confident that if any of you will go into the confessional with me, you will affirm that Mr. Buckle's premises and conclusions contradict your experience.

I think that I need not spend any further time in proving that the question of our free agency, and consequently of our responsibility, is unaffected by such considerations. It rests on distinct evidence of its own, so commanding that it is less influenced by them than the mighty rock is by the ripples of the silent ocean.

There is one question of supreme importance which remains to be determined. If man is responsible, to whom is he responsible?

If the principles of atheism are true, the universe contains nothing but matter, force, and law, and modifications of them. How, out of any combination of these, moral affections, or even life, can have grown, is quite beyond my comprehension; for no atheist would affirm that any of the original constituents of the universe possessed either personality, life, moral affections, or freedom. Yet these exist.

If man consists of nothing but matter, acted on by blind forces, and dominated over by blind laws, he must be incapable of morality or self-sacrifice, and as unworthy of praise or blame as the table before me.

But many atheists are far better men than their principles. Overcome by the stern logic of facts, they admit that man possesses a responsibility of some sort. Although they affirm that there is no evidence that God exists, to whom man is accountable; they do not deny that he is responsible to society and himself. They endeavour to erect a system of responsibility, on the assumption that man is capable of a reasonable self-love. They next endeavour to show that every other principle of morality is nothing but self-love transmuted into some other form. From this it follows that the grandest acts of self-sacrifice are nothing more than transmutations of selfishness. To say the least of it, this is a most startling position.

If there be no God, to whom I am responsible because I am indebted to Him for my existence and every good thing which I possess, it follows that I can only be responsible to myself or to society, as far as it possesses a power to act on my self-love. The expression, "being responsible to oneself," is to a certain extent a misnomer; for it must mean a debt to oneself. Such debts resemble taking money out of one pocket, and putting it into another. When it is said by atheists, that man is responsible to himself, it is intended that there are certain lower principles in human nature which ought to be obedient to the higher. But this idea of "ought," concedes the whole question. Why ought it to be so? If there is nothing in the universe but matter, law, and force, whence came this idea of ought or duty? Our conception of it is the opposite to that of necessary law.

But, assuming for argument's sake a position which I believe to be utterly untrue, that all moral obligation may be resolved into self-love, I ask what possible evidence can I have that I am bound to sacrifice myself for the good of others? If I am only bound to love myself, what right can society have over me, except the law of the stronger? What right can it have to demand self-sacrifice at my hands? It will be replied, that you will best provide for your own happiness by all kinds of virtuous conduct, especially by disinterestedly seeking the happiness of others. It may be so; but supposing that I cannot be made to see this. If virtue is only another form of seeking my own happiness; and if, by defective intellect or other causes, it seems to me that self-indulgence will make me more happy than self-denial, how is any act involving the smallest self-sacrifice to be enforced on me otherwise than by society making me miserable? If this principle be correct, the most virtuous man is he who has the clearest intellect to calculate his own interests.

A great philosopher adduced an illustration of this principle more than 2000 years ago, which proves that it is hopelessly untenable. The ancients feigned that a man named Gyges possessed a ring which, whenever he wished, rendered him invisible to every one, while he retained his powers of vision. Socrates, according to Plato, supposes a man to be in possession of this ring. What influence would it have on his moral conduct if virtue is nothing but self-love? It is obvious that it would free him from all the restraints which society imposes on him; and if there be no God and no hereafter, he would be in a position safely to give the most unrestrained indulgence to his own appetites and passions. It would convert moral obligation into a bugbear, and render society impossible.

But I shall be told that the principle which I am contending against really means that we are bound to seek the greatest happiness of the greatest number, and thereby to insure our own. You see that it is impossible to make a single assertion on this point without contradicting the whole theory. I ask, How am I bound? why am I bound to do this? You say, *we are bound*. Yes, to our own self-love, if there is nothing in the universe but matter, force, and law; though it is incomprehensible how we can be bound over to that. It will be replied, You are bound to other men. Then I reply, There must be something which binds me higher than myself, or than anything originating in myself. If I am bound by a sense of right, then rectitude must be a thing higher than I, who am bound by it; it must exist in something higher than, and independent of, my self-love, and to which it ought to offer itself a willing sacrifice. It is, in fact, I who am bound, which includes my self-love and my entire being. I recognise, therefore, a moral law, which must exist independently of myself, and is invariably and unalterably the same. But I cannot be bound by an abstraction. Abstractions have no existence, except as attributes of concrete things. I infer, therefore, that there must be a personal being, not subject to the changes of my mutability, who is unalterably the same, in whom rectitude and holiness dwell—the living God, the great Creator, who gave me being and a moral nature capable of feeling the obligations I am under to Him.

Atheistic morality affirms that man is responsible to his brother man. I accept the affirmation with all thankfulness. It is the recognition of a great fact, that whether man can reason the matter out clearly or not, a feeling of obligation exists. It is a declaration coming from the inmost recesses of the human heart, which is stronger than all theories, and than all reasonings founded on abstractions. It is inconsistent with the affirmation that virtue is a mere form of self-love, and that man is not a free agent. Yes; man is responsible to society. I accept the truth. Is a stone responsible to society? Does a cat owe obligation to its brother cats? No; therefore there must be something in man which is neither in stone nor cat. But we feel that it is righteous in society to punish those who grossly violate their obligations. It does so daily, either by formal law or by a law equally mighty, though enacted by no Parliament. Is it right to punish a man for what he cannot help? The universal conscience of man answers emphatically, No. Man must, therefore, be a free agent.

It follows that man must be bound by an obligation higher than and external to himself. Consider the expression, *We ought to do so.* What does it mean? The meaning of *ought* is, that a man may leave a thing undone, if he pleases; but that he *ought* not to do so. There is something within him which will reproach him if he does, and say, you *ought* not. There is an obligation before which you *ought* to bow, higher than you. To matter, force, or invariable law the sense of duty or obligation is utterly inapplicable. What owe I to them? There is something within us which points to something outside us, which cannot be generated by their united force.

"*I ought.*" The idea is as universal as man. Even he who in theory denies responsibility, is compelled to use the unwelcome word. To what then does it point? To matter, force, or law, or any of their modifications? Meditate on the mysterious word, for it reaches to the profoundest depths of our being. What does it affirm? *It is right; it is fitting; it is proper; it is your duty.* It may even raise to the greater elevation of the sentiment, "*It is noble, it is lovely so to do.*" When I say, "*I ought,*" I affirm the presence of a power before which everything else, even self, should bend. The feeling, "*It is expedient,*" will not satisfy its demands. It affirms a duty. Must not that duty be *owed* to some one in whom obligation centres, and who has a right to demand self-sacrifice at our hands? Some being therefore must exist who has a right to lay me under obligations. Does such a right exist in my brother man? I may be indebted to my parents. I may be indebted to my educators. I feel under obligation to all who have done me good, and to all in whom holiness and goodness exist. But how can I be under obligation to a man, who is neither good himself, nor has done me good? Yet I feel the obligation. It must therefore centre somewhere. The only foundation on which it can be made to rest, is the Being who has made me, to whom all gratitude is due, whose moral perfections demand my humblest reverence and most devoted love. I can fully recognise the right of Him that made me to say, I demand self-sacrifice at thy hands in behalf of thy brother man, whom I have made also. We can feel that obligation is due to men, because we are all the children of a common Father; but we cannot feel it because we are the children of a common ape.

The feeling, "*I ought,*" proves the existence of *One* outside ourselves, to whom it corresponds, in whom obligation centres, and to whom duty is due. To Him we are all responsible. "*I ought*"—how imperfectly do we succeed in realising the fulness of the conception, and embodying it in practice! I infer from this, that there is a period coming, under the moral government of the Creator, when we shall embody it in a higher and more perfect form. If I am responsible, He will judge me. But He does not judge me here. There must therefore be an hereafter.

Human conduct, viewed by the eye of man, is an entangled web. We cannot determine the precise measure of the responsibility of others. None but He who knows all things can estimate the exact character of our motives, the exact limits of our freedom, or the exact guilt of our conduct. Under every difficulty with which this subject is attended, we may rest assured that the great God will demand of each individual only as much as He has given; and that the Judge of all the earth will certainly do right. Let us remember that to Him we are bound by the highest obligations; that we are His by creation; that we are His by providence, and His by redemption; that these bind us to Him by a moral law, which is recognised by our inmost hearts, and through Him to our brother man; that the Author of our being has the right to call us to account, and that His perfections require Him to do so.

It follows, therefore, that the facts of consciousness and the deepest intuitions of human nature prove that man is responsible to God, and that his responsibility to God causes him to recognise his responsibility to man. Man is a free agent, the voluntary cause of his own actions; and as far as they are voluntary he is accountable for them. "Each of us must give account of himself to God."

CHRISTIANITY IS NOT THE INVENTION OF IMPOSTORS OR OF CREDULOUS ENTHUSIASTS.

BY THE

REV. JOHN GRITTON,

AUTHOR OF "MISSIONARY MONOGRAMS," "THE WORD AND THE WAY," ESSAY ON "MUSIC, AND PAINTED WINDOWS IN CHURCHES," ETC.

Christianity is not the Invention of Impostors or of Credulous Enthusiasts.

THE world was amused fifty years since by clever and well-simulated doubts concerning the existence of Napoleon Buonparte; and within the past five years a scientific and witty writer has called in question the existence of the central orb of our solar system. Possibly the day may come when, in the interests of religious scepticism, some one may endeavour to cast historic doubts on the existence of Christianity, and to blot from the spiritual universe the sun of righteousness.

There will be needed, however, a strange preparation for the process. The myth of the seven sleepers must be transmuted into fact for all nations which have a past, and for all human beings who possess memory; and when the sleeping race shall again open their eyes and take notice of the world in which they awaken, it must be a world in which some destructive process shall have reduced to dust every one of the innumerable monuments and tokens of Christianity which surround us to-day. Human knowledge, and the world on which it exercises its powers, must have each become a tabula rasa; and, when that shall have come to pass, the very process by which only the speculation might become possible will have destroyed the possibility of forming any speculations at all on the then non-existent Christian system.

Ten thousand doubts may arise concerning the origin and character of Christianity, ten thousand speculations may be indulged concerning its aim and results; but the most vagrant flight of the wildest imagination cannot reach to the conception of its non-existence, unless the imagination can also embrace the vagaries of the Hindu Maya, and resolve *all* existence into illusion.

But, short of the denial of its existence, there seem no limits to the doubts which have troubled men with reference to Christianity.

While, however, the difficulties which men entertain concerning the origin of Christianity are very many, they fall under four theories, when classified.

Some conclude that the Christian system is the crystallization and fixture of masses of undefined myth, which have had their birth through long ages; and that the Christ of the Bible is the embodiment of many fancies of men concerning heroism, self-sacrifice, and benevolence. This theory is generally adopted by men who cannot accept the historic verity of the Gospel, and who yet have their moral sense sufficiently quickened to shrink from any implication of deliberate fraud in the formation of a system which everywhere rebukes fraud and condemns dishonesty.

There are other students who hesitate to refer Christianity to deliberate fraud and imposture; and endeavour to explain its origin on the assumption that it is the invention of enthusiasts, whose judgment and con-

Or of Credulous Enthusiasts. 65

science were ruled over by a tyrannous credulity—men who, intending no wrong, yet mistook facts for fancies, and fancies for facts, utterly misapprehended the meaning of events which passed before them; who, being themselves completely deceived, became the unconscious deceivers of the ages which succeeded them.

Others, who are less the creatures of imagination, and are gifted with a truer judgment concerning probabilities, and yet are repelled from the Christian system as a whole, and, unwilling to accept it with all its consequences, are driven to assert that it is the result of imposture—the deliberate misrepresentation of real events, the dishonest record of actual facts, and the wilful invention of words and deeds and persons which might form a conglomeration of truth and falsehood, light and darkness, good and evil, sufficiently consistent to impose on the generality of mankind, but, like all other lies, unauthoritative and barren of good.

The vast majority of those who have read the Christian books, and have applied their minds to the conditions of the great problem of Christianity, are unable to accept either of the three theories stated above, or any possible combination of them. They find that the facts of the case are inexplicable on any supposition but the truth of the records on which the system is founded, and the consequent and necessary truth of the system itself. They feel that crystallized myths, credulous imaginings, and dishonest inventions, separate or in combination, could never have created the Jesus of the Gospels, or elaborated the Christian religion.

This conviction is attended with a deep sense of the loss which men suffer who do not recognize the historic truths of Christianity, and of the danger which they incur by treating the Gospel with neglect, or setting themselves in opposition to it.

These convictions explain our present position. We know that many reject Christianity, and with more or less of deliberation take toward it the attitude of opposers. We believe they are misled and endangered; and we would gladly assist them to reconsider the matter by giving a reason for the hope which is in us.

We may put on one side the consideration of the pure mythical origin of Christianity, except so far as it may be incidentally noticed in connexion with the credulous enthusiastic theory, because as a matter of fact very few attach any importance to it, and those few are mere dreamers who please their imagination with the play of poetic scepticism, and who will not be found in places such as those in which we are met in conflict. Our voices will not reach them, and our time would be wasted in the attempt to penetrate the haunted bowers of their luxurious dilletantism.

Let us pass on to the question whether it be a sufficient account of Christianity to say that it is the invention of credulous enthusiasts.

An enthusiast may have many amiable qualities, and be a very admirable person as to earnestness and singleness of purpose; but in almost every case he will be wanting in judgment, and be subject to the lead of a badly balanced mind. If to these infirmities there be added an easiness of belief amounting to credulity, the result will be that he will believe amiss, and be led to any course of action which may fall in with his views, with no sufficient regard to the justice and uprightness of that course. Such an one might accept a myth as a fact, might mistake a shadow for a person, might elevate a

Or of Credulous Enthusiasts. 67

fellow-creature into a deity, and being thus blinded, might say or do anything which promised permanency to his delusion, or honour to his idol.

Should a number of such persons be possessed by the same idea, and be associated together on the ground of that possession, all their characteristics will be intensified. The delusion which misleads them will be strengthened by the union of so many separate perversities, and their course of conduct will become zig-zag with multiplied crookednesses.

In their work we shall behold abundance of imagination, and but little judgment. Many lights of eccentric genius will sparkle on their way, but the power which could collect them into a focus, and direct them in one steady brilliancy on the path they tread will be wanting. Looking with fixity of gaze on the one end they pursue, they will behold in distorted proportion all the things by which they hurry in their onward course; saying anything which will glorify their idol, they will constantly be betrayed into inaccuracies such as can be tested and exposed by facts which touch their statements at various points; dreamers, and not poets, their work will be rather the rhythmical fantasies of disordered intellect, than the solemn drama in which the unities are preserved, and each circumstance is in consistent relation to every other and to the whole work. We have to deal with the supposition that Christianity is the invention and work of such credulous enthusiasts.

Before we pass to the examination, let it be clearly understood that we mean by Christianity the religion which the books of the New Covenant contain, and that only.

We are concerned only with those things which are

contained in Holy Writ, and we include everything which Holy Writ teaches. We are not concerned with winking Madonnas, ship-loads of pieces of the true cross, or liquifying blood of Neapolitan saints. It is not for us to defend the Pope with his ever erring infallibility, or to excuse priestly assumptions of creative power. "Whatsoever is not to be read (in Holy Scripture), nor may be proved thereby, is not to be required of any man that it should be believed as an article of the faith, or be thought requisite or necessary to salvation."

Was Christianity, as revealed to us in Scripture, the invention of credulous enthusiasts?

We have seen what are the inevitable characteristics of enthusiastic thought, or teaching, or doing. If the Christianity of the Scriptures answers to them, the conclusion may be accepted. Is such the case?

Let it be tested by the character of the central figure of the system, that unique being whom the authors of the Gospel accepted as Master, and worshipped as Lord, whose steps they attended, whose teachings they record, and whose life they have pourtrayed. If the character of Jesus be an invention, and they the originators of it, how comes it to pass that they have marked it with just those qualities which would be expected to be omitted and overlooked by such persons? Take the unity of character in Jesus. On the assumption of His real historic being, and judged by the declared purpose and end of His conduct, is not everything in proportion and order? Think of His dealings with self-righteous hypocrites and heart-broken sinners. Mark His bearing in the presence of the great and mighty, and in the dwellings and haunts of the poor. Regard Him in His relations as Son, brother, teacher, master, and friend. Follow Him into crowds and into solitude. Hear His words to men and His utterances to the Father in heaven. See Him when for others He puts forth supernatural energy, and when for Himself He will not use such powers: is not all consistent with the supposition that He was the God-man, living not only a life with two sides, one towards man and one towards God (which is true of every godly person), but living out two distinct lives in one —never ceasing to be the visitor from a higher world, the sojourner for a time among the abodes of men in man's nature?

Mark the prudence of His teaching in dealing with all kinds of men, and the deep insight He displays into motives and dispositions. How often and how immediately did the human conscience respond to His rebukes, and the human heart answer to His words of kindness and wisdom. Notice again how consistently His teaching is full of the seeds of things—how in dealing with a special case He lays down truths and rules applicable to ten thousand other cases—how in speaking to Jews He enunciates principles applicable to all nations; and while teaching men of the first century, so speaks that nineteen centuries later men turn to His directions for guidance and instruction.

Let it be also borne in mind that this wonderful unity and versimilitude of teaching is not pourtrayed by one hand, and is not the creation of one man's mind. All men, whether gifted or not with critical acumen, recognize that the four books which supply to us all the known facts concerning Jesus Christ, are by different hands—that whether they are the writings of Matthew, Mark, Luke, and John, or no, they are certainly the writings of four persons. Let it be further remembered that while three of the four volumes are largely synoptical, and deal commonly with the same events, they to a considerable extent deal with incidents peculiar to some one of them; and that the fourth, that of John, is totally distinct, and for the most part deals with acts and teachings of Jesus which the other three do not describe. It follows, therefore, that we are met not only by the great improbability that any one credulous enthusiast could imagine or create the unique consistency of the character of Jesus, but by the greater improbability that four more or less independent credulous enthusiasts should agree in their representations, and act so exactly like truthful historians, that only on the assumption that they were such can any plausible account be given of their variances and agreements.

It may be replied that the very acceptance of any teaching which supposes miraculous interference, or which asserts the dwelling among men, and as a man, of a Divine being, is in itself a sufficient proof of credulity and unreasoning enthusiasm. Before this assertion can destroy the force of what has been advanced, it will be necessary, not to assert, but to prove, that miraculous interference is impossible; not to assert, but to prove, that the incarnation of a Divine being is incredible.

Let us now enquire whether other characteristics of the Gospels are consistent with the supposition that they are the invention of credulous enthusiasts, bearing in mind as we do so what has been said with reference to such persons.

The histories on which Christianity is founded do not present to us a person separated from others, and placed in an imaginary locality which the fancy may fix in any continent, or in any part of some immense country, as is the case with Rasselas, the beautiful creation of Samuel Johnson's imagination; nor do they describe events which may be referred to any century at pleasure. The four Gospels, so called, and the book of the Acts of the Apostles, are definite in their chronology and their topography. In the course of the history we are led through the length and breadth of Palestine. Cities and villages, mountains and valleys, rivers and wells, gardens and deserts, are connected with many separate events, and linked one with another in various orders. Minute characteristics of localities are noticed, as well as more general features. The view extends beyond Palestine to Syria, Asia Minor, the Ægean, Greece, Italy, and Spain, Cyprus, Rhodes, Crete, and Melita. The history carries us to Damascus, the Syrian Antioch, Tarsus, the Pysidian Antioch, Derbe, Iconium, Lystra, Athalia, Ephesus, Smyrna, Miletus, Troas, Philippi, Athens, Corinth, Syracuse, Neapolis, the Appii Forum, and Rome. These various places are the scenes of incidents in which Jew and Gentile, Roman and Greek, philosopher and barbarian, play their part. Forms of government, minute distinctions in Roman polity, civic arrangements, and colonial peculiarities, influence the course of events. These events are distinctly associated with persons whose connexion or contemporary existence is asserted. Herod the Great, Herod Archelaus, Herod Antipas, are among the dramatis personæ, as are Pilate, Felix, Gamaliel, Sergius Paulus, Galio, Augustus Cæsar, Nero. If these persons and places are combined with minutiæ of circumstances, what innumerable chances of error will result,— errors such as even fairly instructed, well-informed, and truthful writers might fall into; but if some four or a dozen credulous enthusiasts are venturing into circumstances so complicated,—ignorant, biassed, blinded by prejudice, and easily imposed upon,—cannot any one see that they will blunder hopelessly, and betray their folly at every step? And what are the facts as to these histories? The points in which topographical, chronological, or political mistake has been imputed to the writers in the New Testament may be reckoned up on the fingers. Of those instances some are grounded on mistaken renderings of correct originals, some have been entirely justified by the light of increasing knowledge, and the one or two which remain still open to question are, at the most, apparent exceptions to a clear and marvellous regularity of consistency. Not even now have we summed up the improbabilities which beset the supposition that Christianity is the invention of credulous enthusiasts.

There must be added a thousand confirmations from niceties of speech, dialectical peculiarities, grammatical constructions, and quotations from older writings, both Hebrew and heathen.

Nice and accurate touches as to climate, fruits, flowers, the animal and metallic kingdoms, multiply the chances of error, and, in the same degree, diminish the possibility of any solution but that which recognises the historical truth of the books in question.

There remains one other view of the matter to which we shall do well to pay attentive heed before we give a final reply to the supposition we have been sifting.

Does the general tone of teaching in the Christian books warrant the assumption of their being the invention of easily deceived and unreasonable enthusiasts? Have not sceptics of all schools admitted the fact that the Gospels and Epistles are full of manifold wisdom? Are not multitudes of doubters in this nineteenth century admirers of New Testament morality, even while they reject the miraculous and supernatural elements with which the teaching is connected? Has it not been the aim of doubters in various ages to derogate from the peculiar wisdom of the Christain teaching,—not by questioning its excellence, but by trying to show that Socrates, Plato, Seneca, Aristotle, Homer, Virgil, and others, the wisest men and the deepest thinkers of the human family, have taught as divinely?

A man may turn from the record of miraculous interposition in the Gospels with disdain, but if he have any sense of man's condition, or any appreciation of what is suited to man, can he despise the parabolic teaching of the Gospels, or turn with disdain from the sermon on the mount? He may regard as incredible the records of sight given to the blind, hearing to the deaf, deliverance to demon-possessed bodies and souls of men; or other records, of hungry multitudes fed to satisfaction by a few loaves and fishes, tempests quieted by a word, trees withered to the roots at a rebuke, and the dead recalled to life; but can he deny the wisdom and graciousness of many words put into the mouth of Jesus? Can he find it in his heart to rebuke words spoken to publicans and sinners, fallen women in their misery, and greedy farmers of taxes in their awakenings of conscience?

On the supposition of the existence of a Supreme Being who is at once Creator and Preserver, who rules as a king and loves as a father, can any law to regulate our conduct towards that Supreme Being be stated in words more wise than those put into the mouth of Jesus, "Thou shalt love the Lord thy God with all thy heart, and with all thy soul, and with all thy might, and with all thy strength"? Has moral philosophy or has political economy discovered more fruitful rules as to man's relation with his fellow, than those which are given as the words of Jesus, "Do unto others as ye would they should do unto you," "Thou shalt love thy neighbour as thyself"? Are these utterances credulous, enthusiastic, fanatical? If so, we can but reply, Credulity, be thou my trust; Enthusiasm, be thou my sobriety; Fanaticism, be thou my reason!

Or, to pass to the Epistles : the sceptic may pour scorn on the doctrinal and dogmatic portions of the various letters of Paul, or Peter, or John; he may regard the statements concerning sin, and its removal; the guilty soul, and its justification; the old man, and the new nature, as so many utterances without meaning; but can he venture to include in his condemnation the practical admonitions of the Epistles? Let him listen to the following, and then, with his hand on his heart, condemn them as credulous fanaticism, if he can : "Provide things honest in the sight of all men. If it be possible, as much as lieth in you, live peaceably with all men." "Love worketh no ill to his neighbour, therefore love is the fulfilling of the law" (Rom. xii. 17, 18; xiii. 10); "Though I speak with the tongues of men and of angels, and have not love, I am become as sounding brass, or a tinkling cymbal" (1 Cor. xiii. 1); "We can do nothing against the truth, but for the truth " (2 Cor. xiii. 18); "Let us not be desirous of vain glory, provoking one another, envying one another" (Gal. v. 26); "Let him that stole steal no more, but rather let him labour, working with his hands the thing which is good, that he may have to give to him that needeth" (Eph. iv. 28); "Whatsoever things are true, honest, just, pure, lovely and of good report, if there be any virtue, and if there be any praise, think on these things" (Phil. iv. 8); "Put off all these, anger, wrath, malice, blasphemy, filthy communications out of your mouth. Lie not one to another" (Col. iii. 8, 9); "Let no man go beyond and defraud his brother in any matter" (1 Thess. iv. 6); "Be not weary in well doing" (2 Thess. iii. 13); "Every creature of God is good, and nothing to be refused, if it be received with thanksgiving" (1 Tim. iv. 4); "Shun profane and vain babblings" (2 Tim. ii. 16); "Speak evil of no man; be no brawlers, but gentle, showing all meekness unto all men" (Titus iii. 2); "Let brotherly love continue;" "Remember them which are in bonds, as bound with them;" "Let marriage be honourable in all, and the bed be undefiled" (Heb. xiii. 1—4); "If ye fulfil the royal law according to the Scriptures, 'Thou shalt love thy neighbour as thyself,' ye do well" (James ii. 8); "Let none of you suffer as a murderer, or as a thief, or as an evil doer, or as a busybody in other men's matters" (1 Peter iv. 15); "Giving all diligence, add to your faith courage, and to courage knowledge, and to knowledge temperance, and to temperance patience, and to patience godliness, and to godliness brotherly kindness, and to brotherly kindness charity" (2 Peter i. 5—7); "This commandment have we from Him, that he that loveth God love his brother also" (1 John iv. 21); "Follow not that which is evil, but that which is good" (3 John 11). We have selected, almost at random, these verses from Epistles which set forth in its fulness the Christian system, of which system some men say that it is an invention of credulous enthusiasts. Surely the description *must* be incorrect, the accusation undeserved!

We need pursue this examination no longer. Even should we leave out of question the power of Christianity as displayed in the reformation and sanctification of innumerable hearts and lives of men; even if we put on one side the evidences which might be adduced from the cosmopolitan action of Christianity in every land throughout successive generations, there is enough evidence in the aspect of the question which we have been considering to satisfy us, that, whatever other cause may be assigned for the existence of Christianity, it is impossible to accept the statement that it is the invention of credulous enthusiasts.

Let us then turn to the remaining supposition with which we have to deal. There are men who say that Christianity is a gigantic fraud, the invention of impostors. The upright man is pained whenever, even for lawful ends, he seems to be what he is not. Crooked ways and lying subterfuges are repulsive to him; and if there be a dictum which more than another angers him, it is that "the end sanctifies the means." In the sphere of moral action he agrees with the saying of Burns,

> "An honest man's the noblest work of God."

Such an one will have nothing to do with forgery of history, with falsehood as to persons, places, documents, or doctrines. An impostor is the antithesis of all this. He prefers crooked methods, even when direct courses would equally serve his purpose. He uses the truth only when a lie would be too dangerous. To seem to be what he is, is the supreme misery to which he will descend only when it is impossible any longer for him to seem what he is not. In such a man falsehood will cause no blush, and even that feeling in his heart which is the substitute for shame will be excited only when his lie is detected. He holds that while a blunder is worse than a crime, and dishonesty preferable to virtue, the only really reprehensible thing is to be detected in his wrong doing.

Whatever may have been the starting-point in his downward career, he has come to the level where moral sense is perverted, the conscience gagged, and all those grander aspirations of man which look upward and seek high ends have been dwarfed, blinded, or strangled.

Let it not be replied that this picture is too dark, that a less deep iniquity will suffice for the work contemplated of forging the Gospels or inventing the Jesus of Christianity; for in truth the difficulties in his way are so many, the dangers of detection so abounding, conflicting things to be reconciled and put into shape so numberless, and the things to be burlesqued so sacred, that only a chief of impostors, in whom all fear and shame and right feeling are dead, would dare the difficult task which his ambition or his cupidity might suggest. If the Christian system be the invention of impostors, those impostors are men before whom all the lesser impostors of the world may well hide their faces in envy and admiration.

If it be considered what were the difficulties in the way of the supposed work of inventing Christianity, and how many were the chances of failure, it must be confessed that *all probability* is against the supposition that Christianity is not historically true.

All which has been said in previous passages of this lecture as to the difficulty of keeping up consistency of statement, when the invented history touches so many points in geography, topography, history, and chronology, is applicable in the case now under consideration. So also are all references to minutiæ of political, religious, lingual, domestic, and climatic peculiarity. These re-

78 Christianity not the Invention of Impostors

marks become more forcible when we call to mind that if the Gospels be the work of impostors, they are not the impostors of this century or any century later than the first. The books which we have as our Bible now have been in existence since a period very close to the time when the political and historical combinations therein revealed were existing. It is not the case of a body of competent scholars sitting down in the nineteenth century, collecting around them the libraries of books now existing, which would instruct them in the history, political combination, linguistic condition, and locomotive facilities of the first century; and then, taking a complete view of the whole, inventing a history which should touch all these things, combine them accurately in one narrative, and present to the eye of the most acute and unfriendly critics a picture in which the sharpest gaze could, at the most, detect only a questionable tint or form here and there out of the hundreds of forms in all colours standing out on the canvas.

The invention of the Gospel history, and the consistent connexion therewith of the immense body of dogma, morality, and mental philosophy contained in the historical books and epistles of the Christian Scriptures, would, even under the conditions now supposed, be a greater effort of human sagacity, knowledge, combination, and invention, than any existing monument of human genius.

How much greater would be the marvel, if the Gospel histories, so called, should have been the invention of any man or any possible association of men living at the period with which those supposed histories deal!

Form any supposition *possible* as to the persons who invented, the places in which they carried on their im-

Or of Credulous Enthusiasts. 79

position, their means of information, their political, linguistic, and geographical knowledge, and the suppositions will prove unequal to the weight of the Gospel, if it be an imposture.

If the writers, whoever they may be, do but deal with invented personages, and have but imagined the endless series of incidents which the Christian books record, they must have exposed themselves to detection at ten thousand points.

Consider with what various authors the accounts must agree, and by what an immense series of facts, superstitions, national and sectional views, transitory notions and permanent monuments, the accounts may be tested.

To mention only a few books still extant and available for refutation of mistakes in the Christian writings, let it be remembered that we have the Hebrew text of the Old Testament, the Samaritan Pentateuch, the Chaldæ Paraphrasts, the Targums, the Greek version called the Septuagint, the writings of Flavius Josephus, and of Philo the Jew. Would it be possible for an ideal Jewish character to be imagined and to be described as thinking, speaking, acting, quoting from existing books, dealing with the superstitions of those around him, and referring to the history of the past again and again, and yet to make no slips, and lay the invention open to no well-founded animadversions?

Or take another list of historians, politicians, naturalists, and poets, still remaining, whose works deal with the countries, incidents, climates, superstitions, theologies, moralities, and political conditions which the Christian books deal with more or less intimately: Herodotus, Plato, Livy, Aristotle, Virgil, Horace, Cicero, Cæsar, Lucretius, Juvenal, Tacitus, Pliny, Plautus,

Sallust, Cornelius Nepos, Strabo, Xenephon, Suetonius, Martial.

The chances of detection at the period when the books were undoubtedly committed to the world were numberless, and those chances have been multiplied with the advance of human knowledge and the collection of books in the immense libraries of modern days.

The historical truth of the books of the Christian Scriptures alone has saved them from complete refutation.

Suppose that the Gospels are the truthful records of events, and the Epistles the actual letters which they profess to be—that the writers were recording things which had passed under their own observation in the various countries and places they mention, and all is consistent and satisfactory; but if we reject this solution of the matter, because there is a miraculous element in the history, and a Divine person revealed, we propose a problem, the solution of which would necessitate something contrary to all probabilities and possibilities, something against nature, and not like a miracle, only above nature. We may reject the marvel of the incarnation and the miracles of the Gospels, but we can do so only by credulously accepting suppositions far more difficult of belief than are the facts which they are used to discredit.

In dealing, however, with the supposition of imposture, we are met with moral difficulties which are as much greater than the historical and literary difficulties, as *they* are greater than the difficulties besetting the verity of the Gospel history.

If one characteristic more than another pervades the acting and teaching of the Gospel, it is that of moral goodness. Meanness, hypocrisy, double-dealing, profession of godliness, without corresponding conduct, neglect of the relative duties on which the well-being of families and communities depend, evil thoughts, foolish words, impure actions,—these are everywhere condemned.

Moreover, the morality of the New Testament is not only in accordance with those eternal principles of right, which are so obvious that nearly all thinking men (not biassed and corrupted by vicious living) have recognized them; but in not a few cases, where evil habits and corrupt indulgences had brought in lower standards and more facile rules of conduct, the teaching of the Gospels and Epistles sets up again the true canon, and recals men to the simplicity of a good life. Let any opponent of Christianity, who can do so, point out wherein the moral teaching of the Christian books is such as might reasonably be expected from immoral impostors.

But again, imposture is an essentially selfish thing. Men seek to deceive because they have in view some selfish gratification, some coveted gain, some advantage centering in self.

Is this characteristic evident in Christianity? Is not New Testament teaching essentially unselfish? Does it not everywhere propose the ignorant, sinful, poor, outcast, and perishing, as the objects of attention and concern? Does it not constantly propose the advantage of others as an object to be pursued? Does it not bid us feed the hungry, clothe the naked, entertain the homeless, teach the ignorant, sympathise with the sorrowing, rejoice with the glad, and in all things to bear one another's burdens?

Christianity is the very beginning and basis of a nationality wide as the human race, and all-embracing as the atmosphere which envelopes the whole earth. It is the one system existing among men which gives the higher races of men a benevolent interest in those of a lower civilization and a coarser type, and regards the degraded Hotentot as brother to the Anglo-Saxon.

And, to take another point of view, when the principles of the Gospel are represented as wrought out in human lives, what kind of men are the inventions of the supposed impostors? What are the probabilities of Paul, Peter, John, Barnabas, Philemon, Onesimus, Gaius, being the creation of deceit or imposture?

But, above all, how does the character of Jesus Himself fall in with this supposition? As a boy He grew in favour with God and man. Although conscious of His Divine nature, He was obedient to His mother and reputed father. Among His circle of brothers and sisters and cousins He grew to manhood with no stain upon His character. In fulfilling all righteousness, He condescends to receive the seal of discipleship from His own servant, John. After forty days of fasting, He would not satisfy His hunger in any questionable or irregular way. When tempted to sin, He resisted successfully the allurements addressed to His flesh and will and soul. While continually exercising miraculous power on behalf of others, He suffered hunger and thirst and weariness, and had not where to lay His head. So high and pure and loving were His words, that even His enemies confessed, "Never man spake like this man," and they wondered at the gracious words which proceeded out of His mouth. He healed the broken heart of the widow by restoring her son to life. He comforted the mourning Jairus by calling back his daughter from death. He poured sunlight once again on the darkened home of Martha and Mary by calling back Lazarus from the corruption of the grave.

To the blind He gave the glorious outer world, with the faces of their dear ones. On the ears of the deaf He poured the music of breezes, and voices, and song. He gave to the weak feet strength, to the dumb the power of speech; health to the sick, food to the hungry, and cleansing to the lepers. His days were consumed in labour, and His nights in prayer. To His patience we can trace no limits, to His gentleness no bounds, and to His love no measure. His life is filled with evidences of darkness dispelled from human souls, of ignorance cast out, that the wisdom of God might find a place and throne; of the impure sanctified, and the worldly elevated to the dignity of a God-fearing life; of proud sinners humbled, and trembling sinners comforted; of a life of marvellous consecration, closed by a fitting death of self-sacrifice. Other records there are also, of life purchased by His death, peace won by His soul-agony, liberty secured by His bonds, sin dying in His death, and souls living in His resurrection.

If this character be an invention, it is utterly incomprehensible as the creation of immoral men. They could not have conceived it, nor would they have cared to invent it. Every line of the history would become the severest self-condemnation, every incident a lash on their own shoulders, every parable, appeal, reproof, a scorpion's sting, which would find out any assailable and sensitive point left in their diseased conscience.

Let us consider one more aspect of the matter. The Gospel history has been preached in many lands, and has been addressed to all classes and orders of men. It is a fact, that from age to age, in countless instances, the teaching of Christianity has aroused the conscience of men, begotten in them a sense of dissatisfaction and need, awakened even an agony of desire for purity, holiness, and renewal, and has led them to make sustained efforts to obtain those good things which they desired. It is a fact also, known to multitudes, that within the limits of the books of Holy Scripture these awakened and hungering souls have found the instruction, enlightenment, purification, and satisfaction which they needed. And it is no less certainly true that the uniform result has been that such persons have proved by words and deeds enemies to all immorality. Herein is a strange paradox on the supposition that Christianity is the invention of impostors!

We conclude, then, that Christianity is no such invention. We assert that it is impossible for the Gospel history to have been the work of impostors; and we assert also, that it cannot be the creation of credulous enthusiasts. If these two suppositions be rejected, what other remains, but that Christianity is true?

We have thus far repelled an attack. We now make an onward movement, and challenge men to point out from the Gospels what are the supposed evidences that they are fables and inventions. The experiment has been made, we know, over and over again; and if any one be inclined to try afresh, he will but add another to the mutually destructive schools of criticisms, each one of which has been slain by its fellow, leaving the faith of the Gospel mighty as ever in its power over men for sanctification and peace.

The Gospel is an anvil which has worn out many hammers, a rock which has rolled back ten thousand advancing waves throughout ages of tempest, a river of water of life, which all the dams of unbelief and secularism have failed to stop in its life-bearing and beneficent course.

We commend Christianity to the attention of men because it is true, because the Scriptures of the New Covenant which contain it, and the Scriptures of the Old Covenant, of which it is the logical completion and natural outcome, are evidenced as from God. All the evidences by which any matter can be proved testify to Christianity. Evidences from history, antiquities, national customs, geography, and topography, strengthen it on every side. The work of Jews and heathens, the attacks of enemies, and the apologies of friends, bear testimony to our Christian Scriptures. The buried marvels of Nineveh, disentombed after long ages ; the silent catacombs, opened after many centuries; the awful chambers of the pyramids, penetrated in these later years, have all voices testifying to the historic verity of the Bible. The rock inscriptions of the Sinaitic valleys, the discovered dwellings and temples and stones of Moab and Bashan, are eloquent with varied evidences. The cherished traditions of the Nestorians, the names of passes and mountains and fortresses in Affghanistan, and the documents, habits, and history of the Jewish colony discovered in the interior of China, are all witnessing to the reality and consistency of Bible narratives. In Palestine and Egypt and Syria, each stone has a voice, each mountain an echo, each stream a melody, each city a history, each village a memory; and all proclaim that the Gospel records are true.

The history of Greece and Rome, Chaldæa and Persia, of Tyre and Sidon, Judæa and Egypt, written by unbelievers, such as Volney and Gibbon, is at times expressed in terms which approximate wonderfully to the words of prophetic Scripture; the history as written proleptically in the Bible, and the same history as written by men who hated and sought to discredit the Bible, so strangely according, that the human history might be taken for the Divine prophecy, with but the tenses changed by the "Vav conversive" of time from the future to the past.

So long as the Jordan overflows its banks at harvest from the melting of the snows on Lebanon, so long as the waters of Gennesaret lave the ruins of Capernaum and the hill-sides of Gadara, so long as the Tigris and Euphrates flow by Nineveh and Babylon, and the Nile pours down her fertilizing waters through Goshen to the sea, so long as Kishon waters the foot of Carmel, and Abana and Pharpar make the plains of Damascus the garden of Syria, so long will the waters of earth make harmony to the song that the Lord, even the mighty God, has spoken to us in the books of Moses, by the pen of Samuel, the harp of David, the tears of Jeremiah, the odes of Isaiah, and the visions of Ezekiel;—so long will men confess that the four Evangelists and the writers of the Epistles are true witnesses and inspired teachers.

And what of the voices of the mountains? Who can know the voices of Horeb and Hor, of Carmel and Sirion, of Lebanon and Ararat, of Tabor and Olivet, and yet deny that the Bible is of God?

The Bible is indeed of God—omniscient, eternal, good; and not of men—credulous, dishonest, or mad. And because it is of God it demands of every man that obedience which the creature should render to his Creator, Preserver, Redeemer, Friend.

The words of the Lord are pure words, as silver tried seven times in a furnace of fire. The earth and all the things which are therein shall be burned up, but the word of the Lord endureth for ever.

THE FACTS OF CHRISTIANITY HISTORICALLY TRUE.

BY

B. HARRIS COWPER.

Christianity Historically True.

THE manufacture of history is by no means a modern art, but is one which has been cultivated from an early period. The objects in view have been political, religious, national, or personal; and it must be owned that Jew and Pagan, Mahommedan and Christian, have practised it with more or less success. The science of criticism is now, however, so developed, that the true character of fictitious and of semi-fictitious records can be ascertained with much precision. Hence, while it is difficult to uphold a false history or to launch one, it is a hopeless task to undertake the destruction of a true one. Limited and temporary success is all that the most fortunate can expect. The forgeries of long centuries and various nations have nearly all succumbed to the searching tests applied by modern skill, and have taken their true place in the literature of the world.

Among the books which have been most severely experimented on, we must rank the collection of documents popularly known as the New Testament. This work may be fairly subjected to criticism as claiming to be historical, although its contents comprise epistles, prophecies, and rules of life, as well as narratives in the ordinary sense of the word. The prophecies, rules of life, and epistles alike profess to have an historical basis or framework, and must therefore stand or fall with the rest. As for the narratives proper, they include supernatural occurrences, as well as others, and the supernatural elements are so incorporated with the human story, as it may be termed, that we cannot overlook them. The supernatural features have to be subjected to special investigations, which form no part of the object of this lecture; and yet their position is such that any conclusion respecting the record they are interwoven with will affect their credibility.

In recent times several attempts have been made to disprove the historical character of the fundamental records of Christianity, and men are to be found who doubt whether the New Testament can fairly put in a claim to be a history in the proper sense of the word. The bases of these doubts are mostly theoretical. It is assumed, for instance, that the New Testament has not that amount of literary corroboration which a genuine record ought to have. It is assumed that there is an insuperable obstacle to credibility in the supernatural elements of the book; science, we are told, cannot recognise the supernatural as a reality, and therefore its appearance in a record renders its rejection necessary. Besides, we are reminded of the tendency of men to frame narratives which are mythical; and so powerful and general is this tendency that we have many examples of mythical stories developed out of facts which are altogether transformed, and made to serve purposes to which they stand in no natural relation. Even when there is an historical person as a nucleus for a myth, and he is the prominent figure in it, everything is so exaggerated, that the result is a literary fiction. From such a fiction it is next to impossible to extract the meagre remains of history. Take for example the cases of Zoroaster Krishna, Buddha, or Apollonius of Tyana. How hard it is to separate and bring to light the truth concerning these personages ! With these examples the record of Jesus and His apostles has been compared, and like conclusions have been drawn from it. Zealous and imaginative men have filled in the imperfect outline, have given substance to mere shadow, and have incorporated opinions and suppositions which belong to a later age !

To all these theories we object. We believe the New Testament has all the corroboration required by the nature of the case to justify our strongest faith. We believe that the supernatural features of the record are not disproved by the admission that science cannot deal with them, and we shall continue to believe, until it is demonstrated that science has a right to deal directly with them. Nor shall we fail to bear in mind that science itself must recognise a great many essential elements of the book, even when it turns aside from the supernatural. Our own conviction is, that science is unscientific when it concludes against the supernatural, though we admit that it cannot submit the supernatural to ordinary tests. The truth is, that man can believe in the supernatural, is prone to believe it, and does believe it, and therefore even science must reckon this faith among the phenomena of human nature. He would be a bold man who said that this feature of our constitution is a defect, and that herein our race is so framed as almost universally to believe a lie.

With regard to the mythical hypothesis, it seems that

the best refutation of its application to the New Testament will be to show that there is no room for it in the case. It is excluded by the structure and position of the book, and by the conditions amid which the Christian Church was propagated and established in the world. The demolition of all mythical theories is effected by the same process as that which destroys the objection from want of evidence. This work will be the chief aim of the remainder of the present lecture. The attempt to weaken the history by the allegation that science rejects the supernatural no further concerns us on this occasion, although we must remember the historical conditions under which the supernatural facts of the New Testament appear. These conditions, be it observed, are altogether favourable to our faith in the actual occurrence of the said supernatural events, because we can plead the testimony we have for all facts, whether supernatural or not.

An examination of the New Testament will show that its facts are meant to be taken as historically true.

The form of the book is real and historical. There are four memoirs of Jesus Christ; we call them Gospels. There is a record of the actions of the leading disciples of Jesus, after His departure from the world; this we call the Acts of the Apostles. There are twenty-one epistles, avowedly written to actual persons, relating to real circumstances, and emanating from men who lived in the first age of the Church. Finally, there is a book called the Apocalypse or Revelation, which exhibits indications sufficiently clear to justify our assertion that it claims to be associated with the other writings, historically, at any rate. There are internal marks about these books and documents which show that, though not written by one man, nor in one place, they were composed in a certain

Christianity Historically True. 95

period, and by a class of men who professed to believe and uphold the Christian religion. If these documents, which are so real in form and substance, are merely works of imagination, the conspiracy or accident which produced them is as inexplicable as their silent acceptance everywhere by the Church. Their outward shape, their course of thought, and their grammatical forms and idioms are as purely and perfectly historical as the writings of Plautus and Cicero, Virgil and Horace, Xenophon and Demosthenes, Philo or Josephus; nay, they are as purely and perfectly historical as the works of Chaucer and Shakespeare, Milton and Johnson. Talk of literary corroboration! no documents in existence have it in a higher degree than the New Testament in its form and structure, from beginning to end. This venerable volume could not have been written in any age but that to which we assign it. Its Hebrew idioms, its Syriac phrases, its Alexandrian diction, and its Roman tinge, all point to one source and to one time. Thus we establish its claim to be accepted as an historical monument, and fix the era to which it belongs.

We may go further with our inquiries, and the result will still be favourable to the book. Taking the facts as they stand, we see at once that they belong to a known historical age. The course of the world's history is not absolutely unknown, and we can usually decide whether a record relates to a fabulous or to an historical age. Sometimes there are difficulties, as to the precise chronological position of a work. It is so with Homer, and the same is true of many of the books of the Hindoos and the Chinese, not to mention others. A collection of opinions respecting the age of Homer and the date and character of the events he puts on record in the Iliad, would show diversities of the most startling character. As for the Hindoo books, few indeed of the great Sanskrit writings can be said to belong to an historical age. The most contradictory judgments are formed as to the date of their composition, some placing them two thousand years later than others. Often, too, the form and scene are not at all historical, and all the powers of critics are employed in vain attempts to settle the age even to which they profess to relate. Illustrations are easily accessible, showing the truth of what has been advanced, and its applicability to numerous other so-called records. And, be it noted, that in spite of these tremendous difficulties, not a few of these books are accepted as embodying historical facts. The New Testament scene does not lie in some misty undefined portion of time, the place of which cannot be ascertained, but in a period as historical and as recognisable as that of Queen Elizabeth or Charles the Second.

The geography of the New Testament is historical. It includes empires and kingdoms, provinces and cities, mountains and oceans, rivers and valleys, which are all real and correctly indicated. The smallest villages equally with the largest cities are accurately represented and located. The progress of modern discovery has only tended to confirm the book in its minutest details. This is not usual with mythical and purely fabulous writings, with which, indeed, the rule is quite the opposite. The test is one which cannot be borne by the memoirs of Apollonius of Tyana, any more than by the legends of the Hindoo Krishna. So far, then, the New Testament is historical, and we can appeal to it as a genuine authority from first to last in this respect. Not a single erroneous detail in its geography and topography has been discovered, while it has furnished a clue for the recovery of long forgotten sites. The importance of this whole argument will be best illustrated by reference to a single branch of it, namely, political geography. During the first century various changes took place in the political divisions of countries included in the New Testament narratives. The imperial power of a Cæsar, the caprice of a Herod, and the favour of a state officer, equally sufficed to bring about the transfer of the inhabitants of a region from one governor to another, and to introduce a new jurisdiction, or to cancel an old one. In the case of cities, special privileges were enjoyed by some ; thus, for instance, one was called a metropolis, and another a colony, while peculiar distinctions were borne by men in power, from the highest to the lowest. All these topics come before the notice of the student who criticises the New Testament, and usually his faith is confirmed—it is never shaken by the result. The casual allusions of authentic writers, the technical terms on monuments of stone, and coins of metal, correspond with the intimations of the new Testament in so marvellous a way, that we fairly deduce an argument for its general historical character from these incidental facts.

Intimately connected with our object, also, is the question whether any fictitious persons are to be found in our New Testament. The author of the so-called Life of Apollonius introduced fictitious personages, and in so doing only did what every writer of fiction, epical, dramatic, or historical, from Homer to the latest authors in those branches of literature, has done and been compelled to do. A work of imagination on a large scale with no imaginary characters would be a unique specimen of the creative faculties. Now there is not one character

of the New Testament brought in as historical, which
can be proved to be anything else. There are necessarily some comparatively private individuals, and some
occupying a peculiar position, regarding whom we know
no more than this book teaches. But there are others
about whom we must certainly expect to find some
account elsewhere. The easiest method is to select
these last, and to use them as tests of the accuracy or
otherwise of the scriptural documents. Our position is
that the evangelists and others who wrote the New
Testament, not only bring in historical personages, but
correctly describe them. The royal family of Herod is
accurately introduced, and the personages, as well as the
general designations of its members, are without fault.
The fortunes of this family were very varied, and its
inner history very strange, but the evangelical writers
touch in a ready and accurate manner upon numerous
details extending over more than sixty years. The same
exemption from error appears in the designations of the
Roman Emperors, from Augustus Cæsar onwards, their
subordinates, as Cyrenius, Pilate, Gallio, Felix, and
Festus, Jewish priests, and others. Even eminent
women, as Herodias, Drusilla, and Bernice, are brought
forward in their historical place, and with absolute precision. We might urge the occurrence even of such
names as those of Jesus, James, and John the Baptist, all
of whom are mentioned by Josephus. This might be
done irrespectively of the famous passage (*Antiq*. xviii.
3. 3), in which the last-named writer speaks at length of
Christ, because he speaks of Him elsewhere (*Antiq*. xx.
9. 1). Of the testimonies supplied by Tacitus and Suetonius, by the Emperor Marcus Antoninus, and the brilliant scoffer, Lucian of Samosata, this is perhaps not the

place to discourse at length, though we may refer to them. In like manner we do not now insist on the Christian witnesses, though none but a very unreasonable logic would argue that they are of no value.

Our survey is little more than a bird's-eye view, but it would be incomplete if we observed not the substantial historical incidents which belong to the general records of the time. Even the famous dispute respecting the census or taxing under Cyrenius is scarcely, if at all, more than a question as to a date, and how two statements of one fact are to be harmonised when they seem to be chronologically different. The problem has been boldly grappled with, and among others by professor Zumpt, a German critic, with so much success that the *Quarterly Review* for April, 1871, in an article on his labours exclaims : "Here is a difficulty which but some thirty years ago Dr. Strauss was gloating over and declaring to be entirely insoluble, and now we behold it solved. Here we have another proof that Biblical studies are not, as they were once regarded, a stationary science, but, like all other sciences, admit of progression and increase." This is certainly not a discouraging circumstance, and, remembering that it does not stand alone, leads us to expect the removal of obscurity, in some other cases. Take the statement in Acts xviii. 2, that "Claudius had ordered all Jews to leave Rome." There is, we are told, no certain testimony to that edict, though it is known that the Jews were very severely dealt with by other emperors in that century, and the occurrence is very probable indeed. But there is more than this ; Suetonius informs us that " Claudius expelled the Jews from Rome for constantly rioting, Christ prompting them to it" (*Claud*. xxv.) Here we have a distinct affirmation of the fact that Claudius expelled the Jews from Rome, as we read in the Acts; it is coupled, however, with the curious explanation that Christ was the cause of their expulsion. Perhaps He was. Have we not here a striking comment on His own words, "I am come not to send peace, but a sword"? The Jews at Rome, as we understand Suetonius, discussed the Messiahship of Jesus, debating whether He was the Christ, with so much heat and vehemence, that from words they went to tumult and riot. This confusion exasperated the Emperor, who, in accordance with a popular error, treated Jews and Christians as two sects of one religon, and he ordered that the Jews should not remain in Rome. They left, no doubt, but very likely soon went back again.

On the whole question of the confirmation of the historical character of the New Testament, Mr. Lewin, the diligent author of "Fasti Sacri," may be here quoted. He says, "When the more closely I sift the records of that period, the more at every step I find the sacred penmen confirmed in their most casual and passing allusions to contemporary persons and ancient customs, I necessarily feel that my creed rests on no insecure foundation, that it is not the cunningly devised fable of an after age, but is part and parcel of actual history. . . . I believe that many who indulge in scepticism, do it, not from conviction, but from never having seriously addressed their attention to an inquiry into the truth." Mr. Lewin speaks not without a good reason in the shape of a volume of 500 closely printed large octavo pages. He who can refute the witnesses adduced in that work will have done much to overthrow the historical claims of the New Testament. An ambitious and learned unbeliever would immortalize himself if he succeeded in destroying the testimonies of that one book. But before he attempts it, let the would-be destroyer carefully consider what he undertakes.

The task of overthrowing the course of proofs upon which we stake the credibility of the New Testament cannot be so easy as if we addressed men's credulity, and not their intelligence. We have no relics surrounded with mystery, and held in reverential awe. If we showed you the stone which they exhibit at Toulouse, as the one which killed Stephen, you would not admit it as a proof of his martyrdom. If we took you to Rome, to the Church of St. Mary the Greater, and showed you the holy manger, the cradle, the hay, and the swaddling clothes, and the relics of five of the holy Innocents, you would not look on them as weighing a grain in the scale of evidence. It would be labour lost to exhibit to you the milk of the blessed Virgin, the wood of the cross, the shroud in which the dead Christ was wrapped. You would shrug your shoulders at the relics of Sts. Peter and Paul, Philip, James, and Bartholomew; at the head of St. Matthias, and at the arms of Matthew and Luke. This is but a fragment from a single list of the articles displayed at a single church in Rome. We have the same contempt for it that you have.

In like manner we do not ask you to explore, with pilgrims of easy faith, the places where, in Palestine and elsewhere, they pretend to show the identical spots where all the chief transactions of the life of Jesus occurred, and wind up the exhibition by pointing out His footmarks!

We have something much more satisfactory to bring before you. Such is the correspondence between the New Testament representations and the ascertainable facts. The antipathy which prevailed between the Jews and the Samaritans is sufficiently verified by passages from Josephus. The popularity and splendour of the temple and worship of Diana at Ephesus is attested by ancient writers, and demonstrated by recent excavations on the spot. The condition and state of Athens are shown by other witnesses to be correctly set forth in the Christian Scriptures. And so of other things. Our foes have failed to discover the unhistorical, and have been driven or shut up to general expressions of discontent, and to assaults upon the miraculous elements. But surely it is no light argument in our favour that we can confirm the incidental statements of our book to such an extent, that of those which belong to ordinary history, very few remain unconfirmed, and none are known to be fictitious. It may be said that in a few instances there are chronological or other differences of detail between what we read in the New Testament and in the works of some other writers. Nor do we care to deny that it is so, because it remains to be shown that our book is less credible than the others, and that it is wrong wherever it does not perfectly coincide with them.

There is another reason for the truly historical character of the Christian Scriptures, arising out of their moral tone and the impression they produce. From first to last there is an uniform avoidance of mere rhetorical phraseology; all is calm, and dignified, and natural. The idea of producing the studied "effects" which characterise all writers of fiction, is never entertained by the evangelical penmen. The things which are peculiar to Christianity are so interwoven with the characters and details which may be called external, that the result reminds us of the warp and woof of a textile fabric. As these cannot be separated without destroying the piece, so will it be if we seek to extract from the New Testament the purely Christian element, and to leave the secular.

That the veracity of the Christian writers is a reality is to be inferred from their constant attitude in relation to truth and its kindred virtues. They inculcate sincerity and honesty of the most absolute description; the practice of hypocrisy, fraud, and lying is prohibited in the most solemn terms, and denounced in language of terrible power and significance. Christians are exhorted to put away lying, and to speak truth to one another; it is declared that liars are excluded from all the blessings offered by the Gospel in this world and in that to come, and Jesus is represented as asserting that Satan is the father of lying. On the other hand, the commendations paid to truth and sincerity, the inducements offered to men to make them true, and the representation of God Himself as absolutely true, are equally unqualified. To all which we ought to add the reiterated affirmations of the writers and speakers, that what they say is true. So much in favour of truth is scarcely possible in a book which is framed in falsehood and deceit. Consistently to sustain these professions of truth would not be within the power of any band of impostors. But these men held fast their profession, and bequeathed their book to the world as true. To suggest that they were mistaken is to imply that they were insane; and, in truth, the suggestion itself is not strongly rational, because a body of men, not one, but several, must have laboured under a delusion respecting a supposed train of occurrences extending over many years, and in which they were personally concerned. The suggestion also encounters the difficulty originated by the pervading tissue of known historic fact, and the impracticability of placing a finger upon any ascertained fiction.

Let us now take a somewhat different position, and see what there is outside the book in favour of our opinion. The adversary must in all honour concede our first two propositions, namely, (1) that the existence of the Christian records can be traced back to a date very near to that which we ascribe to them, and (2) that the earliest witnesses for their existence believed the facts set out in those records. The proof for these two is identical. To establish it we need not begin with the much maligned Eusebius of Cæsarea, who, as a compiler of ancient history, occupies an important place from a purely secular point of view. We can dispense with Athanasius, and Lactantius, and Cyprian. We have older witness than Origen, and Hippolytus, and Clement of Alexandria. Tertullian is not indispensable for our purpose. The labours of the chronicler, Julius Africanus, and of the historian, Hegesippus, may be passed over as no more essential than those of Papias. All these and a hundred more venerable names, though dead, yet speak, and proclaim themselves witness for the facts of the Christian's Book; but we may fearlessly pass beyond them, assured that the nearer we come to the source of its light we shall not be the more involved in darkness.

Plunging at a bound across seventeen centuries, we find on every hand Christian communities. They are to be seen on the northern shores of Africa, and in the valley of the Nile; they are scattered over Palestine and Syria; they spread away into and across the vast plains of Mesopotamia; they are sprinkled along the coasts and among the provinces of Asia Minor, from east to west, in Smyrna and Ephesus, as well as in less populous cities; they are numerous in Macedonia and Achaia and other Grecian provinces; they are planted in Italy, with Rome as their centre; they are distinguishable in Gaul, and indeed are more widely extended than the Roman Empire. All this is the work of little more than a century; and all these churches believe the facts recorded in the New Testament! Who can so much as imagine all these myriads deceived? Among their leaders and ministers were men who had been Jews and Pagans, but who had been convinced that Jesus was the Christ, and that what was told of Him and the apostles was true. There were men of learning and philosophers, who had submitted to the evidences which they at first had only despised. We cannot think that light arguments persuaded Athenagoras of Alexandria, Tatian of Syria, Bardesanes of Edessa, Theophilus of Antioch, Melito of Sardis, Justin Martyr of Samaria, Sixtus of Rome, or Irenæus of Lyons. Yet we find them one and all, with many more, associated with the Christian flock as believers in the facts of Christianity. If their sincerity is not attested by their conversion, nor sealed by the blood of those who died for Christ, their knowledge of the facts of the New Testament, and their avowal of belief in them, is demonstrated by their simple profession.

Observe also that these early churches accepted certain institutions which were commemorative of some of the cardinal facts of the New Testament. They had the rite of baptism; they were familiar with Sunday as a memorial of the resurrection of Jesus from the dead; they observed the Lord's Supper, as a memento of His crucifixion; and, we may add, the Easter festival itself can be traced back at least to the middle of the second century. The grandfathers and grandmothers of those who kept these feasts might many of them have been living when Christ died upon the cross; and we know that some of them conversed with men who knew the apostles. It is difficult to see what place there is for imposture, delusion, or myth, in the presence of these facts. The hypothesis of a combination of leaders to deceive the people is simply impossible. Not only were these leaders too numerous, but too many interests were at stake, and too many eyes were upon them; nor were the people all fools or knaves.

That the New Testament facts were publicly extant is proved by other forms of evidence. The books in which they are composed were in existence and were circulated. They are mentioned by some Christian authors of that age, and were used by all. They lie at the foundation of all the earliest Christian literature now extant. Their influence and very form moulded the thoughts and language of Irenæus, Justin, and others already named, as well as of Polycarp, Ignatius, and the rest. The documents were necessarily published and common in Greek; they were translated into Latin, and into Syriac, and were partly extant at least in the Hebrew of that time. The whole civilized world therefore had ample opportunity of refuting them if untrue. But from none, whether on the banks of the Nile or of the Jordan, the Euphrates or the Tigris, the Tiber, the Rhone, or the Hellespont, did there sound forth a protest against the substantial truth of the Christian Book.

Narrowing our range as we advance, we come to the

very borders of the apostolic age; but even there, in the scanty literary remains which have survived the ordeal of modern criticism, we find the same unfaltering witness to, and acceptance of, the facts of Christianity. The beautiful letter to Diognetus, the vigorous but eccentric document called after Barnabas, the gushing utterances of Ignatius, and the admirable counsels of Clement, are unanimous. Clement, in fact, belongs to the apostolic age, and he bears brilliant testimony to Jesus and His apostles, Paul, for example, whose first Epistle to the Corinthians is explicitly quoted. Clement is the link which connects with Christ and the New Testament the chain of evidence which extends to our own day. Of this chain every link is uniform, complete, and radiant with light. It lays hold on Christ the rock of ages; it has sufficed to sustain the faith of His Church from the beginning; and as generations pass new links are added. God be thanked, the longer it lasts and the longer it is, the stronger it grows. The variations of the needle which points to the pole are far greater than those of the witness which points to the Saviour.

At a very early date men arose who put a peculiar explanation on the facts, or associated them with other facts and speculations. Hence came what we call heresies. These began in the lifetime of the apostles, as we may gather from the New Testament. It is palpable, however, from all the evidence we have, and some of it very ancient, that these heresies affected the reality of but a small number of the facts recorded in the Christian records. Even the one which regarded Christ as not a real man in flesh and blood, is not essentially adverse to our view, because the question raised was one of interpretation. It was admitted that Jesus appeared as a man, and as a human being appeared to teach, and so of the rest; and this was a recognition of the historic facts. So strange were the theories advanced by some founders of heresy, that we cannot avoid thinking they would gladly have rejected, had it been possible, not a few of the incidents set forth in the New Testament. That they had that book is known in regard to some of them who accepted it in a form more or less entire. The rejection of parts implies the existence of the whole, and does not imply the rejection of historic statements so much as rejection of authority. Some of the earliest commentators on the Gospels were heretics, of whom Basilides was a notable example, living as he did early in the second century, and was born in the first.

That the prevalent belief which we find so widespread in the second century, and even before, was no idle assent to a myth, may be inferred from other facts, to which we appeal in support of our argument. Nobody can trace Jesus and the apostles to an earlier date than that the evangelical writers refer them to. Therefore, if the records were untrue or mythical, they must not only have originated in an historical age, but very soon indeed after, nay, almost before, some of the alleged writers were dead. Observe, too, that no one can trace these narratives to any original source, except the country from which they may be said to have all emanated, although not all written in Palestine. Bear in mind, also, that the acceptance of the evangelical story and Epistles was fraught with consequences far more serious than we can easily realize, and that therefore belief, as a rule, must have been the result of powerful conviction. Put all these things together, and you will perceive in them a fresh group of reasons in favour of the historical veracity of the New Testament.

It is just possible that some might here urge as an objection the case of the so-called Apocryphal Gospels, respecting which we have been told that they are as ancient as the Canonical Gospels, are as well attested, and were equally received in the early Christian Church. Each of these assertions is incorrect; 1, they are not so ancient; 2, are not as well attested; and, 3, were not equally received in the early Church. The earliest extant author who refers to apocryphal books is Irenæus, far on in the second century; but it is said such documents were used before his time, which is very likely, in fact is certain, because he himself tells us so. From him we gather the important fact that the spurious and fabulous books were the production of erratic heretics. An attempt has been made to find quotations from Apocryphal Gospels in Justin Martyr and Ignatius, but with very unsatisfactory results. What Clement of Alexandria calls the Gospel according to the Hebrews, seems to have been a modification of one of our Gospels; and the same may have been the case with others. But one fact results from all inquiries, and it is that the apocryphal books were imitations of the canonical, were intended to supply supposed historical omissions, or were meant to be the vehicle of peculiar doctrines; all which proves them the less ancient. As to their being well attested, nothing of the kind appears in those examples which we possess, but very much to suggest that they are considerably more modern, and are not attested at all. Of their acceptance by the churches, the less said the better; because we have no proof of their reception as authorities by the early Fathers or the early

Church. Not one of them ever found its way into the canon; they either perished, like the heresies which produced them, or took their place among avowedly legendary literature. Some of them may be mythical, in the loose sense in which the Life of Apollonius is so; but they occupy a very different position from the myths of Greece, Italy, and India.

The historical character of the New Testament has been assailed on the ground of the alleged silence of contemporary historians. To this we have already referred; but we must mention it again in order to add some things which come in better here. In the first place, no writer can be found from whom we might justly look for mention of some of the facts, who does not mention them. It is a curious circumstance that there was no writer of the history of that period from Velleius Paterculus, who concluded his work in about A.D. 30, to Josephus, who wrote not less than sixty years later. For the great events of that long period we are dependent upon other sources. We are told of Philo; but Philo was not an historian in any proper sense; he lived in Egypt, and died before any of the Christian Scriptures could have been circulated. Not one of his extant works brings him into contact with such movements as the introduction of Christianity. About A.D. 40 or 41 he went to Rome on a mission connected with the Jews, his countrymen; but there was nothing in that to call for any allusion from him to Jesus and the apostles. His object was such that, as a prudent man, he would say nothing of Christianity, whatever he might know. In the meantime Philo is a valuable witness in our favour in several respects. He mentions various facts which are noticed in the New Testament as belonging to the

Christianity Historically True. 111

history of the period; he confirms the New Testament representations of the condition of the Jews and of the state of opinion among them; and his use of Greek words aud phrases, which are peculiar, harmonises extensively with the same things in the New Testament.

With reference to the assertion that the writers of the Christian Scriptures are not mentioned until long after they must have been dead, we may safely say that it is no real objection at all. If the principle were applied to other writers, as a test, a large number of the most generally received would have to be rejected. It would be so with the two most recently named in this lecture. Velleius Paterculus may possibly be alluded to as a man, but not as an author, by Tacitus; and it is probable that he is meant in a passage of Priscian, in the fourth century. This is all the ancient external testimony we have for him. The name of Philo and his journey to Rome first appear in Josephus, some fifty years after his death; but even Josephus mentions none of his writings. The second to speak of him is Justin Martyr, another fifty years later; and the third is Clement of Alexandria, fifty years later again. We may well ask the man of little faith why he accepts Velleius Paterculus and Philo, but refuses Matthew, Mark, Luke, and John, Peter and Paul!

Another point of considerable importance is the silence of the adversaries of the Church. Whatever objections to details and principles were made by Julian and Porphyry, Celsus, and the rest, we search in vain for any intimation that they denied the historical basis and framework of the New Testament. These were no ignoble and ignorant opponents, but men of position, ability, and learning; yet they shrank from uttering the broad denials which are so current in our day. Julian was an emperor, and in him centred the last hopes of the old paganism; and surely, with all the resources of the age at his command, and all the will required, he would have discovered and proclaimed the fact that the Church was founded upon a fable, and that there was no place in history for the records of the New Testament. He adopts a different course; he recognizes Matthew, Mark, Luke, John, and Paul, by name as writers, but he assails their doctrine, he rejects the supernatural. The cases of Porphyry and Celsus were similar. We fail then to find any intimation that any of the earliest opponents of Christianity occupied the position which we are attacking to-day. Their very silence is eloquent. If we are told that the Christians burnt the books of their enemies, we may say that this was not till a comparatively late period, and we are sorry that Christians followed the bad example set them by their persecutors. In the meantime we have still so many arguments in favour of Christianity in very early writers, and so many replies to the objections then advanced, that we know perfectly well what the unbelievers of those ages had to say. It does not appear from any extant records that the Jews attacked the New Testament on broad historical grounds, any more than the Gentiles did.

Both Jews and Gentiles allowed the Church to spread its Scriptures far and wide, without an attempt to expose their now supposed unhistorical character. No one can say they were slack in their attempts to destroy the rising faith. The new doctrines were mocked and ridiculed and held up to scorn; the believers were branded as ignominious apostates; bonds and imprisonments, exile and the arena, fire and sword, were their

Christianity Historically True. 113

portion; the pride of the Cæsars frowned upon them; the vanity of the philosophers despised them; the bigotry of the Jews was bitter against them; the very superstition of the multitudes was in a fury with them; the satirists lampooned them; the orators denounced them; the priests hated them; the judges condemned them; and the wild beast or executioner despatched them. You know the result. The more they were afflicted the more they multiplied, and the blood of the martyrs was the seed of the Church. The Christian books remained unrefuted, and the imperial edicts were unable to suppress them. They went abroad, were copied, and translated, and men at all risks believed, and loved, and obeyed them. Throw yourselves into these circumstances, and realize, if you can, the possibility of a shameless fiction surviving such an ordeal, and gaining new power from day to day. It is not the way of men to accept in vast numbers, and to retain amid such risks, stories for which there is not only no foundation, but the exposure of which is an easy work. We seek in vain for any parallel to the case of the early Church, and we may safely affirm that the phenomenon is explicable only on the principle that the record on which it depended was historically and divinely true.

That record is still extant, and it invites investigation. It is willing to undergo, as a book, all the legitimate tests to which a book can be subjected. It requests the philologist to analyse its language, the archæologist to explore its references to works of human skill; the botanist and zoologist to indentify its references to animal and vegetable life; the historian to investigate its allusions to contemporary history; the Jew to try its indications of Hebrew customs and opinions, laws, and traditions;.

the Gentile to search into what it says of the idols and worship of the heathen; every man who is a competent authority on any alleged fact in its pages, and by their verdict it is willing to be judged.

It has been thus tried in every generation; it has passed many times through this manifold ordeal; it is passing through it now. But while the fashion of the world has been changing, and the wisdom of the world has varied from age to age, faith in the New Testament as both true and the word of the Lord has remained, and is destined to abide for ever.*

* It will be recollected that Gilbert West, an accomplished sceptic of the last century, set himself to apply the ordinary laws of evidence to the New Testament record of the resurrection of Jesus Christ; the result was the restoration of faith, and a book in defence of the records of the resurrection. Dr. Johnson says, "When West's book was published, it was bought by some who did not know his change of opinion, in expectation of new objections against Christianity." To this anecdote another, no less famous, may be added. It is related of Thomas Lord Lyttelton, that "in early life he had been led to entertain doubts of the truth of revelation; but a serious inquiry into the evidences of the Christian religion produced in his mind a firm conviction of its Divine authority, in which he persisted to the end of his life. He gave a public testimony of his attachment to the cause by a 'Dissertation on the Conversion of St. Paul,' printed in 1747, which is justly regarded as a masterly performance."
—*Rose's General Biographical Dictionary.*

SCIENCE AND SCRIPTURE NOT ANTAGONISTIC, BECAUSE DISTINCT IN THEIR SPHERES OF THOUGHT.

BY THE

REV. GEORGE HENSLOW, M.A., F.L.S., F.G.S.,

LECTURER ON BOTANY AT S. BARTHOLOMEW'S HOSPITAL.

Science and Scripture not Antagonistic, because distinct in their Spheres of Thought.

PART I.

INTRODUCTORY.

The Objects of Science.

IN order that there may be no misunderstanding as to the proper usage of terms, it is desirable to state or define clearly, at the very outset of a disquisition, any expressions about which a discussion may arise. On the present occasion, the two mentioned in the subject of this essay are not difficult to define. *Scripture* is synonymous with the Bible; while by *Science* is meant the investigation of facts and phenomena recognizable by the senses, and of the causes which have brought them into existence. Hence Science endeavours to trace out the laws which govern the changes they may undergo.

The objects of scientific research are so numerous, that it is necessary to divide and subdivide them into many departments: thus we have natural, experimental, physical, social, and other branches of science too numerous to mention.

If we consider the objects of a few of such branches, selecting, for example, *physical* science, and of that, the study of electricity and magnetism, we should probably find that the phenomena presented by these subtle forces were first examined solely for the love of acquiring knowledge; but a great practical result issuing from them is Telegraphy. Or, if we turn to *chemistry*, there is scarcely a single art or manufacture that is not largely indebted to that branch of experimental science; while a knowledge of the laws of health, and the practical endeavours to furnish the conditions requisite for their action, both internally and externally to our persons, is largely aided by familiarity with chemical science. Similarly, the investigation into the laws of heat have aided mankind to an immeasurable degree by the application of steam.

It will appear from a few considerations of this sort that we may regard scientific pursuits, or rather the motive for pursuing them, from two points of view.

On the one hand, it is solely from the love of and thirst for knowledge, without any reference or definite idea as to the probability of that knowledge bringing forth some practical result: for example, it is not clear how the spectroscopic analysis of the light of a nebula can be of any practical use to mankind; nor how the structure of the fishes of an ancient geological period is at all likely to assist pisciculture at the present time.

On the other hand, branches of science may be pursued with a practical motive only, as when physical laws are studied in engineering, chemistry for improvements in candle manufacturing; vegetable physiology for the application of its principle in the cultivation of plants, whether agricultural or horticultural.

Now it will hardly be maintained, certainly not by

any liberal-minded and intellectual person, that Science should not be studied unless it can be shown that the pursuit leads to some practical end. The desirability of studying some branch merely as an intellectual stimulus is so generally recognised, that it would be waste of time to argue against such gross utilitarianism. Admitting the recognised love for Science, and the delight in pursuing it, as a natural and wholesome impulse, it seems strange that any persons should be found at the present day who can condemn the pursuit; for it is but one form of the *search after truth.*

The naturalist, for example, on investigating the laws which govern the development of animal and vegetable life, does no more than examine as accurately and carefully as he can the animals and plants brought under his notice, and then traces the laws governing the changes which take place in their forms and structures, and the laws governing their development and reproduction. If he cannot discover the cause of any phenomenon completely, he uses such knowledge as he possesses of similar or analogous causes, and by means of it supplements this unknown cause by a certain amount of reasonable and probable grounds of conjecture, and so frames an hypothesis or theory, holding it, however, with a light hand until he acquire more knowledge, and so discover the entire and proper cause, *i.e.*, if his suggestion shall have ultimately proved wrong.

Science, in its development under man's study, cannot advance at all without such theories and hypotheses; they are the temporal stepping-stones to knowledge, to be shifted or abandoned as soon as the right road is discovered.

It is a proof of ignorance of the method of progress

of all kinds of science, if any one ridicule and condemn such theories. They frequently appear absurd to the uninitiated; in fact, it may be generally stated, that what persons do not understand they are strangely inclined to despise. Not being scientifically trained, they do not appreciate the difficulties encountered by the scientific investigator, and they cannot understand why he does not put before them at once absolute and positive reasons at every turn of his scientific enquiries.

They are apt to scorn and scoff at the results which he has arrived at by long and tedious processes of reasoning, merely because they seem to them, *à priori*, absurd; simply because they do not tally with their own ignorance. The most flagrant example, and now a matter of history, was the case of Galileo; how, when he stoutly maintained that the sun did not go round the world to produce day and night, the inquisitorial powers condemned him to recant; but truth would not be thus chained down, and so, rising from his knees, he said "Ah! the earth moves for all that!" Well knowing this, men still hoot and scowl at theories even now, which are in advance of, if not contrary to, early received or traditional belief. They will not take the trouble to give five minutes' investigation into the subject, or make the slightest attempt to follow the line of thought which the scientific man has been patiently, it may be for years, closely and unintermittently pursuing, his sole object having been to elicit from nature her voice of truth.

In thus alluding to objections raised by certain non-scientific persons against science, their animadversions would seem to be directed against certain departments of science; for one does not often hear of any serious opposition, *i.e.*, to chemistry, electricity, botany, or to social science, the object being generally supposed at least harmless, if not beneficial; while in the last-mentioned case, the object of men of known philosophic characters is esteemed good, as aiming at the well-being and improvement of social condition.* But the science which seems to have called forth the greatest amount of ridicule, abuse, and opposition, is *Geology*, coupled with the doctrine which has partially grown out of it, viz., evolution of living things, and as an extension of that doctrine, according to some theorists, the origin of man himself.

It will be necessary to consider wherein the objection lies, and if possible to meet it.

Now, to do this, we must first consider the scope, of Scripture, for it may be stated at once that the objection appears to lie in erroneous and preconceived ideas derived from Scripture, that is, the Bible.

Having done this, I shall return to geology, and then bring Science and the Scriptures face to face.

PART II.

THE SCRIPTURE, OR THE BIBLE.

With regard to this book, the following facts are so well known and so easy of proof, that we need not stop to discuss them: That half of it was written in Hebrew, and that the greater portion of that half concerns the history of the Jews, a race of people still existing, and

* It is true there are certain special pleaders for social science, falsely so called, but they are pleaders for the guilty, not the innocent.

who cherish that portion of the Scriptures which refers to them with the most jealous care. The other half was written in Greek, and consists of a few memoirs of a most remarkable man called Jesus Christ, who, as these memoirs detail, promulgated not exactly a new religion, but one of a more comprehensive and liberal kind than that taught in the Old Testament, and which was for the Jews' special benefit, but which they have rejected. Moreover, the religion of Jesus Christ is identically the same with that advanced by several writers, whose epistles are bound up in the same volume with the memoirs alluded to. It is not that each individual writer has advanced *his* view of what religion or morality should be, but that each and all have described and enforced the same religion advocated by Jesus Christ. Observe, too, that this religion has something in it which appeals to the intuitions, feelings, and reason of mankind; that wherever other so-called Christian teachers have endeavoured to advocate it *aright*, it has been accepted. The result is, that Christianity, together with its aberrant and semi-Judaistic form, Muhammadanism, which includes base concessions to man's weakness, inadmissible however in the pure teaching of Christ, has occupied an immense area of the world.

Now, if we inquire into the nature and scope of Christianity, we shall find that, in the first place, it may be described as an effort to restore to a recognised position of superiority those virtues which, until Christ came, had been relegated to an inferior place: the virtues of charity, gentleness, kindness, mercy, pity, meekness, and the like, having been despised of men; while mere animal or physical courage, if sufficient, could make a man a god.

Secondly, self-sacrifice for others was to be a leading feature, instead of selfishness; and to do to others what we should wish them to do to us, was to be the guiding rule of our life.

Thirdly, every form of uprightness, honesty, probity, truthfulness, and the like, were strictly enforced.

Surely it is hardly needful to pursue this subject, for the more we unravel the precepts and the principles of the Gospel, the further do we advance from any supposed injurious contact with science. For the object of this essay is not to propound or display the system of Jewish or Christian morality, but to endeavour to discover any discrepancies between them and science. This cannot be done. Everything shows that their *spheres of thought* are totally distinct. On the one hand, science has for its object the knowledge of the material world and all upon it, *i.e.*, the development of the human intellect. On the other hand, the Scriptures unfold the method of improvement of human morality. The one makes man intellectually wise, the other renders him spiritually good.

Science aids him to benefit his physical and social condition of life on this earth. Religion improves his moral life here, and fits him for eternity.

Having thus seen that the objects of science and the Scriptures are totally distinct, let us now consider some of the statements made by certain critics of the Bible, before returning to the only point where there would seem to be any real disagreements, viz., between geology and the first chapter of Genesis.

The first objection, and a very old one, is, that it is frequently inaccurate when scientific facts are alluded to. This objection has almost been withdrawn by opponents themselves; for it is so clear that *appearances* are alluded to, and *not absolute facts*, that the object of the allusion is in no way impaired by the substitution, and that, as a matter of scientific fact, the writer had no intention of displaying his knowledge, that the objection completely loses its force. Hence, to say that the sun stood still is paralleled by our own expression, the sun rises and sets. Moreover, a strictly accurate expression would have conveyed no meaning to the people who witnessed the sight. Had Moses said, for example, "Stand still, thou earth!" for the earth was apparently at rest, no arresting its motion would have been perceptible. On the other hand, many expressions, which must have seemed perplexing to people at the time, have since been proved to have been correct ; such, for example, as, " My doctrine shall drop as the rain, my speech shall *distil* as the dew" (Deut. xxxii. 2). Compare with this the common but erroneous expression, "The dew falleth." "The wind whirleth about continually, returning again according to his circuits" (Eccl. i. 6). No one then knew that winds are portions of cyclones, and also travel in circuits round the poles of the earth.

Again, Job says, chapter xxvi., verse 7, "He hangeth the earth upon nothing; He maketh weight for the winds." Wind was not known to have weight until Priestly invented the barometer, and the weight of air is now measured by that instrument. Again, in chapter xxxviii. 31, Job asks, "Canst thou bind the sweet influences of the Pleiades?" It is now pretty satisfactorily established that the Pleiades form the focus of our system; that just as our planets revolve round the sun, so the sun, *together with* all the members of our system, revolve round the Pleiades.

In Deut. xxxii. 24, we meet with a strictly true and scientifically accurate expression of physiology, "They shall be *burnt* with hunger, and devoured with burning heat." The consumption of the body by hunger is as strictly a burning as a coal is burnt in the fire!

Such are a few of the strictly scientific expressions in the Bible; and what is particularly worthy of note is, first, that their accuracy could not have been known at the time they were written; and, secondly, the popular expressions of to-day are far more inaccurate, yet we never call them in question, because their use never misleads, but conveys the meaning intended by the speaker. For example, to speak of roots of a potato; the dew falling; thunder affecting ale; the sun rising and setting.

With regard to the fact of inaccurate expression being found in the Bible, it is most important to remember that the Scriptures were never intended, nor their writers inspired, for the express purpose of teaching astronomy, geology, physiology, or any other science. Nevertheless it is both interesting and useful to observe how Scriptural expressions are found, after all, to agree with the discoveries and deductions of modern science.

PART III.

GENESIS COMPARED WITH GEOLOGY.

There are a few preliminary remarks to be made with reference to the language of Scripture, as well as to our translation, or the received version; not to add the various interpretations of its meanings, which will preclude all idea of any *à priori* certainty as to an absolute and indubitable meaning being always capable of extraction.

In the first place, one of the most obvious facts noticeable in Scripture is its utter want of any scientific precision in its use of terms. Whenever a scientific fact is introduced, it is in popular language, and such as would be understood by a person living at the time in which it was uttered. This is no more than might be expected. Science did not exist in the days included, not merely by the Pentateuch, but even during that of the entire Bible itself. Moreover the writers, not giving any exposition of science, never aim at expressing themselves scientifically.

This unscientific but popular style is very observable in the frequent use of terms without any definition: as in the case of the *soul* and *spirit* of man; consequently it is next to impossible to secure an accurate comprehension of their meaning in each case.

A word closely concerned with the subject herein discussed may be mentioned as an example; viz., the "firmament." Again, we cannot distinguish between "Created" (*Bara*), and "made" (*Asah*). Though there are these two distinct words, yet we are quite unable to discover whether there be really any *absolute* distinction between them or not.

With regard to our received version, it is most unfortunate that the same word in the original frequently receives more than one rendering in English: thus the words διαβολος and αγαπη have each more than one rendering; while ἀγαπᾶν and φιλεῖν are translated alike.

Lastly, the great diversity of meanings which different persons put upon the same passages, and which have given rise to as many sects in the Church of Christ, ought to be sufficient to prove that we cannot necessarily expect an unmistakable rendering everywhere in the words of Scripture.

We cannot, therefore, be too cautious in adapting a scientific value to any particular passage of Scripture: for an argument based upon such a rigid interpretation as we may give it would fall to the ground, from the fact that the passage being unscientifically expressed could not bear so severe a strain upon it.

An illustration of this may be seen in theologians adapting the meaning of indefinite time to the word *Yom*. For, when geology had advanced sufficiently to be able to show incontestably that, whatever the "days" of Genesis might mean, they could not possibly signify that the world was created within the space of six literal days, theologians, finding they must yield to scientific discoveries, immediately adopted the above interpretation, resting their belief upon the expression, "One day with the Lord is as a thousand years." But, if the chapter be read without any reference to geology, and the first three verses of the second chapter be carefully compared with the fourth commandment, I think no one would ever dream of giving such a rendering to *Yom*. The simplest rendering, and the most natural one, is an ordinary day, and nothing more.

Now, the question at once arises, Is there any possible reconciliation between the days of Genesis and the ages of geology? I believe there is, though wherever one cannot feel positive, it is far better to confess our ignorance, and wait for more light, rather than to force an unnatural meaning upon a passage, where no such interpretation was intended.

In the first place, the evidence of geology is too plain to be refuted. It is no use abusing science, nor persecuting the geologist any longer, much less dreading him as encroaching upon, if not undermining, the long-cherished belief derived from erroneous scriptural interpretations.

I, for one, prefer to believe my rendering of Genesis to be imperfect, rather than regard geological time as wrong. I feel that my convictions, based on the study of the structure of the earth, are more sure than my interpretations of the fragmentary notices handed down in thirty-one verses of Scripture.

But again I repeat, I do not believe there is any disagreement, and for the reasons which I shall now proceed to give.

First, let us endeavour to arrive at some at least probable meaning of this word day.

I *know* it was *not* a day.

I at once feel inclined to speculate as to what these days mean; but, at the same time, I am bound to recognize the fact that I can but speculate, while I am thankful that no part of my morality, no part of salvation, depends in the slightest degree upon the questions connected with the origin of the world. I can perceive clearly that the real object of Scripture has, so to say, nothing to do with the first chapter of Genesis, and so I am indifferent as to whether my suppositions be true or not.

We have seen sufficient of the objects of Scripture to know that they are for the good of man, for the development of his morality and religion; and though we may find an account of the creation, it matters not whether we understand it, or fail to do so, that is, so far as the good of our souls is concerned.

Let us now enter upon a short enquiry as to the probable meaning of the word "day."

The first thing I notice is that the writer could not have been present, nor a witness of the progress of creation. No man was alive. How, then, was a knowledge acquired?

On reading the injunctions from the Lord so frequent during the times of the kings of Israel and Judah, there is the frequent expression, "Thus saith the Lord," and then follows the actual words as uttered. It is not so here. The expressions used are of a descriptive style, as if from an observer or listener.

May not, then, these descriptions be of views brought before the writer's eye during six distinct *nightly* visions? It is not out of keeping with God's methods of instruction to adopt dreams and visions, while the remarkable expression that the evening and the morning were a day seems to lend countenance to the idea; for the views would be, so to say, daylight views, though seen in a dream at night, that is, between evening and a morning.

I offer this to be accepted or rejected as any man thinks best, and as the only interpretation that I can suggest. It is worth while observing, if this was the origin of the days, and if the seer was left to make his own observation, and to draw his own inferences from the sights presented to him, describing only what he saw and heard, that there is nothing of the nature of *falsehood* either *here* or in the fourth commandment, any more than in the words, " Sun, stand thou still."

If in either case the expressions were used for the purpose of teaching science, it might perhaps be considered so; as this however was not the case, neither the one nor the other convey any falsehood. "For in six days the Lord made heaven and earth" might be paraphrased somewhat as follows: In the period of time represented or included within those six visions of the Creator. In fact, here, as in other instances of Scripture, *appearances* take the place of scientific descriptions of facts, and do duty for them. As long as no one could appreciate the science, and while the appearance would convey any lessons more truly than strictly scientific or accurate expressions could do, then the best way to convey the truth intended is clearly by means of the appearances rather than the actual facts.

In suggesting the hypothesis that the seer was presented with six panoramic views of creation, I would add that they would only be such as he could see at one glance. There is no necessity to believe, even if it were possible, that he saw the whole of the surface of the globe at each time. The brief description of each day either preclude this ideas, or else he described but a very small portion of what he saw. I should rather feel inclined to think he wrote down the most conspicuous features of the landscape which met his eye, not recording anything that was not obviously exhibited: for example, no mention of fishes is made, though we know they existed in large numbers, and many of great size, at a very early period of the world's history.

Let us now consider the first chapter of Genesis, and see if it be really possible to draw at least some parallel between it and the discoveries of geology.

The very first verse has called forth much discussion. Some persons, still clinging to the idea of six literal days, fancy that the whole of geological discoveries are included, or rather passed over, under that first verse, and that a new world arose out of its chaotic dissolution.

I see no warrant for that idea whatever. I rather would suggest that it is a sort of heading to the account about to follow; just as we adopt some expression to convey the general meaning of a chapter in a book. Or it may have been a preliminary protest against the idea of a self-existing world without a personal God.

At all events, I fancy I see so close a parallel between these days of Genesis and periods of geology, as to lead me to require no such hypothesis as the one mentioned above.

One more remark upon the scope of geology. Geology proper, or uniformitarian* geology, does not profess to go beyond objective facts, or to attempt more than reasonable deduction. Speculative geology, however, embraces much more than this, and ventures to treat of the early cosmical conditions.

We must remember, however, that all theories about those supposed conditions are purely hypothetical, and must be held accordingly with a light hand in proportion to the want of strict evidence.

Now the generally accepted theory is the "nebular," viz., that our system, *i.e.*, the sun and all its attendant planets, was once a vast nebula, or an immense volume of incandescent gases. This by condensation would produce light and heat. At that time the earth could have had no "form" whatever. As soon, however, as one special condensation had produced the earth, apart from the greater condensation forming the sun, and a terrestial revolution had begun, "day and night" must

* This word implies that the processes of change which are going on now have ever been the same through all ages of the world.

have followed. In other words, as soon as the earth had ceased to be a self-luminous star, and had become an opaque, non-luminous body.

Before proceeding further, let the reader note the extreme brevity of the account in Genesis; for the successive conditions of the world were probably at first gaseous; secondly, that of a star; and lastly, that of an earth.

Incandescent vapour first gives light. (Compare Genesis i. 3.) The earth was next self-luminous; this condition appears to have been passed over in Genesis; but the next period, *i.e.*, as soon as the crust was formed, may possibly be referred to indirectly by the establishment of day and night (verse 5).

The subsequent condition supposed by geologists is, that an envelope of dense vapours, of steam, salt, etc., with various gases, surrounded the crust until it was cool enough to allow water to rest upon it. The atmosphere, when even this had taken place, was probably for a long period dense and vaporous, such as may be that of Jupiter at the present day. The salts, etc., in this atmosphere would gradually subside, and be absorbed by the water, which would now become salt, at the same time clearing the atmosphere, (firmament?) which would bear the lighter vapours only above it.

Now, some such appearances as suggested by this hypothesis may have been presented to the seer;[*] for it is impossible to be quite certain of his meaning in the 6th verse. It looks as if he were merely alluding to the clouds in the air and the sea below; but who can tell he may not be describing other appearances in ordinary

[*] May not the fact that prophets were called "Seers" before the time of Samuel lend some countenance to the supposition that visions were the usual means of communication from God to man?

language, totally different from, but bearing some general resemblance to, ordinary atmospheric phenomena.

We must always remember what I have already insisted upon, that scientific expressions in Scripture are often, if not always, descriptive appearances of facts, but not the actual facts themselves.

The next phenomenon is the rising of land out of water, and is a fact which I think on reflection will show how true it is that appearances are only described. If an island rose out of the sea, it would cause the water to rush away from it, and might easily give the appearance of the land being immovable, while the water fell away.

Geology, as usual, states the absolute fact, irrespective of appearances, and tells us it is the land which has risen, while the sea has simply retired to the lowest levels.

Geology now believes the world to have had a sheet of water all over it, and the seas to have been formed by the refrigeration of the shell, whereby it has become wrinkled by contracting, the wrinkles giving rise to mountains, and the depressions to seas. Here therefore, as before, there is no real contradiction to science in the words of Scripture.

Now the next verse (11) brings us to contemplate vegetation. What has geology to say on this subject? With regard to vegetation, we know that at one period of the world's history we have discovered a very great deal more than of any other period, and moreover vegetation is found in all parts of the world, being stored up in the form of coal. We are not without evidence of plant life during other ages; but no discoveries have been made of anything like the enormous profusion of that particular period.

It must always be remembered that negative evidence is very weak in geology; from the very nature of the case we should expect much more evidence of marine life, as indeed is the case, than of any other. Nevertheless it is a very remarkable fact that one epoch should have revealed to us such a vast amount of evidence of vegetable life. Again, we must remember that this vegetation is by no means the first instances of life. Every class of animal as high as reptiles have been found to have existed before or during that period. Animal life is a proof in itself of the necessity of vegetation, which must have existed, though the evidences yet discovered are exceedingly scanty. This is not to be wondered at, seeing probably about the ten thousandth part of the world only has been searched (Huxley).

Now, then, we are in a position to ask, "Does the carboniferous flora, to which I have been alluding, represent that mentioned in verse 12?" It may or it may not. At least there is no disagreement.

We now come to the most difficult part of all, the 14th to 19th verses. It is quite evident that some light, visible only to the earth for twelve hours, existed before, otherwise day and night could not have been established on the rotation of the earth (recorded in verse 4). The interpretation, hitherto given to explain this are probably very wide of the truth, such as a larger amount of carbonic acid and vapour in the air, which it is supposed had hitherto obscured the sun. This can easily be shown to be absurd; or, again, that the earth was lighted by auroras. I might suggest another perhaps equally erroneous, that the condensation of incandescent vapour had taken far longer time with the sun than with the earth, and it might have had no appearance until the fourth day of a sharply-defined orb, as it is now.

But it is better to confess our ignorance, and to believe, that had we seen it as the observer saw it, or did we know all, the description of the fourth day would be perfectly clear. As it stands, however, geology has nothing to offer either for or against it. Now let us pass on to the 20th verse; here we suddenly find ourselves introduced to moving, that is, creeping creatures and fowl, while the word whale is a mistranslation, the Hebrew word (*Tannin*) signifying a "sea monster," probably not that cetacean at all. Let us compare this account with what geology has to reveal. As a matter of fact, an enormous number of reptiles of all sizes existed abundantly, some of them attaining gigantic dimensions, and well deserving of the name of sea monster, some being forty feet in length, with jaws six feet long, and more than 180 large teeth. These monsters appear to have been accompanied not only by strange birds, quite unlike modern types, but also by flying reptiles, varying in size from a few inches to twenty feet across.

Now a person taking a survey of the world at this period, he could not fail to be struck with the vast and numerous forms of reptilian life associated with many strange and large fowl, by which term he would probably include the winged reptiles alluded to.

Again let us ask the question, Does geology contradict Genesis? The answer is that the creation of the fifth day agrees marvellously well with the *Mesozoic* age of geology, or the "Age of Reptiles" as it has been called.

We have but one more day to consider. On this are brought forth living creatures (not described as *moving* observe, a term which is more expressive of unwieldy reptiles). "Cattle" are mentioned, "beasts of the earth," and "creeping things," as apparently distinguished from the sea monster of the fifth day. What has Geology to say? that after the age of reptiles had passed away, there followed a long period represented to us by a series of "beds" containing great and numerous successions of quadrupedal life. The first totally unlike the present existing races, but gradually approaching the form and structure of existing beasts, till at last they appear identical. And what is more significant is the fact that the evidence of man's existence has been found associated with the latest series, not in a separate deposit of a later date than those containing extinct forms, but accompany them in such a way as to necessitate the belief that he was one of the creatures which appeared together.

Had he a separate day, according to Genesis?

The sixth day witnessed the in-coming of man, as well as the beasts of the field.

Do Genesis and Geology agree, or does Geology run counted to Genesis?

Thus far I trust the reader will not hesitate to reply that there is no contradiction whatever.

PART IV.

THE DOCTRINE OF EVOLUTION.

There yet remains, or rather has lately risen in the minds of some, a new doubt with reference to Science, and that is whether the Doctrine of Evolution or Development of life will not prove to run counter to the history of creation as given in Genesis.

Let us turn to Genesis: with reference to creative facts, we find no explanation whatever as to the process of creation. The bare fact only is stated in the words God "created" (*Barah*) or "God made" (*Asah*); no perceptible difference being discoverable between these words. Moreover nothing is told us whether the "heaven and the earth" were created out of nothing or out of pre-existing matter.

Now we must carefully observe that there is a second kind of expression used in this same first chapter of Genesis, with reference to creation; namely, "*Let* the waters and the earth *bring forth*." We have here the imperative mood, and the use of such expressions can only imply other agents than the speaker. The inference, therefore, seems to be that secondary agents, represented by the water and the earth, are here enjoined to carry out the will of the Lord.

The conclusion one can only arrive at is, that both expressions are of equivalent value; so that when nature produces any effects, those effects are due to the will of God, while the latter of the expressions strongly encourages the idea of secondary intermediary agents, rather than direct creative fiats. The notion of the evolution of living things arises from an impartial study of nature; and whatever be the cause of it, the probability of the truth of evolution far outweighs the idea that every animal and plant has been respectively due to creative fiats. It would be out of place to give any lengthy evidence of the truth of evolution; at least up to, for I believe it is not inclusive of man, the truth of evolution is a moral conviction; and if Genesis does not palpably refer to it, it at least lends it encouragement by the frequent use of the imperative mood, as quoted above.

Even with regard to man, Genesis only says man was created out of the dust of the earth: but all animals are so likewise. There is neither assent nor denial of evolution of man. Reason, however, while recognizing the fact that man's body cannot be separated from the higher order of animals entirely, yet perceives that in his entirety constitutes a different family: yet in his intellect he is so far in advance, and in his morality absolutely severed, that the gap between him and them cannot be accounted for on any principle of development at present known; and gives us altogether the idea of some special interference.

Now this is also, as it seems, told us in Genesis. The unusual expression, "Let us make man," implying, as I believe, that interference; while the "breath of life which causes man to become a living soul," may, I also believe, be seen in his morality, which *does* completely sever him from all other animals.*

The general result, then, at which we have arrived, is, that while Genesis may not forcibly bear witness either to geology or evolution, it in no way contradicts them; nay, rather the reverse, it appears to hint at both. On the other hand, the evidences of geology, and the truth of evolution, which have been acquired from a close tudy of natnre, cannot now be gainsayed. The more one studies nature, the more one feels convinced that had we perfect knowledge of all things, the harmony between Genesis and geology, and between the processes

---

* See Mr. Darwin's Descent of Man, "Man alone is moral."

of creation recorded in Scripture, and evolution, would be perfect and absolute.

I trust I shall have now succeeded in this brief review of Genesis and geology to prove that the charge of being incorrect brought against Scripture is unfounded.

Once more, bearing in mind that the object of the Scriptures is the elevation of the moral character of man, let us see if nature, scientifically considered, lends other aid to support the truthfulness of Scripture than is to be found in its harmony with Genesis.

The first thing which strikes the student as soon as he has acquired a considerable range of knowledge over the several departments of nature, is the grand *unity of principle* which pervades the whole. Let me illustrate this. If we take all the vertebrata, or animals which possess a "backbone," whether we examine living or extinct forms, we find they are all constructed on the same identical plan of type.

The homologous parts are marvellously modified to suit the different kinds of habits. Thus the arm and hand of a man, the fore leg of a horse, the wing of a bat or bird, the paddles of a whale, are all modifications of one and the same organ. Similarly all the other members of the different types; so that all living creatures can be reduced to a few, say about five, fundamental types. The same fact is applicable to plants, both to the vegetable kingdom as a whole, as well as to the separate organs of an individual plant; leaves, scales, petals, stamens, etc., being all modifications of the same thing, and reducible to one type.

Unity of plan with diversity of result is to be seen everywhere running through nature. Now read the Scriptures. One God is enforced throughout: " Hear, O

Israel, the Lord your God is one Lord;" "Thou shalt have none other gods but me." Again, "God is Love;" and the various phases of Divine attributes, mercy, justice, benevolence, are but differentiated forms of one and the same power typified in love. Again, note how unchangeable are the laws of nature; and so God says of Himself, "I change not;" "I am not a man, that I should lie; or the son of man, that I should repent." "What a man soweth, that shall he also reap," is expressive both of the laws of nature as of morality.

The humble and pious mind cannot fail to feel, if not to see, that there is an ever-abiding presence of a conserving power; and if we turn to Scripture, we are there told that it is "in Him we live, move, and have our being."

Nay, more: the catastrophes of nature, the physical evils which surround us, the troubles, toils, cares, and anxieties to which we are born, and if not those of our own causing, are as much a part of nature as they are necessary for the moral growth of men. They constitute the "inideal"* conditions by which man is surrounded while resident in this world for a disciplinary process to fit him for eternity. Turn to the Scriptures, and we find it to be the same God who there declares it to be His will; for He says by Isaiah, "I cause good, and I create evil."

On the other hand, regarding nature apart from physical evils, we see the abundant harvests and the rich fruits of the earth poured forth in plenty; her corn, wine,

---

* The words "*inideal*" and "*inideality*" are suggested to express the relative state of perfection of this world, and that the *ideal* is never reached.

and oil, iron, gold, and silver in abundance, and all other things to the hand of man that he requires; and we cannot but bless that bountiful nature who gives so much to her patient toiler—man.

Turn to the Scriptures, and we find God not only described as the God of nature, and the "giver of all good things to man," but also "the abundant Rewarder of him that doeth right." On the other hand, just as an earthquake may seemingly ruthlessly destroy the fair cities of men, or a tempest deprive him of his expected harvests; so is God described as the "Revenger of all them that do evil."

Now in these few contrasts we have seen that while nature, on the one hand, seems to pour forth the utmost of her bounties; on the other hand, her forces sometimes become pent up, and then suddenly burst forth and destroy all her intended offerings to man.

What is the meaning of this seemingly capricious conduct? Let us first note our own inward consciousness as to the relationship in which we stand to nature.

First, we can recognise this imperfect inideal condition of things, and we can imagine and long for a state of existence free from all care whatever, from the most trivial to the most agonising terror, distress, or pain.

Now, I see nothing in nature which responds to this yearning for a happier state of things; I am driven, then, to the conclusion that this feeling ever rising in my heart does not arise from experience. It is inborn, and craves for a response from nature. If I cannot get rest and perfect happiness here, I shall surely obtain it elsewhere; then it must be that *I shall live again*; that is the discovery at which I am compelled to arrive, while conscience, arising at my disobedience to law, leads me to think that my state here is probational only, and that if I live according to the light I possess, it will be well with me hereafter.

Now let us turn once more to the Scriptures, and we shall find that all will become clear. These natural yearnings receive their promise of reward. The conditions which the blind soul had faintly traced in the glimmer of light received from nature alone are there revealed; and we rise from that book convinced of its truth from the harmony between its teaching and those of nature. The cravings of the heart and the deductions of the intellect are there found revealed and made plain. Aye, and what is more, our conscience has accused us again and again for having broken nature's laws, and we knew not how to compensate nature. In Scripture we find they are God's laws, and we crave for pardon.

He tells us He has pardoned us; for His Son has died that we may live!

Henceforth let us study the Scriptures in conjunction with nature, being well assured now, that the more we know of each, the greater will be their harmony. And that while we do our duty, living in hope and faith, we shall not fail of that heavenly reward which is the only solution of the great problem of life; the only clue to unravel the apparently inexplicable mystery of physical evil.

THE MORAL TEACHING OF THE OLD TESTAMENT VINDICATED.

BY THE

REV. J. H. TITCOMB, M.A.,
VICAR OF ST. STEPHEN'S, SOUTH LAMBETH, AND RURAL DEAN OF CLAPHAM.

The Moral Teaching of the Old Testament Vindicated.

IN introducing this subject to your notice, gentlemen, I mean to take three things for granted: first, that I am not to be held responsible for the views of other people, but only for my own; secondly, that you are all sincere inquirers after truth; and thirdly, that no one desires to raise a false issue upon the question which is to come under discussion.

Let me commence, then, by plainly stating what it is I have to do. I have not to argue whether a Divine revelation be, in itself, either possible or probable. The position is simply this: Here is a volume, called the Old Testament Scripture, which we Christians receive as containing a revelation from God to man. Against that opinion you, on your part, may have a hundred different arguments; but it is only with one of these that I am now concerned; viz., those difficulties of belief which arise out of its moral teaching. You tell me that, scattered up and down this volume, there are some parts so inconsistent with pure morality, as at once to disprove its derivation from a holy God. My business to-night, therefore, will not be to prove that a revelation exists, but, taking this book into my hand, which professes to contain such a revelation, I shall have to vindicate its teaching as consistent with the moral being of the Deity.

That is, I think, a fair statement of the case. Consequently, if, in the discussion which is to ensue, any gentleman confuses the debate by introducing into it irrelevant matter, I shall immediately ask the chairman to interpose.

One thing further by way of preface. I charge you to be true to the dogma that aboriginal man was a naked savage, who, passing through a long course of barbarity and moral debasement, came only gradually into a state of respectable civilization! This may sound strange and very unexpected. Yet you cannot refuse to accept the position. It is the chosen ground of modern scepticism, and therefore no unbeliever has a right to move from it.

1. Do not suppose that we ourselves believe in this origin of man. On the contrary, we maintain that he was primevally good and noble; formed, both mentally and spiritually, in the image of his great Creator. At the same time we believe in a mysteriously permitted fall, which not only resulted in man's moral degradation, but, curiously enough, brought about a state of society harmonizing, in a great measure, with your own conceptions of the subject. Why that fall from original perfection was permitted by a wise and holy God, and all its consequent train of evils allowed to be introduced into the world, is a question upon which you will, perhaps, expect me to say a few words. You will observe, however, I am not called upon, under the terms of this lecture, to expound the difficulty, but only to vindicate the character of the moral teaching which it involves. Now on what ground do you impeach this?

If I maintain that the possibility óf the moral fall of a finite being from his first created perfection is and always must be an inevitably necessary postulate in the conditions of his personal freedom, you may argue that I limit the Divine omnipotence. I reply that it is no impeachment of omnipotence to say that God is Himself limited by certain immutable laws of truth, which are among the essential ingredients of His own self-existence. For example, no one can fairly impeach God's omnipotence because He is unable to make two and two equal three. In the same way, no one can do so, if, in creating finite moral agents subordinated to His own government, it was impossible for Him to have made them as omnipotent as Himself. Had that been so, it is true they would never have fallen. But then it would have been the multiplication of separate Gods, not the creation of dependent moral agents ; and that is so self-contradictory as to be utterly inconceivable.

This necessary condition of things, then, was as much the outcome of an eternal and immutable law belonging to the Divine self-existence, as the law which makes one less than two, or the part inferior to the whole. Now, you must not rise up, here, gentlemen, and dispute the existence of God altogether. For, observe, *that* is not the question to-night. You are consenting to examine now a certain Book, which professes to contain a revelation from God. The argument is not whether this revelation be either possible or probable; but whether, on the assumption that the Bible be such a revelation, its moral teaching in the Old Testament does, or does not, violate the essential conditions of Divine Love, Truth, and Holiness.

. Perhaps you tell me that "the creation of man, with a

foreknowledge of his fall, involving the deliberate introduction of all its conseqent miseries into the world, *does* impeach the Divine love." You say that, "if such a contingency were necessarily possible, and still more, if it were foreseen, it could not have been consistent with Infinite Love to have given those evils any opportunity of bursting forth; that God might have interposed by His omnipotence to nip them then in the bud, and so have preserved all things pure and perfect and happy; and that a book which gives such a different account of things cannot be a true revelation."

I reply, that if we were fully acquainted with the facts of the moral universe,—if we knew for certain every part of the Divine administration throughout a multitude of other inhabited worlds than our own,—if every other providential dispensation, and all their diversified relations to those of our own world, were plainly within the field of our view, and everything presented just the same sin and misery in those worlds as in ours, then this reasoning might be very plausible and good. But seeing it is not so; seeing that we know only a part of the case; that possibly there may be many hidden relationships between other worlds and ours, of which we are entirely ignorant, and which, if thoroughly understood, might convert these objections against the love and goodness of God into arguments of an altogether opposite nature, I have a right to disregard them as involving hasty and unnecessary conclusions. Let me illustrate what I mean. You might argue, in the same way, at first sight, that the creation of man, having nerves which are exquisitely sensitive to bodily pain, and their exposure, notwithstanding, to the action of fire, is quite inconsistent with the character of a God of goodness and love. Think only of the miseries which have ensued from burnings and scaldings, and of the horrible agony suffered by the human body in consequence of the delicate organisation of its nervous system. You may say, "How can you talk to us of a God of love when He has made man thus, and exposed him to all these evils?" Yet you know well enough, gentlemen, that the sufferings thus permitted by God's providence do indirectly promote the general happiness of mankind, even though it be at the expense of many burnt and scalded individuals. For were our bodies not thus sensitive to pain, we should have no warning against danger, and might be injured in our limbs and lives perpetually before we had time to avert the misfortune. If, then, there are evils in the *natural* world, which thus serve the purposes of an ulterior and general benevolence, why may not the same principle be supposed to exist in regard to the *moral* world? Why should not the miseries which the fall of man has introduced among ourselves stand exactly in the same relation to other created intelligences as the burnings and scaldings of individual sufferers do to the general community around us, who thus mercifully learn and profit through the ill-fated experience of others?

The doubt you feel on this question, therefore, is not any necessary and inherent difficulty in the moral teaching of Scripture, but simply one which arises from the imperfect consciousness of man respecting the entire administration of God's moral purposes throughout other portions of the universe.

2. Time allowing me to say no more on this point, I now come back to that from which I just diverged, viz., the effects of the fall of man in the moral deterioration of society.

No one can read the early part of the Old Testament without seeing that, after the fall of man, the world became morally and socially degenerate. In regard to *material* civilization, it was some years before a city was built;* and still longer, probably centuries, before any portion of mankind had ceased to live in what is popularly called a stone age, or learnt the use of metals and musical instruments.† In regard to *moral* civilization, barbarity and lawlessness seemed to have grown worse and worse. Beginning with the murder of Abel, it went on through a long period of violence and vice, which culminated in an age when, to use the words of the Bible, "the wickedness of man was great in the earth, and the imagination of the thoughts of his heart was only evil continually;" ‡ and again, when "the earth was corrupt before God, and filled with violence." ǁ You certainly cannot be scandalised, gentlemen, at this picture of the world's early history; for, though you start from a different origin of it yourselves, yet your own theory of man's primeval savagery exactly squares with its main outlines. Here we stand, at all events, on a common platform. All is confusion, brutality, and disorganisation.

3. Coalescing, however, at this point, we are doomed in a moment to part company. For when we go on to read in Scripture that God "repented He had made man," and that He destroyed the whole race, save one family, by a flood, you at once impeach the moral teaching of the Bible, and say "that this representation of an infinitely wise, perfect, and unchangeable Deity is utterly incredible; and that a book which thus describes a disappointed

---

* Gen. iv. 17. ‡ Gen. vi. 5.
† Gen. iv. 21, 22. ǁ Gen. vi. 11.

Old Testament Vindicated. 151

God, whose only remedy lay in destroying the work of His own hands, cannot be a true revelation."

You applaud the sentiment! Yes, gentlemen. But that only shows how thoroughly we understand you, and how little we are careful to blink the apparent difficulties of the argument. Do you suppose that *you* are the only person to whom this language has proved perplexing? Do you think that *we*, who believe, have not as intelligent a perception of Scripture difficulties as yourselves? The difference between us is, that *you* read the words in question under the light of modern knowledge, just as if they had been addressed to men of the 19th century; whereas *we* read them (according to all fair laws of criticism) under the light of the age in which they were delivered, and just as the men of that uneducated and uncivilised period would alone have been able to understand any revelation of the Divine mind upon this subject. Had words of an abstract and philosophical character been employed instead of this simple idea, "*God repented that He had made man,*" they would have been totally unsuited to the moral and intellectual consciousness of so degraded and demoralised a race. The choice, therefore, of imperfect terms of speech like these must not be attributed to the fact that they properly represented the action of the Divine mind; but that they formed the most ready vehicle of thought through which even the least approximation to the truth could address itself to the perception of such people. You will thus perceive in a moment, gentlemen, (if you only take the trouble to throw your minds into the circumstances under which Scripture describes the revelation to have been communicated,) that the low and immature form of this statement was but an inevitable condition of the case, arising from the impossibility of any more abstract and philosophical conceptions being understood at the time.

4. But this is no answer, you will tell me, to that impeachment of the Divine benevolence which sprang out of the destruction of the human race by a flood. Certainly not, for we must take one thing at once. Am I to understand you, however, as saying that a God of love and mercy had absolutely no moral right thus to destroy His own creation on account of its prolonged and inveterate self-corruption, after He had warned it, and been patient with it through centuries of protracted long-suffering? Are there not stages of moral evil, even in the present day, which show themselves absolutely irreclaimable by any remedies known to man; crimes so deep and inveterate that neither mercy nor remedial treatment will stop them? Now you will observe from the narrative that this was just the case here. Long-suffering had reached its utmost limit; corruption and rebellion had left only one righteous family. Hence, if permitted longer, the very last remnant of goodness would have perished out of the earth! What! Do you mean to tell me that it would have been consistent with perfect love to allow the last spark of moral goodness to become extinguished? Are all the resources of love and mercy to be spent upon the wicked, and none to be exhibited for the protection of the righteous? Are there not some periods and cases, even within our own experience, when severe judgments on hardened criminals become conservative of benevolence and kindness toward the innocent? Would any just government allow assassins to go through a country committing murder and rapine upon the population, and corrupting the vitals of society, without feeling it a duty to interfere on behalf of the virtuous? The cases are exactly

analogous. Only, in this instance, the government was God's, and the corruption, instead of being partial, was all but universal. Look at the case fairly in this light, gentlemen, and your impeachment of the Divine goodness hopelessly falls to the ground.

5. Let us now pass on to the picture which the Old Testament gives of the state of the world after that awful period. Such was the depravity of human nature, consequent upon its first moral fall, that we find evil soon reappearing, and again becoming dominant. Witness the enormities related of Sodom and Gomorrah, the dissolute and disorganised state of the Canaanitish nations, and even the violent and licentious condition of Israel under the Judges. Indeed, it scarcely seems too much to say, from a careful study of this part of the Old Testament, that there was as low a level of general morality, and as little respect for human life, and as much barbaric cruelty, as still exists in the heathenism of Asia and Africa. And here you will be pleased to recollect, gentlemen, that when we Christians recognise this low moral condition of the primitive races of mankind, we are brought on to the same platform as yourselves, who hold that the origin of all moral and material civilization may be traced through a passage over debased periods of history which were marked by uncontrolled licentiousness and uncivilised barbarism.

Well then, that being so far agreed upon, only see how such a condition of things must have necessarily affected the composition of a book which professes to contain a Divine revelation to man. The position is this: "Given a state of degraded barbarism and imperfect moral perceptions, to raise it to one of elevation."

One thing, by a law of common sense, is clear: that,

unless the God who is supposed to have bestowed this revelation had absolutely forced the recipients of it into a compelled state of blameless obedience, the degraded age in which they thus lived must have largely qualified the nature and degree of their moral rectitude. Yet, I presume, no one who is here this evening will dare to rise up and argue that it could ever have been consistent with the genuine idea of moral progress, that mankind should be forced into holiness, just as lunatics are into quietness, by means of handcuffs and straight-waistcoats. You might as well call the lions in our zoological gardens tame and domesticated animals, or the cotton looms of Manchester moral agents, as evil men good, when only made so compulsorily after that fashion. Any such idea as that, is, I am persuaded, far too unphilosophical and unreasonable to satisfy either the intellect or the moral sense of an audience such as this. If you assume, for the sake of argument, therefore, as you have now consented to do, that a revelation may have been given to man, I am sure you will allow that it must still have left him exposed to his natural struggle with debased passions, and to the necessary influences of that imperfect civilization by which he was surrounded. Consider these circumstances. According to your own belief, as well as ours, if revelation came to man at all, it must have first come to him at a time when his naturally uneducated instincts were those of cruelty, treachery, and licentiousness. What impeachment, therefore, can be honestly brought against the purity of the revelation itself, if its effects upon the lives of such men was not to give them all an instant and immediate emancipation from their antecedent corruptions? On what fair ground could you expect the moral advancement to be anything else but slow, partial, and progressive? Why should you be staggered, if, in a book which professes to record the history of men who received a Divine revelation under such circumstances, you should find it still impregnated with many of the old underlying elements of evil? Unless moral rectitude had been perfected in such persons by irresistible compulsion, how, in the name of common sense, could you expect to find them rising up erect into a sudden and fully developed state of holiness, untouched by sin, and unaffected by their lack of pure civilization? You have, therefore, no right to find fault with the morality of the Old Testament on account of the occasional crimes or imperfect rectitude of some of its chief heroes. You have no reason to be surprised, for example, that Noah and Lot should have become intoxicated; that Jacob should have lied, or cheated his brother Esau; that Moses should have committed manslaughter; that Jael should have violated hospitality by an act of treacherous murder; that some of the judges, otherwise remarkable for the heroism of faith, should yet have been men of occasionally uncontrollable passion; and that even David, while in the main a man of honour, after God's own heart, should have nevertheless been tainted by corruption, and tempted to adultery. If revelation raised these Scripture heroes in many particulars above their natural level, it is no proof of its falsehood that it did not raise them up equally in all other particulars. It must be remembered, too, that the sins just mentioned are simply chronicled as matters of fact in the pages of a book which contain Divine revelation, and are no part of the revelation itself. Indeed, considered as a history of the past, it is one great merit of the Old

Testament that it furnishes us with a gallery of characters for instruction, which are often as much intended for our warning as for our instruction; that it does not bring before us mere ideal figures which never existed, like the beatified ghosts of many modern biographies, but living men and women, with all the blots and blurs of a fallen manhood, just as they still cling to them, even under the most favoured circumstances. You must also bear in mind, gentlemen, that, according to your own creed, everything, both in physical nature and in moral progress, was being slowly evolved under a law of successive developments. We ask you, therefore, to be consistent with your own position; and to admit that, even though a revelation came in for the purpose of aiding that development of moral progress, it must nevertheless have necessarily been hindered in its purifying effects by the general depravity of those primeval times. Under which circumstances we contend that your satire upon the imperfect morality of many of the Old Testament characters is neither consistent with your own theory, nor is it philosophical, or just, or wise.

6. If you could prove to us out of Scripture that God is represented as approving of these outbreaks of sin in His servants, we would allow you to triumph; we would acknowledge the justice of your allegations. But did He? Where is it said that God approved of Noah's drunkenness, or of Lot's incest, or of Jacob's polygamy? The most you can say is, that God is not represented as having made any coercive interference to prevent them. But this only proves that the moral elevation of society, in an age so unenlightened and uncultivated, was one of such extreme difficulty as to need the greatest toleration and longsuffering. The fact is, that Scripture

represents the moral government of God, at this period, as the working out of the problem already stated:— "How shall a Deity, whose being is infinitely holy, elevate a race of men who are living in an age of semi-barbarism and of corruption?" How was He to do it, without adopting one of two courses?—either forcing them irresistibly to do what was right, having no respect to their personal sense of responsibility; or else patiently allowing time for the gradual evolution of their higher moral life, through periods of permitted imperfection? The first of these courses, as I have already remarked, would have been no more a *bonâ fide* subjugation of moral evil, than the caging of wild beasts in our zoological gardens, or the handcuffing of maniacs in our workhouses, would be the genuine elevation of soul-debased natures. Hence, the action of Divine revelation on man must be sought for in the second course. And that is why evils of a social character, which are now universally reprobated, were, in those early times, permitted with a long-suffering tolerance which is not granted at present, since the world has grown up into a higher and purer civilization.

Take polygamy and slavery, for example, both of which found temporary provisions of a remedial character in the law of Moses, in order to soften their evil tendencies, and minimise, as far as possible, their corrupting influences upon society. Remember, you are not to tell me that God was responsible for these uncivilized institutions, because, in an age of uncivilization, He patiently bore with such evil manners, and, instead of sweeping them away at once, enacted remedial laws which gradually prepared the way, by moral rather than coercive means, for their final and perpetual extinction. The Scriptures might have represented Him as meeting these existing evils by arbitrarily enforcing upon His church the highest social morality all at once. But if so, it would have been against all the analogies of nature and providence, in which we see slow evolutions and progressive development to be one of God's invariable and established laws. That He should be represented, therefore, here as following the same order, meeting social evils as they existed, and making the revelation He gave to man, not, in the first place, a means of their sudden and complete expulsion, but of their gradual and progressive purification; this, so far from being an argument against the Old Testament, ought to be distinctly one in its favour, inasmuch as it harmonises with all the other methods of the world's administration.

7. And here, gentlemen, let me call your attention to the fact that your attacks against Divine revelation are singularly shifting and double-sided. For while, on the one hand, you thus accuse it of imperfection because it represents God as being too tolerant and long-suffering toward evil, you turn round and attack it still more violently because it represents God as being, in other particulars, far too severe and relentless against evil. You point, for example, to His destruction of the Canaanites and the Amalekites as specimens of His providential judgments, which were unjustly tyrannical and cruel, and utterly inconsistent with a moral governor whose nature is that of love and goodness. Thus it would appear that nothing suits you. One moment you tell us that our God was over-gentle, and even time-serving, because He did not sweep away polygamy and slavery at a blow; at another moment you accuse Him of cruelty and injustice because He cut off wicked nations, which were on the

point of corrupting His church through sins far deeper and more hateful. But "wisdom is justified of her children." There is no real discrepancy between these two apparently opposite courses of God's government. They are alike founded upon grand ulterior purposes of love and goodness to man; purposes which, though not transparent on the surface, are yet plainly discernible upon calm and close inspection.

No one can possibly shrink more than I do from those Divine injunctions which the Old Testament records concerning the massacre of whole cities and peoples; for I hope I have a heart, gentlemen, which is quite as far removed from all sympathy with savage and brutal bloodshed as any of your own. I stand in imagination, indeed, amidst those scenes of terrific slaughter, and as I listen to the shrieks of helpless women and children, mercilessly sabred or speared, I lift up my eyes to heaven, and exclaim, "Can this be Thy work, O merciful Father? Surely, oh, surely, these murderers have mistaken their self-barbarity for a Divine commission. Only in their own envenomed passions can they hear that voice, which they pretend or think comes from Thee!" I suppose such are the first instincts of every feeling heart in this day of 19th century civilisation.

But need I remind you that it is also part of our 19th century civilization to be the disciples of reason as much as of feeling; and that each of these ought to have its legitimate sphere in our estimate of the interests of humanity? Need I tell a reflecting and thoughtful audience like the present, that, upon the assumption of there being a God who is the Supreme Governor of the world, reason should carefully discriminate between His moral right to annihilate nations which are incurably corrupt, and His moral right to make their fellow-creatures the executioners of that destruction? The two questions are perfectly distinct. First, then, let me ask whether the Old Testament ought to be rejected as a true revelation, because it assumes the moral right of Deity to annihilate nations which are incurably corrupt?

This was exactly the case before us. These nations, according to the statements of Scripture, were hopelessly corrupt. They were spared for centuries, through Divine long-suffering, because "their iniquity was not yet full." (Gen. xv. 16.) The question therefore arose, whether, when thus hopelessly incurable, they should be still spared, seeing that with this prolongation of mercy they would soon corrupt all others less degenerate than themselves, until the earth became, as it had become previously before the flood, one seething mass of moral impurity, threatening the final and complete extinction of all goodness. Here I ask again, as I did before, Are all the resources of love and mercy to be spent upon the abandoned, and none to be exhibited for the protection of the more virtuous? Do not judgments of the severest nature against the former, often practically prove conservative of benevolence and kindness towards the latter? Is not this reasoning the very basis of all just moral government in our most civilized communities at present? The great difference between the two cases is, that in our own sphere of government we apply the principles only to individuals; whereas in this the larger sphere of Divine government the principle is applied to nations. But in either case the principle is the same.

Perhaps you say, "No; there is this great difference of principle; that *we*, in the case of individuals, discriminate between the old and young, between the more

Old Testament Vindicated. 161

hardened and more innocent; whereas God, in the case of these nations, made no discrimination, but involved all persons, without exception, in one wholesale slaughter. Was that consistent with mercy or justice? The reply to this question is entirely dependent upon the degree of moral abandonment into which these nations had fallen. The question is, was the case such that the children of these criminals, if spared, would certainly have grown up, like their parents, perpetuating the same contagion? Is it not a fact that bad qualities are transmitted from father to son, and intensified after several stages of transmission; so that where parents have proved ineradicably evil, there, by the simple law of inheritance, the evil not only remains, but grows worse and worse? And is it not a law of the world (account for it how you will), that some degraded races are destined to extinction, as the only means of getting rid of the curse which they inflict upon society? I therefore argue, that, just as in the destruction of a wild beast's lair, the young leopards or panthers naturally and inevitably fall with the older brutes, so, in the inexorable necessities of this dreadful case, the children and their parents required the same treatment. You will remind me, perhaps, of the possible amelioration and improvement of this younger race under the process of education. Yes, gentlemen; but that is an element of modern civilisation which, in this period of the world's history, had not been developed. All such gentler and more noble methods of the moral government of the world, of course, formed part of God's ulterior designs; but these were then as necessarily reserved for the future as the genial warmth of summer is ever kept behind during the snows and blasts of winter. If, therefore, the annihilation of these refuse nations was at all consistent with the essential principles of Divine love and mercy to others, it follows that the inclusion of the young with the old cannot fairly be objected to, when taken in connection with the low and imperfect development of the moral training of a corrupted world.

And this brings me to the next question—Must the Old Testament be rejected as a true revelation, because it represents God's destruction of these nations as ordained through human executioners?

The real answer to this query lies in the uncivilised character of those times; in the fact that no nation then upon the earth had any natural reverence for the sanctity of human life taken in war; so that those massacres, which to our refined sense of feeling are deeply revolting, were in those days among the necessary accompaniments of conquest. It was a period of horrible barbaric cruelty, when captives taken in war were generally slaughtered. Not only in those remote ages, but even long after the introduction of a much higher civilisation, the same barbarities in war have been frequently chronicled in secular history, and of which many instances might be given if the case required it. In employing this method of national judgment, therefore, although there was no *elevation* by God of the moral sense of Israel, yet there was no actual *deterioration* of it. Revelation in this respect did nothing, it must be freely granted, towards the world's social amelioration or moral advancement; it simply used the debased practices of war as it found them, leaving its own ulterior purposes of reformation in the background. It worked through the existing evils of an uncivilised age, in order to clear the ground for future action by which society might, upon the whole, be more quickly raised to a purer and higher level. In the light of subsequent and grander revelations, no one can justify this kind of agency as good. More correctly speaking, it was the employment of a popular evil for the suppression of evils still greater. Considered in strict propriety, and under our present high civilisation, war, under any circumstances, is an evil. Yet, as a means of eliminating greater evils, and as links in that great chain of events by which the moral government of God is conducting mankind, through successive steps of discipline, to a future period of renovation, I can see nothing which makes it unreasonable that ultimate good should have been worked out through processes of this terrible nature, without any impeachment of God's holiness. The more so because all these cases, in which man was appointed to be the executive of God's magistracy, were accompanied by other ordinary laws of duty, which counterbalanced their tendency toward ferociousness, and which really marked a very great advance in the moral education of the world. Consider only for a moment or two the inspired humanity with which the law of Moses gradually indoctrinated Israel in other respects, and which afterwards found expression even in war time; as when Elisha rebuked the king of Israel, saying, "Wouldest thou smite those whom thou hast taken captive with thy sword and bow? Set bread and water before them, that they may eat" (2 Kings vi. 22). Consider, too, the ameliorated conditions under which the common practice of slavery was regulated. For example, the servitude of *Hebrew* men and women was compulsorily terminable at the end of six years, and possibly sooner, if the year of Jubilee intervened, when there was a general release (see Ex. xxi. 2, Lev. xxv. 40); and not only so, but it was forbidden to be used with any severity, " Thou shall not rule over him with rigour, but shalt fear thy God" (Lev. xxv. 43). Even with regard to *foreign* slaves, the Hebrews were also educated into a spirit of far greater tolerance and humanity than the world at that time understood; for if a master ill-used one of them, even to the blinding of an eye or the knocking out a tooth, it was a law that the slave might instantly claim his freedom (Ex. xxi. 26, 27). Were you aware of that, gentlemen? Whereas if the slave died, his blood was to be avenged on the master (Ex. xxi. 20).* Who can read of these things without noting the gradual elevation which it fostered?

Read again those injunctions in Exodus, which taught the sacredness of personal property,† pity for the helpless,‡ kindness to enemies;§ again, those precepts in Leviticus, which taught reverence for parents,|| kindness to the deaf and blind,¶ the sin both of secret malice and of wilful vengeance;** reverence for the aged, and†† hospitality to strangers;‡‡ and, once more, those precepts in Deuteronomy, which taught Israel that their property should be placed at the disposal of poor travellers and neighbours,§§ and that they should observe the strictest impartiality and justice in the judgment of criminals.||||

In this way, gentlemen, (if you will only take a calm

* Slaves might also, if well conducted, share the inheritance of the family (Prov. xvii. 2). and even marry into the family (1 Chron. ii. 35).

† Ex. xxii. 1 –15. ¶ Lev. xix. 14. §§ Deut. xxiii. 24, 25;
‡ Ex. xxii. 21—27. ** Lev. xix. 17, 18. xv. 7—11.
§ Ex. xxiii. 4—6. †† Lev. xix. 32. |||| Deut. xxv. 1—3.
|| Lev. xix. 3. ‡‡ Lev. xix. 33, 34.

and dispassionate view of the subject,) you may see that, while revelation represents God as employing the barbaric custom of war then in vogue among men, for the purpose of destroying certain incorrigibly corrupt and corrupting nations, which were lying in and about Canaan like festering ulcers, and which were threatening to eat out the moral life of a people who had received a deposit of supernatural truth for the gradual regeneration of the whole world; it yet consistently carried out this design by exhibiting, from the very first, certain principles and precepts of moral action, which, like germs of a higher civilization, were to be developed slowly and gradually until they should at last find their full expansion in the 19th century of our own era.

Such is a brief outline of the thoughts which satisfy my own reason upon this difficult subject, and which possibly may modify even if they do not satisfy yours.

8. Let us now pass to two or three other points. There stands, for instance, in immediate connection with this, the curse of Noah upon Ham, the father of Canaan, (for so the Septuagint reads it,) on account of his indecent treatment of Noah during his helpless state of drunkenness; upon which Lord Bolingbroke says, "This curse contradicts all our notions of order and justice. One is tempted to think that the patriarch was still drunk, and that no man in his senses could hold such language, or pass such a sentence." But allow me to observe that the justice or injustice of Noah, in thus condemning a whole posterity for the offence of one or two progenitors, is not the real point at issue. Suppose, for argument's sake, we admit that the patriarch was personally vindictive in his anger. Revelation merely records the fact, without the least record of a justification of it. The only difficulty consists

in this; that, whereas Noah would then have uttered an intemperate and unjust sentence, it nevertheless should have proved true; implying that God confirmed the wish, and acted upon it. Yet why should that conclusion be drawn? Is not this making a perfectly gratuitous difficulty for the sake of attacking Scripture? For what evidence have we to prove that exactly the same course of events in the future history of the great Hamitic family would not have taken place, even if Noah had never uttered this curse? None! The only remarkable feature in the case is, that what Noah may have uttered with intemperate and unjust violence, should have thus, unconsciously to himself, been an actual portrait of the pending and unfulfilled future. To say, however, that the curse thus uttered mysteriously fitted into the truth of coming events, is one thing; to affirm that the shaping of those events was *caused* by the curse, is quite another thing. In the latter case revelation might, perhaps, be impeached; in the former there can be no impeachment; it is only an illustration of the marvellous manner in which God can exhibit by things, evil in themselves, deep truths, which are, nevertheless, as cause and sequence, quite unconnected with one another.

9. "Well," you say, "but what about Abraham being tempted of God to immolate his son Isaac for a burnt offering? How can you believe in a revelation which presents you with a God so cruel and bloodthirsty as that?" This would indeed be a formidable difficulty if we were really obliged to regard God as intending the immolation of Isaac; or even if we were obliged to believe that Abraham set about the work as meaning to offer a propitiatory sacrifice. But so far from this being the case, the whole narrative, carefully considered, shows that

neither of the views can be true. For *on God's side* it is certain that the sacrifice was not meant to be actually offered; otherwise, it would not afterwards have been forbidden. This fact alone proves, as plainly as it is possible, that the command was nothing but a temporary discipline of Abraham's faith and obedience, with a view to test his intuitive perception of the Divine mind, and to bring out the strength of his character. *On Abraham's side*, the case is fully as clear. For previously to this strange command it had been distinctly said, " In Isaac shall thy seed be called" (Gen. xxi. 12). Abraham, therefore, who fully believed that promise, was not at all solicitous about the issue of the command. In fact, he penetrated the Divine motive, and realized the secret object of his trial. Isaac could not have been meant to be a real burnt offering, otherwise the word of promise would have failed—" In Isaac shall thy seed be called." Hence Abraham went to Mount Moriah in the full assurance of faith, either that the death of his son would be countermanded, as soon as he showed himself willing to stand the test; or else that, if it were momentarily permitted, his son would afterwards be restored to life (comp. Heb. xi. 19). In this way the patriarch's intuitive perception of Divine truth rendered the act free from criminality; and Scripture, when properly interpreted, lends no sanction to the idea, that, in setting about the work as he did, he had the least notion of offering up Isaac as a propitiatory sacrifice for sin. The truth is, that however much it may strike *you* in the light of one of those human immolations which the surrounding heathen practised, it was not only no such thing, either on God's part or on Abraham's, but only a test on one side, and an exhibition on the other, of a splendid and triumphant faith. I submit that this is an unanswerable reply, and I challenge you to give me a rejoinder.

10. You remind me there are other points remaining. Of course there are; and more than I shall have time to deal with. If I cannot take them up, therefore, separately, let me supply you with at least one or two canons of criticism under which they may severally be resolved. I would say,—

(1.) "*Do not expect that every sentiment in a book written by inspiration must necessarily itself be inspired.*"

I suppose no thoughtful person can have carefully read his Bible without occasionally finding places in which he has been constrained to say, "Surely this sentiment, though recorded under Divine inspiration, was not itself inspired." Gentlemen, nothing is ever gained by refusing to look at difficulties fearlessly and honestly. It would be of no use for us to come here and skim them over as if we were ignorant of their force, or afraid to meet them in argument. My mission would be vain to-night, if I were to allow any of you to go away saying, "He did not fairly put himself in our place," or, "He avoided the points which he did not know how to answer."

Time presses, however. Hence I only offer you this cautionary criticism as a key for the explanation of certain difficulties which you can use at your own leisure. I say there are sentiments recorded in Scripture by Divine inspiration, which were not themselves inspired at the time of their original utterance. Take, for example, the sayings of the three friends of Job; concerning whom God declared by express revelation that "they had not spoken the thing which was right" (Job xlii. 7). Now, from this declaration there is an obvious denial both of the inspiration and infallibility of at least some portions of those nine chapters of Job which contain their speeches. Not that, in writing out and recording those speeches, we think the sacred penman himself was uninspired; for we believe that it was sometimes as much a part of inspiration to record errors as to preserve truth. It is under this canon of interpretation that we class the song of Deborah, in which she glorifies treachery and assassination; yet the glorification of a treacherous lie could be no part of inspired truth; inasmuch as "it is impossible for God to lie" (Heb. vi. 18), and "He cannot deny Himself" (2 Tim. ii. 13). Still that furnishes no evidence against the inspiration of the book from which it is taken. For though Deborah was not inspired when speaking, yet the sacred writer may none the less have been inspired to chronicle her utterance. In other words, the book *containing* a revelation cannot be impeached because it records sayings which, though historically correct, are not so morally. As another illustration, take the complaint of Jeremiah when he cursed the day of his birth. "Cursed be the day wherein I was born" (Jer. xx. 14). Even the most reverent believer has a right to pause at this place, and say, "Could the prophet have been inspired in thus murmuring? Was it not rebellious discontent against his heavenly Father?" Note the logical distinction, however, which exists between the fact that Jeremiah uttered this sentiment out of his own wicked heart, and the fact that he was inspired to embody it afterwards in the midst of true revelations from God. We say we believe it to be often the part of Divine inspiration to record error as well as truth; chronicling error as something uttered, not because the Spirit of God approved of it, but because it was a commentary upon human weakness and ignorance.

I believe this canon of criticism is perfectly sound, gentlemen, and that it will help you, if you wish to be helped, over many apparent difficulties.

11. Now take another. (2.) "*Do not expect to find every action of inspired men in the Bible necessarily performed under the guidance of God; for at the moment of that particular act the Divine inspiration may not have been upon him.*"

For example, take the case of David's feigning himself mad in Gath, where he behaved himself in the most deceitful and disgraceful manner (1 Sam. xxi. 13). No one supposes that because the inspired historian relates this, that David was therefore under an inspiration to do it. On the contrary, we see at a glance that it was opposed to God's moral law, and a mark of unbelief in God's providence. Hence we immediately distinguish between its uninspired origin and the inspired narrative which records it.

In the same way, when we find Samson cohabiting with the Philistine Delilah, or Jephthah sacrificing his daughter in obedience to a rash vow, the book which records these acts may be written by inspiration, albeit these men were under no inspiration at the time of their committing those unworthy deeds. This canon of criticism will clear away many difficulties. Amongst others it will remove that horrible stumbling-block over which you so often make merry; I mean the treatment of the Midianitish people by Moses, when he slew all save the virgins, whom he permitted the Israelites to keep for their own depraved purposes. As far as I understand this conduct, gentlemen, I see no evidence in the account to show that Moses was here acting under any Divine order. The fact is recorded as history; and Moses was inspired to record it; but it does not follow that he was also inspired to give that order.

12. And now let me briefly note a third and final canon. You may not admit it, or if you admit it you may laugh at it, but as a matter of Biblical critism, and of Hebrew composition it is simply indisputable :—viz., "*That Jewish writers were frequently in the habit of attributing to God Himself the evils which He permitted in His Providence.*"

Let me first give you one undoubted illustration. "Shall there be evil in a city, and I have not done it? saith the Lord" (Amos iii. 6). The morality of the Old Testament might indeed be truly impeached, if this were intended to teach that God was the actual author of evil. Indeed, the notion is so preposterous, that nothing but the glaring impossibility of such an idea could have permitted this Jewish method of phraseology to approximate so apparently close to it.

Falling, however, as it did, within this well-known line of Hebrew style of composition—viz., that what God was known to have *permitted* without any arbitrary intervention of providence, He was often said to have *done*—that statement of the prophet Amos was liable to no misconception. We ourselves, in these western countries, may pronounce such a method of speech both awkward and loose; but in eastern lands, our own more precise and formal habits of expression are not by any means the law. You are not, therefore, to deny this Jewish style of writing, because it does not square with your own laws of thought. You must accept it as a peculiarity of the country to which it belongs, and of the nation in which it was followed, where verbal criticisms, like those in vogue among ourselves, were altogether unknown. And this being so, it supplies us with a canon of Scripture criticism which at once takes off the edge from several serious impeachments of the moral teaching of the Old Testament. Thus, in 2 Samuel xii., 8, God is actually described as saying to David, " I gave thee thy master's house, and thy master's wives into thy bosom ; " words which appear to make the Deity responsible for David's concubinage; and which, although unsuited to *our* methods and habits of speech, were, nevertheless, perfectly well understood by the Hebrew nation. So in that passage where the Lord is represented as sending forth a "lying spirit in the mouths of the prophets " (1 Kings xxii. 23). According to the accurate phraseology of western countries, this language seems appalling; but, under the familiar canon of criticism to which I now refer, it becomes easy and unimpeachable The same is to be said of the corresponding scene in Job i. 6—12. In both these places we have merely. certain conceptions of moral truth thrown into a dramatic form, for the sake of impressiveness, rather than the record of historical facts. Criticised with literal rigour, the language in each case may be made to prove that God holds communion with evil spirits, which is contrary to the whole tenor of Scripture; but, properly interpreted, according to the genius of Hebrew literature, they are free from any such impeachment.

In concluding this address, let me now very briefly sum up the principles which I have been applying to the solution of Old Testament difficulties :—

(1.) Omnipotence cannot work contradictions.

(2.) The constitution of moral beings having a perfectly free agency, without any possibility of falling, would be a contradiction.

(3.) The revelation of God's moral nature and pur-

Old Testament Vindicated. 173

poses, in any abstract and philosophical language, would have been utterly incomprehensible by the demoralised and uncivilised races of primitive mankind.

(4.) Long-suffering mercy toward the wicked, unlimited by protection and preservation of the righteous, would be a violation of Divine goodness.

(5.) The infliction of pain and suffering wisely conserve the purposes of ulterior and general benevolence.

(6.) Obedience to Divine law, enforced by arbitrary coercion, can never constitute moral elevation of character.

(7.) The raising of degraded and uncivilised races to moral purity must necessarily be the result of slow and progressive evolution.

(8.) In the process of this evolution we may expect to find the patient endurance of some evils, accompanied by remedial measures for their final extinction.

(9.) We may also expect to find a severe extermination of other evils, when those evils are otherwise ineradicable.

(10.) In the union of this patience and severity the moral character of Divine government is shown by the ordination of a concurrent set of laws, which tended to humanise, civilise, and purify the heart of man.

(11.) Divine inspiration has often directed the record both of sentiments and facts in the sacred books of Scripture which were, in themselves, not only uninspired, but untrue and improper.

(12.) According to the genius of Hebrew literature, God is often said to have done what He *permitted* in His Providence to be done.

I have now finished, gentlemen. I have attempted no flowers of rhetoric. I have made no effort at fine writing. My object has been to reason rather than expatiate. I think, too, in common candour, you must allow that I have shrunk from no difficulty; and that I have abstained from everything which would intentionally wound your feelings. Let me express the hope, therefore, that in the discussion which is to ensue, you will, on your side, be equally cautious and respectful.

THE METAPHORICAL LANGUAGE

APPLIED TO

GOD IN THE OLD TESTAMENT.

BY THE

REV. R. B. GIRDLESTONE, M.A.,

AUTHOR OF "THE ANATOMY OF SCEPTICISM," "THE SYNONYMS OF THE OLD TESTAMENT," "DIES IRÆ," ETC.

The Metaphorical Language applied to God in the Old Testament.

IT is to be observed at the outset that our subject does not give rise to any discussion as to the fact of God's existence; it deals only with the peculiar mode in which His character and work are set forth in a collection of Hebrew books which we call the Old Testament, and which are the common property of Jews and Christians. The writers of these books generally proceed on the hypothesis that God exists, and that any person who denies this truth puts himself in an abnormal position, and abrogates some of the highest functions of his nature. Hence it is that we find no demonstration of the being of God in the Scripture, but simply an account of certain things which He is supposed to have said and done. I must take it for granted, therefore, at least on the present occasion, that there is a God, and that the Old Testament professes to be a statement of facts and truths issued by His authority; for it is from this point of view only that the subject before us can be fairly approached. And I cannot but notice, in passing, how fitting and natural it is, if there be a God, that He should take some means of making known to men His ways and His intentions. Strange indeed would it be if century after century were to pass away, and the silence of heaven remain unbroken. Strange if He, who has given us so many means of communicating with one another, should be either unable or unwilling to hold intercourse with His creatures. If my reason and conscience convince me that there is a God, my heart pleads for a Revelation ; nor does it plead in vain.

Premising, therefore, for the sake of argument, that the Old Testament is to be regarded as in some sense a revelation of God's truth, we have to consider the metaphorical language used concerning Him in its pages. Now, as a general principle, it will be granted that a teacher must adapt himself to the capabilities of those who are to be instructed. There is, however, a special difficulty in the present instance, owing to the gulf which exists, or which is supposed to exist, between man and God. Let us try to estimate the nature of this difficulty. I believe that there is a great deal of truth of which we can have no clear cognisance. Not only are we hindered by limitations of space from knowing what is going on in other worlds, and by limitations of time, from knowing the unrecorded events of the distant past ; but also our means of apprehending that which is near and which is present are exceedingly restricted. The senses are the windows of the soul, whereby various phases of the outer world command an approach to our consciousness ; but they are surrounded by *barriers*, which prohibit the entrance of all other external things except those which are capable of giving an impression through these particular channels. It may be that if other organs, other vehicles of perception, other avenues of consciousness, were bestowed upon us, a great deal of creation which our philosophy barely dreams of would be laid

God in the Old Testament.

open before our astonished minds. It has been said that the microscope practically furnishes us with a new sense. Certainly it introduces us to an aspect of the universe with which we should be otherwise unacquainted, and has thus become the vehicle of a new revelation. Yet it would have been absolutely useless unless it had been adapted to the organ of sight, whereby alone the wonders unfolded by the microscopic lens are brought within the range of our apprehension. Now supposing that we are not at present constructed to receive full, clear, and direct communications from the Author of our being, then in order that He may come in contact with our understandings, He must needs adapt Himself to our existing faculties. If I wish to speak to a deaf man, I must accommodate myself to his defects, and use the language of gesture; and if a blind man wishes to read, he must learn to read raised type with his fingers. In the one case the eye has to do the duty of the ear; and in the other the sense of feeling has to make up for the loss of the sense of sight. And so, if that Being, who is the source and centre of all existence, is to speak to man, He must adopt human language; He must talk as a man to his brother; the Infinite must unfold Himself in terms of the finite.

Still it has been affirmed that much of the language applied to God in the Old Testament is so material, not to say carnal, as to be utterly inapplicable to a spiritual being. The argument would probably run thus: "God, if there be a God, is not a material being; but the Bible represents Him as if He were; therefore the Biblical account of Him is not to be trusted;" or else: "God is in some parts of the Bible described as spiritual, in others as material; but both cannot be true; therefore the Bible is inconsistent, and its account of God is not trustworthy." Certainly there is some *prima facie* ground for such a line of reasoning. For what are the facts? Let us look them fairly in the face. We find frequently in the Old Testament bodily organs, together with human actions and feelings, attributed to God. He is said to see, to hear, to smell, to blow; He is described as having a terrible voice, a mouth, nostrils, lips, breath, a mighty hand, an outstretched arm, palms to his hands, a back. He is said to have rested and to have been refreshed after the act of creation, to have walked in the garden, to have come down to see the Tower of Babel, to laugh, and to awake like one out of sleep. He is described as a man of war, and is said to have a sword, a bow and arrows, and a glittering spear, as well as a shepherd's rod and staff; He rides upon horses, and on the wings of the wind, and has thousands of chariots. We are told that He appeared to Abraham, that He brought him forth from his tent on one occasion; that He went His way after a conversation; that He was actually *seen* by the elders of Israel, and that He spoke face to face with Moses. Again, He is said to have made coats of skin for Adam and Eve, to have taken off the chariot-wheels of the Egyptians in the Red Sea, and to have cast great stones upon the enemies of Israel. Once more, we read that He tempted Abraham; that He sought to kill Moses; that He repented of having made man; that He was weary with repenting (Jer. xv. 6); that He hardened the heart of Pharaoh, king of Egypt, and the heart of Sihon, king of the Amorites; that He was provoked to wrath; that He is furious (Nahum i. 2, 3), and takes vengeance (Ps. xcix. 8), and that He was capable of being actuated by fear (Deut. xxxii. 27).

God in the Old Testament. 181

Is such language as this consistent with the spirituality of God? Does it convey a faithful representation of the Divine Being, and one which commends itself to an enlightened mind? Before hastily replying in the negative, we must consider, first, that the books of the Old Testament are very *ancient*, and were addressed primarily to a people whose standard of mental cultivation was not exactly what ours is. Some accommodation to their point of view was manifestly necessary. Secondly, they are *oriental*, and a highly figurative style is much more common in the East than in the West. Thirdly, many of the most peculiar of the metaphorical expressions above instanced occur in the *poetical* parts of the Old Testament, and for these a greater latitude of expression may legitimately be allowed. Fourthly, we only read the Scriptures in a *translation*, which, however excellent, fails sometimes to convey to our minds an idiom which is natural and simple in the original. Fifthly, if the ways and doings of the Divine Being were to be expressed intelligibly, it must needs be by the use of metaphors taken from human nature. Our language relating to things unseen and abstract is generally drawn from the analogy of things visible. Thus the word "language," which I have just used, is derived from *lingua*, a tongue; and the word "derive" signifies, literally, the tracing of the course of a river. When we speak of even-handed justice, dogging the footsteps of crime, of the strong arm of the law, of the iron grip of oppression, no one is foolish enough to suppose that justice has a hand, the law an arm, and crime a foot, any more than he would imagine that a field can laugh, or that the wind has an eye, and the storm a bad temper, when we speak of a smiling landscape, of the eye of the wind, or of a furious storm. These are simply figurative, or, if you will, anthropomorphic ways of expressing things.

Now it cannot be doubted that this pictorial and concrete style is very telling and effective. In fact, it is one of the secrets of true eloquence; for the more we clothe things in language derived from human attributes, instead of wrapping them up in metaphysical abstractions, so much the easier is it to strike home to the hearts of our hearers. And if this be so, why should God debar Himself from the use of human metaphor for the purpose of expounding those ways which, when regarded in the abstract, are past finding out? Why should He not talk to us, His children, in a style suited to our comprehension, and attractive to our minds? All true greatness is near akin to simplicity; and it seems to me that there is nothing more worthy of Him, whose judgments are far above out of our sight, than that He should use human beings as His messengers, human language as His vehicle of communication, and human metaphors as exponents of His character, attributes, and actions.

It must be observed, moreover, that the anthropomorphic expressions given above are not presented formally by the sacred writers as a complete account of the nature and attributes of God; on the contrary, I have had to read the whole Old Testament through to find them, and have culled them from various parts, and arranged them under various heads as best I could. The Hebrew writers have abstained from giving us any such disquisitions on the essential nature of God as might gratify the curiosity of an inquiring intellect; or any such pictorial descriptions as could feed an excited imagination. Thus, when the elders "saw the God of Israel" (Exodus xxiv. 10), *what* did they see? We are not told. When the prophet heard the still small voice saying unto him, "What doest thou here, Elijah?" he hid his face in his mantle, and saw nothing. When Isaiah "saw the Lord sitting upon His throne," what sort of a vision was vouchsafed to him? Something which made him feel his sinfulness and impurity, but we are not told what it was. And so when Ezekiel had those marvellous visions, which are described in his prophecy, there is no formal description of the appearance of God Himself. The human feelings, words, and deeds ascribed to God in the Old Testament are nowhere set forth as an account of what He is in His essential Being, but are simply introduced into the sacred record in order to give us some practical and intelligible idea of His relations towards the human race.

This point has been well put by one whom I can never name without reverence, the late Mr. Isaac Taylor, in his "Spirit of the Hebrew Poetry." After remarking that the writings of the Old Testament are symbolic in their phraseology and style, he observes that they are the fittest possible medium for conveying the truth concerning the Divine nature. We find in them, he says, not a crude theology, adapted to the gross conceptions of a rude people, but *an ultimate theology* adapted to the free use of all men, in all times, and under all conditions of intellectual advancement. "Age after age, these writings have met and satisfied the requirements of piety and of virtue; it has been so as well among the most highly cultured as among the unlearned, to whom they have imparted whatever it is needful and possible for man to know concerning God, the Creator, the Ruler, the Father, and concerning that life divine, the end of which is the life eternal." "Scientific theology," he continues, "professes to regard the Divine nature and attributes as its centre; and from that centre (supposed to be known) inferences in all directions are logically derived. But the very contrary of this is true of Biblical theology; for the central area of Biblical Theism is the human spirit, in its actual condition, its original powers, its necessary limitations, its ever-varying consciousness, its lapses, its sorrows, its perils, its hopes and its fears; its misjudgments, its faiths, its unbelief; its brightness, its darkness; whatever is lifelike in man, and whatever portends death." In this respect, Isaac Taylor truly says, Biblical writers differ from all other teachers, ancient and modern. They speak of God, not as an abstract Being, but in His relation to man. If for a moment they utter what appears to be an abstract proposition concerning Him, they invariably bring it into contact with the spiritual wants of man. Thus the Psalmist says, "Great is the Lord, and of great power, His understanding is infinite." Here are three abstract propositions, but let us note the company in which they appear. Before them come the words, "He healeth the broken in heart, He bindeth up their wounds." Here this infinite Being is brought into close contact with the sorrowful. "He telleth the number of the stars; He calleth them all by their names." Here His omniscience is put in a practical form which impresses itself most vividly upon the mind. Then comes the verse already cited, and it is immediately followed by another concrete and figurative, but intensely practical, aspect of His character: "The Lord lifteth up the meek, He casteth the wicked down to the ground" (Psalm cxlvii. 3—6). Now what a good *working conception* of the character and attributes of God we obtain from these four verses! How much more intelligible and practical than a string of abstract metaphysical propositions would have been! Nor is this a solitary instance. I could readily recite a hundred passages equally effective; in fact, the Bible is studded over with these gems of thought, all clear, sublime, practical, and —may I not add?—in accordance with the demands of the human consciousness.

The truth is, that when we begin to speculate about God, we get lost; and the longer we labour to grasp a scientific theory of the Divine Being, the deeper we plunge in the mist. But the Hebrew writers make short work of philosophical theories, and confine themselves to categorical statements in figurative language. Who, for example, can realize the omnipresence of God, or His omniscience? Who can grasp the conception of a conscious Being pervading all existence? It is hard indeed when we begin to reason upon the matter philosophically; but it is propounded intelligibly, and commands our instant assent, when set forth in such words as the following:—"The eyes of the Lord are in every place beholding the evil and the good." "Thou knowest my down-sitting and mine uprising; Thou understandest my thought afar off. Thou art about my path and about my bed, and spiest out all my ways. If I ascend up into heaven,.Thou art there; if I make my bed in Hades, behold,—Thou. If I take the wings of the morning, and dwell in the uttermost parts of the sea, even there shall Thy hand lead me, and Thy right hand shall hold me. If I say, Surely the darkness shall cover me, even the night shall be turned into day. Yea, the darkness is no darkness with Thee; the night is as clear as the ..."; the darkness and light to Thee are both alike."

Such is the method by which God lodges a right conception of His attributes in the heart of man. Other modes might be devised which would appear more scientific and philosophical, but can any be found which is more effective and more thoroughly adapted to the wants of the world?

A careful consideration of these and similar passages of Scripture will lead us to the conclusion that the Hebrew writers stand alone as the teachers, not merely of monotheism, but of the spirit-stirring belief that God is not far from every one of us, and that His nearness has for its object the elevation of man to his true position. The heaven is God's throne and the earth is His footstool, but "to this man," He says, "will I look, even to him that is poor, and of a contrite spirit, and that trembleth at my word." He inhabits eternity, and dwells in the high and holy place, but also "with him that is of a contrite and humble spirit, to revive the spirit of the humble, and to revive the heart of the contrite ones." Passages such as these are like a stream of light and heat sent down from heaven upon the dwelling of the humble worshipper. Whether he be one who turns the soil for his daily bread, or be the occupant of a professor's chair, it will be the same theology that he hence derives.

Nor is there the slightest fear lest these strong figurative expressions concerning God should be misunderstood by a thoughtful reader. When the Psalmist says, "The Lord is in His holy temple, the Lord's seat is in heaven, His eyes behold, His eyelids try the children of men," no one would go away with the impression that the Lord's presence is confined to some particular building, or that He has a literal and material seat or throne, or that He has eyes and eyelids. He would rather understand that whilst the Lord is dwelling in an atmosphere of holiness, and occupying the infinite space of heaven with His presence, and ruling all the heavenly bodies with His power, He yet has time and thought to observe the characters and conduct of men, singly. The dropping of the eyelid for the purpose of reflective scrutiny would indicate to him God's determination and a power to look through disguises, and rightly to discern the thoughts of the heart. Again, when the reader meets with the precious words, "Underneath are the everlasting arms," it would not occur to him that God had arms, but he would un-understand that the Divine Being is one able and willing to support those who lean upon Him and trust Him, under all circumstances and throughout all time. Once more, when one reads the words, "I have graven thee on the palms of my hands," who would argue from them that God had palms to His hands? Certainly no one in his senses. The inquirer would soon find out their meaning, viz., that God will never forget the wants and interests of His people, who are as close and as present to Him as they would be to a man who had written their names on the palms of his hands.

I need not, however, press such points as these. They must be manifest to every reflective mind. Let us rather advance to what is, after all, the most important consideration; viz., that the human metaphors whereby the nature and doings of God are described in the Old Testament are not only the best available means, but, when taken in conjunction with the rest of the teaching of Scripture, are fully adequate to effect their purpose.

We sometimes speak of God as bare spirit, and as separated by an infinite gulf from the material universe; but we must take care not to draw false inferences from such a statement. For who can venture to draw a definite boundary line between mind and matter? Who can determine the exact point at which spiritual existence ceases to hold relationship with material? There are some, indeed, who go so far as to tell us that mind is only a mode of matter, and that consciousness results from certain dispositions of the physical forces which run through the universe; whilst others hold that matter is the product of mind, that even the created human will and intellect are constantly showing their superiority over earth, and that consequently the First Cause of all things visible and invisible must have generated the material out of the spiritual. Certain it is that there are traces of unity and of design in the natural world which lead many to believe that it proceeds from one intelligent Being, who, forasmuch as He is not revealed to any of our senses, may be regarded as a spirit. If this be allowed to be true, at least for the sake of argument, then we should reasonably expect that the most spiritual part of creation would, to some extent, express the nature, the character, and the attributes of the Creator. Now the highest, the noblest part of the known creation is man—am I taking too much upon myself in saying this?—and if so, it is in man especially that we must look for the characteristics of God. As in each one of us the limbs are intended to express and develop into action the feelings and intentions of the heart and will, so we may conceive that the human being, holding, as he does, the highest rank in the visible creation, is so constituted as to exhibit, at least, the germs and rudiments of the attributes of his Creator; and thus, to revert to an old saying, though nature (*i.e.*, the purely material world) conceals God, yet man reveals Him. Nature obeys, but man commands;

nature is silent, but man speaks; nature is almost monotónous in its regularity, but man is constantly adapting himself to new circumstances. The points in which the lower animals rise above the inanimate world are just those in which they resemble man; and the points in which man exceeds the qualities of the lower animals are those in which he approaches the nature of God. As there is such a thing as a correlation of physical forces, according to which the laws of light, heat, and motion are regulated on analogous principles, so there is a correlation of moral and spiritual forces, according to which human faculties, human thoughts, human feelings, and human actions afford some analogies whereby we can discern the nature of that Being who is the source and spring of the human race.

This is the secret of the anthropomorphism of the Old Testament, and is implied in the first page, where we read the glorious words, "And God said, Let us make man in our image, after our likeness." Man is here regarded as God's offspring. If we could find a perfect man, not only sound in body, but also pure in heart, keen in understanding, strong in will, firm in purpose, and sublime in unselfishness, then we should have, at least in h:s moral and spiritual functions, the best possible image of God. If the child is the truest representative of the father, then man, when seen at his best, must be the fairest representative of God; and even human nature, as we observe it now, with all its faults, furnishes far better illustrations of the Divine modes of feeling and action, than can be obtained from any other source.

Whilst, however, human actions and thoughts and words are the best terms in which to unfold the working of the Divine Being, yet they need to be counterbalanced by other expositions of His nature. We need to be taught, as the Old Testament teaches us, that God's ways are not our ways, neither are His thoughts our thoughts; and that, as the heaven is higher than the earth, so are His ways than our ways, and His thoughts than our thoughts. We need to be reminded that we cannot by searching find out God; that we cannot find out the Almighty to perfection; and that, while much is revealed to us and to our children, there are still secret things which belong only to God. The outward and visible universe is but a part of His way: but "the thunder of His power, who can understand?"

In accordance with these necessary precautions, the *differentia*, so to speak, of God, those points in which He differs from man, are dwelt upon at various times in the Old Testament; and it will be observed that the difference lies not in their moral or intellectual qualities as such, but in the intensity of these qualities, and in the mode in which they work. Love, long-suffering, purity, holiness, compassion, will, determination, understanding, and wisdom, stand for the same kind of attributes in God as in man. But they differ in their fineness and perfection, and also in their durability and extension. Thus man's love is fleeting, but God's is everlasting; a mother *may* forget her child, but God will not forget; man gets faint and weary in well doing, but God fainteth not, neither. is weary; man has a limited intelligence, but there is no searching of God's understanding; man may be great, but there is no end of God's greatness. In a word, take a fully developed man; intensify all his moral and intellectual qualities infinitely, take from him all those material limitations which make him a creature of time and space; regard him as an absolute, eternal, omnipresent, spiritual being, the essence of all that is pure and holy and loving. Picture up such a being as having created the universe; as having appointed and carried out all the details of every part; as sustaining all things from moment to moment; as the source and fountain of all forces, whether physical or spiritual; as the real agent of all things, even where secondary causes are at work; as the founder of the human race; and as claiming the affection and obedience of those whom he has thus brought into existence, and whom he has endued with free will, and with various spiritual faculties. You will then have the sort of picture which the Old Testament presents of God, viewed in relation to man.

The Jews, if they believed their Old Testament, must have had a truly spiritual conception of God. He was revealed to them as an unseen spectator of human action, giving to each man a time of probation. "Behold, I go forward," says Job, "but He is not there; and backward, but I cannot perceive Him: on the left hand, where He doth work, but I cannot behold Him: He hideth Himself on the right hand, that I cannot see Him: but He knoweth the way that I take: when He hath tried me, I shall come forth as gold" (Job xxiii. 8—10). He is *absolute*, doing whatsoever He pleases and thinks right in heaven and earth (Ps. cxxxv. 6). He is *infinite;* the heavens cannot contain Him, though He fills all heaven and earth with His presence; "It is He that sitteth upon the circle of the earth, and the inhabitants thereof are as grasshoppers; that stretcheth out the heavens as a curtain, aud spreadeth them out as a tent to dwell in; that bringeth the princes to nought, and maketh the judges of the earth as nothingness." Well may He ask the question, " To whom, then, will ye liken Me, or shall I be equal? Lift up your eyes on high, and behold who hath created these (stars), bringing out their host by number, calling them all by their names, by the greatness of His might, for that He is strong in power; not one faileth." (See Isaiah xl.)

The Jews were not taught to regard Jehovah as their own peculiar Divinity, on a par with the gods of other nations. He was not the God of the Jews only, but also of the Gentiles, for their idols were really no gods. He is described as the God of the spirits of all flesh, *i.e.*, the central force, or the essence of forces (for this seems to be the meaning of the Hebrew name for God), through whose agency spiritual life manifests itself, more or less, in all men (Num. xvi. 22; xxvii. 16). Though He was in a peculiar sense the King of Israel (1 Sam. xii. 12), yet He was also to be feared as King of nations (Jer. x. 7, 10), not only because He is the Creator, Preserver, and Lord of all, but because He divided to all nations their inheritance upon earth (Deut. xxxii. 8; Jer. xxvii. 5).

Again, the Jews were especially guarded against the entertaining of any material notions of God. They were taught that He was a Being whom they had not seen, and therefore they were not to attempt to make an image of Him. An appeal, indeed, had been made by Him at Mount Sinai to their sense of hearing, but not to their sense of sight. They had heard a voice, but had seen no form (Deut. iv. 12, 19, 32—36). They were taught that He was not confined to any locality; that their approach to Him was to be spiritual, and depending upon distance; for however far they were from their native land, they could find Him, if only they sought Him with all their heart (Deut. iv. 29). Though high up, and far above out of their sight, He was very near the contrite heart (Isa. lvii. 15); and the only thing that kept Him apart from them was their sin (Isa. lix. 2). The most holy place in the tabernacle and temple, where He dwelt between the cherubim, was not regarded by them as His local habitation. It was simply the place where the priest should bring the sacrificial blood, which was the sign of their sin, into contact with the ark containing the law, which was the sign of His holiness and love. The symbolic actions of the priest represented God's nature and dealings, but there was no one definite created object which represented the Divine Being Himself. All was dark within that veil, because He could not be unfolded to their sight (2 Chron. vi. 1). Clouds and darkness were round about Him, because the true full light was not yet revealed. When King Solomon was dedicating an earthly abode to God's honour, he spoke of heaven as the real dwelling-place of the Most High, but added, what we all feel to be true, that the heaven and the heaven of heavens could not contain Him (2 Chron. vi. 18).

Such are the safeguards provided in the Jewish Scriptures to counterbalance, to qualify, and to expound the anthropomorphic language in which the dealings of God are set forth in other passages.

There are two truths with regard to the Divine nature which are taken for granted in Scripture; one is, that whatever powers man has, those God must necessarily have too. The faculties of the creature exist in the Creator, because the cause must always include the elements of the effect. This point is brought out forcibly in the ninety-fourth Psalm, where we read that certain oppressors of the widow, the fatherless, and the stranger, imagined that the Lord did not see what they were doing. How does the Psalmist argue the matter? He appeals to their reason: "Understand, ye brutish among the people, and ye fools, when will ye be wise? He that planted the ear, shall He not hear? He that formed the eye, shall He not see? He that teacheth man knowledge, shall He not know?" Similar questions might be raised with regard to all the faculties and powers in human nature.

The other truth is, that though God has all the powers which man has, He does not exercise them through the fleshly or material instrumentality that man requires. Thus Job asks God, "Hast Thou eyes of flesh? or seest Thou as man seeth?" (Job x. 4). Man, as at present constituted, cannot obtain knowledge of the material world except through the corporeal organs, nor can he think, reason, feel, or imagine, without a material brain. But we gather from Scripture that the results which we thus obtain through such elaborate and delicate instruments as the eye, and the ear, and the brain, are attained by the First Cause of these organs without any such instrumentalities. This is natural, and is only analogous to the differences which we see between the strong and the weak, between the learned and unlearned upon earth. I may leap over a deep and wide ditch, but I tell my little child that he must go all the way round by a bridge. I may work out a mathematical problem in my mind, but my child must go through an elaborate process on his slate so as to produce the required result.

Let me give two instances which may illustrate this truth. In Deuteronomy i. 33, God is described as going before Israel to search out a place where they should pitch their tents. This is a process with which every traveller in the East is familiar. I well remember how,

God in the Old Testament. 195

when I was travelling through the Holy Land, some one used to be sent forwards, as we approached our resting-place for the night, to search out a suitable place where we should pitch our tents. But would the Jews, on reading the above passage, imagine that God had to look here and there before resolving where they should pitch? No. They would only learn that the most fitting resting-place was always found for them by God, and that they were led to it, not fortuitously, but under the guidance of His providence.

Again, we read in several places that God *repented*. Are we to suppose from such passages that He was really sorry for what He had done, and that He had confessedly made a mistake? Surely not. They simply mean that the same result was attained by God, as would have been produced by repentance in man's case. If corresponding results had been arrived at under human government, we should have said that they sprang from repentance, and therefore the word is fitly used with regard to the Divine action. But lest we should interpret the word too literally, and should imagine that God not only arrives at the results which repentance produces, but also goes through the process of repentance, as it is exhibited in man, we find that in the very chapter in which God is described as repenting that He had made Saul king over Israel, it is recorded emphatically, that "the Strength of Israel will not lie nor repent; for He is not a man that He should repent" (1 Sam. xv. 11, 29, 35). Thus the one passage is checked and counterbalanced by the other. And so we shall find it in other instances, which at first sight might present some difficulty.

I feel bound here to remark on one passage which

cannot have escaped your notice. You remember that when Moses, feeling that his faith needed to be confirmed, prayed to God, saying, "I beseech Thee, show me Thy glory," the Lord is represented as answering, "Thou canst not see my face: for there shall no man see me, and live." But He added, "I will make all my goodness pass before thee, and I will proclaim the name of the Lord before thee; ... and I will cover thee with my hand while I pass by: and I will take away mine hand, and thou shalt see my back (or that which cometh after me), but my face shall not be seen" (Ex. xxxiii. 18—23). Now it is manifest that this passage must be considered as modifying what would otherwise be the literal interpretation of Exodus xxiv. 10, 11, where we read that the elders "saw" the God of Israel. We cannot suppose that they could have higher privileges than Moses; we may therefore conclude that the vision or sight of God referred to in the twenty-fourth chapter was akin to that spoken of in the thirty-third. But the question arises, What, after all, did they see? and what did Moses see? I have already pointed out the impossibility of answering this question. Considering that God is constantly set forth as an infinite spiritual Being, He cannot have been beheld in His essential attributes by the naked eye; but those privileged persons may have seen some symbol or symbols of His varied attributes; if so, it would be clearly understood by the spectators that they *were* symbols. We are told that the Lord descended in the cloud, and stood with Moses on Mount Sinai, and proclaimed the name of the Lord. "And the Lord passed by before him, and proclaimed the Lord, the Lord God, merciful and gracious, long-suffering, and abundant in goodness and truth, keeping mercy for thousands, forgiving iniquity, and transgression, and sin, and that will by no means clear (the guilty)." What a noble name! what sublime attributes! These were impressed upon the mind of Moses, apparently in some outward and visible way, whether through symbolical representations or otherwise. Then it was that there passed before him One whom he was withheld from looking upon face to face, but whose retreating form he was permitted to behold. This form was probably like unto that of a son of man, clad in robes of majesty and glory. Such may have been the nature of the vision, if we take the words literally, and believe that Moses actually beheld the back of God. But it is possible that we should understand by the *face* of God his essential Being, and by the *back* that which proceeds from Him, *i.e.*, the results of His attributes, and the workings of His goodness. These may have been unfolded in visions to the favoured few, who were, thus enabled to realize the Divine attributes, not indeed as they are in their essence, but as they are exhibited in God's dealings with His people. They saw the Back, not the Face; the results, not the processes.

There is one other point with regard to our subject which must not pass unnoticed, namely, that God condescends in the Old Testament to make use of the terms of *human relationship*, in order to set forth the family bond which exists between Himself and the children of men. Amongst the gifts bestowed upon the human race, none is so great or so beautiful as *love*. This precious gift is nurtured in us from infancy; it branches out in many directions, and links us with the past, the present, and the future generations. Most wonderful and interesting it is to turn to the Old Testament, and find there that whatsoever is pure, and noble, and spiritual in social intercourse, in friendly relationship, and in family life, is adapted to set forth the varied aspects of the connection which exists between God and man. And well may it be so; for what are these social and family bonds but developments and representations of some of the elements in the nature of the Divine Being? What are they but broken lights reflecting the nature of Him, whose essential attribute is Love?

The most familiar example of this truth is that which affirms the Fatherhood of God. It is sometimes asked, If God is the Father of the human race, who is its mother? But such a question shows a misunderstanding of the Biblical use of the word Father when applied to God. They are the spiritual, not the material aspects of Fatherhood which represent God's relationship to man. He is called Father, because He is the source of all human life by creation; because He is the sustainer and educator of men, working *on* them and *in* them, either directly or through physical and social agencies. "Have we not all one Father?" says the prophet, "hath not one God created us?" (Mal. ii. 10). "Thou art our Father," says Isaiah, "We are the clay, and Thou the Potter, and we are all the work of Thy hands" (Isa. lxiv. 8. See also Ex. iv. 22, and Deut. xxxii. 18). "The Lord thy God supported thee, as a man doth support his son" (Deut. i. 31). "Thou shalt also consider in thy heart, that as a man chasteneth his son, so the Lord thy God chasteneth thee" (Deut. viii. 5). These are some of the senses in which God is described as assuming the fatherly relation in dealing with His people. And has He not also in His heart that peculiar tenderness which belongs to a mother? Yes. He says to Israel, "As one whom his mother comforteth, so will I comfort you"

(Isa. lxvi. 13). But you will say that love can exhibit itself in a still stronger form; for the conjugal relationship is more intimate than the parental. Well, God accepts it. In Isaiah liv. 5, we read these marvellous words, "Thy Maker is thy husband;" and in Jeremiah iii. 14, "I am married to you;" and in Hosea ii. 19, "I will betroth thee unto me for ever."

And now I must draw to a close. I have endeavoured to show that the Old Testament speaks of God in human metaphor, not only because this was the sole mode of approach to the intellect and heart, but also because of the near relationship which exists between the spiritual part of man and the nature of God.

Regard the body with its material organs,—the hand, the eye, the nostril,—as the symbol and expression of the powers and emotions of the inner man; and you will have taken the first step necessary for the understanding of Bible metaphors. Assume that these powers and emotions of the human spirit are of the same kind, though differing in their extent and mode of working, as those which God includes within His nature; and you will have taken the second step. Imagine a perfectly wise, pure, and loving man; strip off from him all that is material, all that is conditioned by time and space, all that involves limitation and restriction; then the mental and moral residuum gives you a rudimentary conception of the God of the Old Testament; and thus you will have taken the third step. Conceive this Being as acting through the so-called laws of nature, which are simply the expressions of His will; so that whatever *they* effect, *He* may be said to effect. Conceive also that He has not restricted Himself to those physical ordinances which we regard as immutable, but that He has reserved to Himself the right and power of superseding them, or of acting in advance of them on due occasion; and you will have reached a fourth step. Such a view of the Divine Being as you will thus attain will not only enable you to interpret rightly many passages of the Bible which would otherwise prove a stumbling-block, but will help you to realize the grandeur of human nature, its possibilities in the unrevealed future, and its capability of becoming the dwelling-place of the Divine Being Himself, who, as some of us believe, has taken the manhood into the Godhead.

We are all constantly in danger, either of running into materialism, which is idolatry, or else of having such vague and abstract views of the Divine Being as tend to put Him far away, and practically result in atheism. The Old Testament provides against both of these dangers. It shows that God is a spiritual, not a material Being. It shows also that His life is closely akin to the spiritual side of ours, and that He is not far from every one of us; for in Him we live, and move, and have our being, and as even heathen poets have said, "We are His offspring."

Brother men! Let us *own* Him—Let us *claim* Him —as our Father!

MIRACLES AS CREDENTIALS OF A REVELATION.

BY

DR. GLADSTONE, F.R.S.

Miracles as Credentials of a Revelation.

IF towards the close of the Roman Empire a Christian advocate had stood up in some Hall of Science in Egypt, Greece, or Italy, and had appealed to the testimony of miracles, he would have found his audience more ready to admit them as facts than as credentials. A Jew present might have allowed that Jesus of Nazareth healed many sick persons—indeed, the writings of the Rabbis admit it—but he would have contended that these wonders were performed by diabolical or at least magical power. A devotee of the pagan religions might have put Jesus alongside of Æsculapius or Hercules among the multitude of heavenly powers; and the mass of hearers, credulous or incredulous, would have classed the narratives of the Christian with the tales told of the oracles, the story of Apollonius of Tyana, and the magic that was pouring over the Roman world from Syria and the more distant East.

If some preacher of righteousness in the dark ages had talked of the Bible miracles as credentials, he would have met with little encouragement from believers, and little opposition from sceptics; for stories of portents, occult influences, the power of words, or strange transmutations, were swallowed without thought; astrology, alchemy, and magical medicine, were the sciences of the day: but whether the wondrous deeds were attributed to divine or to infernal power, whether the miracle-workers were to be canonized or burnt, depended upon whether they gained the endorsement or the anathema of the Church. Verily in those ages faith in God was weak, but faith in the devil was marvellously strong.

But as I stand before you this evening the whole aspect of the argument is changed. Hercules and Æsculapius died long ago; some of us have crawled into the hollow under the statue of Isis at Pompeii, from which the concealed priests uttered the oracles; Apollonius is a romance; we have ceased to believe in magic, or to burn sorcerers; while as to the devil, he is both dethroned and laughed at; and though a personal Satan keeps his place in the general creed of Christendom, few believe that his power extends beyond the realm of mind or spirit. The objection urged now against miracles is not so much that they are inconclusive, as that they are incredible; and many Christians as well as sceptics find that the miraculous histories of the Bible are not helps to their faith, but difficulties in its way.

The advance of natural science is the principal, though not the only, cause of this change of view. And it is because I am a scientific man, and therefore capable of appreciating the difficulties of the case, that this subject has fallen to my lot. I can indeed sympathise with every doubter; between the faith of my childhood and my present convictions there lay a chaos of scepticism; in one of my earliest essays I wrote of the "dread uniformity of nature's laws;" and if that presses heavily now on the mind of any of my audience, he shall not hear from my lips any light or unfeeling word. I may add, however, that it is many years since I came to the principal con-

Miracles as Credentials of a Revelation. 205

clusions I mean to express to-night—conclusions which have remained with little modification, though I have since studied Professor Baden Powell's "Order of Nature," and many other writings on various sides of the controversy.

How is it that this advance of science, this triumphal progress of modern discovery, has affected our views of miracles? It is not that it has taught us the existence of natural laws, or revealed to us an order in nature. This was recognized long ago. From time immemorial men knew that the sun rose and set regularly, and that the moon went through certain regular phases; and thousands of years ago attempts were made to calculate such apparently irregular things as eclipses. Polytheistic nations may indeed have thought that one god interfered sometimes with the proceedings of another, but the worshippers of the one Jehovah at least believed Him without a rival, and held it as one of His most ancient and most solemn promises that "while the earth remaineth, seed-time and harvest, and cold and heat, and summer and winter, and day and night, shall not cease." This fore-ordained order of events was personified in the Greek and Latin mythologies as Moira, or Fate; and taking rank as a deity, her influence appeared so irresistible, that the question arose whether Fate was subject to Jupiter, or Jupiter to Fate. The philosophers of Greece recognized just as fully the order of nature, and as far back as Pythagoras the word Kosmos, beauty and order, was used to signify the universe. It became the term commonly employed, so that to a Greek the two ideas glided into one, and Kosmos was afterwards defined as "the connected system of all things, the order and arrangement of the whole preserved under the Gods, and by the Gods." And not very different from this, except in the use of the singular for the plural, are the words addressed by a Jewish sage to the Almighty, "Thou hast ordered all things in measure, and number, and weight."

Of course we understand the laws of nature incomparably better than the Greeks or Jews did; many things that once seemed to break the harmony have now fallen into their proper places, and large regions of phenomena hitherto undreamt of have been opened to our gaze. Gradually the mechanism of the great universe is being made clearer and clearer to the human intellect. We trace the continuity of its several parts; we believe in the indestructibility of matter, the transformation of force, and the conservation of energy. Such faith have we in the analogy of nature, that in our laboratories we often predict "measure, number, and weight," before we try the experiment, and even foretell the boiling points and other properties of compound bodies that have never yet been produced. Yet, while holding that the amount of energy in the universe always remains the same, we believe not in a ceaseless round of phenomena, but in a certain slow progress towards perfection; and we understand, or think we understand, more and more of the origin of things, and the various stages of development by which the objects and living beings around us have come into existence.

But the great influence of modern science on this question of miracles has not arisen from the additional proofs that the proceedings of nature are orderly, so much as from the perception that those proceedings are independent of the interests of men. The progress of knowledge has abolished the belief in portents and omens. If a comet shook its dreadful sword, if a coronet of red flames sprang up from the northern horizon, or if the heavens rained tears of fire, it was thought to presage some dire calamity, but now we compare the flashing of the aurora with the trembling of our magnetic needles, and we calculate the orbit of the comet, or the return of the shower of shooting stars. It is true that nativities are still cast, and fortunes are told, but only in the dark corners of European society. The progress of science, too, has exorcised nature, and showing that "all are but parts of one stupendous whole," it has left no room for the freaks of evil spirits. Science has taught us, moreover, that nature is "no respecter of persons," and is unmoved by fear, or love, or pity. The benevolence or religious worth of a Christian visitor is no protection to him in the wards of a fever hospital, and the agony of a thousand men, women, and children made no difference to the heeling over of the *Atlantic* when she struck on the Sambro Rock.

Yet, while science asserts that the course of nature does not turn aside for the benefit of men, Christianity maintains that it has been sometimes so turned aside, and many intelligent Christians believe that it sometimes is so still.

"Incredible!" cries Hume. "We have this only on human testimony, and it is far more in accordance with experience that human testimony should be false, than that miracles should take place." More in accordance with your experience and mine no doubt; but to assume that miracles are contrary to universal experience is to assume the point at issue. Hume's argument would leave it impossible to believe in any extraordinary event in past history. But I will not repeat the various answers which were at once given to this sophistry, but content myself with the words of John Stuart Mill:* "All which Hume has made out, and this he must be considered to have made out, is, that (at least in the imperfect state of our knowledge of natural agencies, which leaves it always possible that some of the physical antecedents have been hidden from us,) no evidence can prove a miracle to any one who did not previously believe the existence of a being or beings with supernatural power; or who believes himself to have full proof that the character of the Being whom he recognizes, is inconsistent with his having seen fit to interfere on the occasion in question."

There are doubtless some in my audience who do not believe in any God at all. To them of course miracles have no meaning: if they saw with their own eyes multitudes fed with a few loaves and fishes, or a dead man raised to life, it would be simply an unaccountable perturbation in the movements of that lifeless, though self-originated and self-sustained, machinery of the universe. I must leave such, merely asking them to listen to an anecdote. "In the society of Baron d'Holbach, Diderot proposed one day to nominate an advocate of God, and they chose Abbé Galleani. He seated himself, and began thus: "One day, at Naples, a man of the Basilicate took in our presence six dice in a box, and betted that he would throw six. I said the chance was possible. He threw it a second time immediately after: I said the same. He put the dice into the box three, four, five times, and always threw six. 'Sangue di Bacco,' I cried, 'the dice are loaded!' and so they were. Philosophers, when I consider the order of nature ever renewed, its unchangeable laws,

* System of Logic, Book III., c. xxv., § 2.

its revolutions always constant in infinite variety, that single chance which preserves the universe such as we see it, returning incessantly in spite of a hundred million other possible chances of perturbation and destruction, I cry, 'Assuredly Nature is loaded.'"

Among those who believe that "nature is loaded," we sometimes meet with persons who say that God must always have acted in such and such a prescribed manner. These men belong to the Greek period, and like some of the old theologians, have decided the question between Fate and Jupiter, in favour of Fate, or like some of the old philosophers, have personified Necessity, and then fallen before the phantom of their own raising. But a comparison with the Greeks is too complimentary; these persons remind me rather of that fly, who, sticking head downwards on the beam of a steam engine, discoursed with quiet confidence to a coterie of brother flies, about the limited capacity of Watt.

But there are earnest men who, without saying "must" or "must not" to the Supreme, deny to man the right of thinking of God's procedure in nature as ever in any way different from that in which we see Him ordinarily acting, and they remind us that He is the unchangeable One, and that with Him there is "no variableness, neither shadow of turning." This objection may be, and often is, the offspring of faith, scientific and religious; and it certainly merits a careful and serious reply.

Will any one who feels this difficulty pass with me from the inanimate to the animate creation? We shall find there the old physical forces in full play, but regulated and modified in their action according to new physiological laws unknown in the mineral kingdom, but equally orderly, equally constant, equally divine. We shall observe, moreover, the indications of mind, thought, purpose, will. Even in the lower animals around us, our dogs, horses, or singing birds, we unhesitatingly recognize a freedom of choice, and a spontaneousness of action; we are pleased or angry with them, we punish or reward them. If, after studying the inanimate world, we turn to consider our own minds, we feel still more that we have passed from the domain of mechanism to that of motive, from necessity to liberty. We find ourselves weighing reasons, choosing between different courses, and then— altering the ordinary course of nature. Thus I am free to lift this piece of paper, or to let it lie; but if I lift it, my will has counteracted the law of gravitation. It is true I can influence the course of nature only within certain limits; and can do so only by taking advantage of the natural forces themselves; it is true also that I cannot destroy matter, but I can change its mode of combination; it may be true, likewise, that to increase or diminish the amount of energy in the universe is beyond my power, but I can and do transmute one force into another, and vary their direction.

In close analogy to this perturbing influence of our human wills is what may be conceived to take place if the Supreme Will works a miracle. It is not necessary to suppose that there has been in any instance either the creation or destruction of matter or energy, but only some new distribution of force ;* yet it is a necessary part of

---

* Of course this remark is not intended to exclude the idea of an original act of creation. In this connection the following passage of the great Leibnitz may be read with interest: "According to my opinion, the same force and vigour remains always in the world, and only passes from one part of matter to another, agreeably to the

the conception of a miracle that this interference with the ordinary course of nature shall be such as man is unable to effect.

We have already thought of the universe under the simile of a machine; let us look at the machines of men. One day I stood in the cathedral of Strasburg before the famous clock, and watched it steadily marking the seconds, minutes, hours, days of the weeks, days of the month, phases of the moon, etc., when suddenly the figure of an angel turned up his hour glass, another struck four times, and Death struck twelve times with metal marrow bones to indicate noon; various figures passed in and out of doorways, the twelve apostles marched one by one before the figure of their Master, and a brass cock three times flapped its wings, threw back its head, and crowed. All this was of course as much a part of the designer's plan as the ordinary marking of the time; and in like manner there is no reason whatever against conceiving that the introduction of new movements in the great machine of the universe may be part of the working out of the great Designer's plan: in fact, that the apparent suspension of a law of nature is only the coming into operation of a higher law.

I am not, however, content to speak of nature as a machine invented, made, and set going by God. The analogy may perhaps hold good so far, but then it breaks down; for our machines are sustained in action by the physical forces themselves, and so they cannot serve as

laws of nature and the beautiful pre-established order. And I hold that when God works miracles, He does not do it in order to supply the wants of nature, but those of grace. Whoever thinks otherwise must needs have a very mean notion of the wisdom and power of God."

an explanation of the orderly action of these forces. It seems to me more philosophical to conceive of the material universe as one expression of the Divine thought, the orderly action of the Supreme will; and thus the "laws of nature" become simply the methods in which He chooses to act.

There is a similar, though of course inferior, order in the actions of men. I watch my neighbour for several days, and see that every morning, whether fine or wet, he leaves home for the city, and that he returns again in the evening. This is the first law at which I arrive. But after a few days I find there is a break of a day; this occurs again shortly afterwards; and presently I have to correct my idea of the law of his movements, for I find it to be this:—for six days consecutively he goes to work, but not on the seventh day. And so the summer and autumn pass, and the winter comes on, and I am gaining great confidence in the formula by which I express my neighbour's movements, when one morning I find the course of six days is broken. I discover, however, a reason for this: Christmas is come, and among the blessings it brings is the release from daily toil. Well, I must interpolate this annual festival in my formula. Again the order of my neighbour's procedure seems perfect, when suddenly there is an unexpected break, and on inquiry I learn that one of his family is ill: new circumstances have called in action another motive, and anxious love has broken the order of his daily life.

Just so in the procedure of God it is the occurrence of new, though perhaps foreseen, circumstances which supplies the motive for the miracle. The Christian theory is, not that a miracle is an effect without a cause, but

Miracles as Credentials of a Revelation. 213

the consequence of the coming in of a new cause.* I proceed to explain what this new cause is.

Among the few points on which Christians, Jews, Mahometans, Buddhists, Sun-worshippers, Brahmins, Fetish-worshippers, Deists and Secularists are all agreed, is this,—men are not as good or as happy as they might be. There is found everywhere a longing for something better, some remedy for evil, or, at any rate, some relief from suffering and sorrow. Among the commonest beliefs of man is that in spiritual beings, and in the existence of the soul after death; and among his strongest instincts are those of prayer and worship. Sometimes this need expresses itself in confident appeals to some deity; at other times it cannot advance beyond that which the poet laureate describes:

> "So runs my dream: but what am I?
> An infant crying in the night,
> An infant crying for the light,
> And with no language but a cry."

But, friends, when the baby cries, the mother's arms are stretched forth in the darkness to soothe its fears or to supply its needs; and so men have believed that when they cried, a heavenly Father has responded to their cry, and come to their help.

Yet is it true? Does the Almighty really care for men? May it not be that this religious instinct, unlike other instincts, is doomed to perpetual disappointment?

Or, granting that He may have broken the silence, in what way has He spoken? Has He revealed Himself solely to the individual inquirer, or has He sent a message to a particular race of men, or to the whole

* *Vide* T. Brown, Mill, Bushnell, Duke of Argyll, Warington, etc.

human family? Many men have put in their claims as His messengers; but there are lunatics and fanatics abroad, not to speak of designing impostors, and we do well to ask the credentials of every professed ambassador from the court of heaven. Indeed, the divergence of their statements obliges us to do so. Which religion are we to follow? Are we to fall back on ancient tradition, or rely on modern utterances? Are we to listen to a book or a priest? If a book, shall it be the Bible, or the Vedas, the Zendavesta, or the Koran? If a priest, which deity of the pantheon shall he represent? Are we to believe, with the Christian Scriptures, that God Himself is "waiting to be gracious," or are we required to propitiate His favour as other religions teach? And when we come to practical morality, are we to guide our lives by the teaching of Buddha, Confucius, or Jesus of Nazareth?

It is no part of my intention to speculate on the various ways in which the Supreme Being might have confirmed His message either to the individual recipient, or to others; "His ways are higher than our ways;" but I think that there are two conclusions which will be generally accepted by those who have given any attention to the subject. First, that if a revelation is given, there are good reasons why some authentication should be given with it. Secondly, that if He should choose to accompany the revelation of His will with some departure from the ordinary course of nature, it would be an effective way of accomplishing the purpose. There would, indeed, be certain advantages attending such a mode of attestation: it would attract and rivet attention; it would be comprehensible by all, the ignorant as well as the learned, the debased as well as the pure in heart;

and there would be a certain congruity between the message and the seal; for a special revelation of Himself is a departure from God's ordinary course of action, and partakes itself of the nature of miracle.

It is, also, no part of my intention to consider what kind of evidence has been offered by the various religions in the world, or whether, indeed, they have offered any evidence. There is one religion with which we are specially interested: it is that which, whether true or false, is professed by the most civilized nations, and believed by many of our greatest thinkers; one which powerfully influences modern thought, and affects us all, whether we accept it or not. This religion has a long history, which is inextricably intertwined with narratives of miracles;* and I propose glancing, with you, at these narratives, and observing what purpose is assigned to such departures from the ordinary course of nature. It need make no difference to our inquiry whether we believe them to be literally true, or coloured exaggerations of real events, or fabulous as fairy tales: what we have to find out is the motive assigned for their performance; and then we have to judge for ourselves whether this motive is sufficient to render credible a departure from the ordinary course of God's proceedings in nature.

Fortunately, in regard both to ancient Judaism and to Christianity, which was developed from it, we have documentary evidence; and we may fairly accept these

---

* There are three Hebrew and three Greek words principally employed in the Bible, which are rendered in our English version by "miracles," "marvellous works," "wonders," and "signs;" terms which are applied to the same events, regarded, however, from different points of view.

writings as representing the opinions of the founders and early teachers of the two systems.

The sacred books of the Jews commence with some fragmentary records which profess to carry the history of man up to the earliest period. These are followed by a tolerably consecutive history of their nation from the time of their great progenitor, Abraham. At first, it is stated, the one true God spoke to this Eastern sheikh and his descendants, but no attestation was given beyond the family itself, as indeed it was not needed. When, however, the Hebrews were to be delivered from their slavery in Egypt, and to be raised into a nation, we read of a marvellous outburst of miraculous power, all in connection with their great leader and lawgiver, Moses. He is first convinced of his Divine commision by means of a miracle ;* and he is empowered to perform miracles in order to convince others;† then the relative control over the forces of nature possessed by the God of the Hebrews and the Gods of Egypt is submitted to the arbitrament of miracle;‡ a series of wonders are wrought in order to deliver the chosen people from the house of bondage, to preserve them in their long pilgrimage through the Arabian desert, and to convince their degraded minds that Jehovah was indeed the God, and that the statutes and commandments which He gave through His servant Moses were to be kept.§ The Jewish history proceeds to describe the invasion and the gradual subjugation of Canaan, and still we meet with miracle apparently to secure the allegiance to God of that people who were the repositories of His revealed law. Sometimes, as in the case of Gideon, miracles

* Exod. iii. ‡ Exod. v., *et seq.*; see vii. 9.
† Exod. iv. § Deut. iv. 32-40.

Miracles as Credentials of a Revelation. 217

were wrought first to fortify the faith of a hesitating leader, and then to show the people that it was really "the sword of the Lord" that gained the victory over the hosts of the Midianites.* We read at length of the tribes being welded into a nation living in tolerable security, and worshipping the Lord; there is no rival deity, and no fresh revelation, though Divine poems are composed and sung, and there are few or no miracles. But presently the kingdom is rent in two; the southern portion retains the worship of Jehovah, at least in outward form; there arise many prophets, but there is no need of confirming their testimony by miracles; only towards the close of the kingdom of Judah we meet with a miraculous deliverance from an invading foe, and a sign given to confirm the monarch's hope.† In the northern kingdom, however, it was far otherwise: for political reasons Jeroboam set up an idolatrous worship of the true God within his own dominions, and instantly a prophet is sent to denounce the sacrilege, with the credentials of a double sign.‡ Half a century later King Ahab, through his marriage with Jezebel, introduced the worship of Baal, and immediately a mighty prophet, Elijah the Tishbite, proclaims a drought in the name of the Lord God of Israel, and soon on the summit of Carmel the gauntlet is thrown down, and the rival claims of Jehovah and Baal are decided by the wager of battle.§ But indeed the whole history of this great reformer of Israel, and his successor, Elisha, is a series of miraculous events. When the Jews were carried captive to Babylon, we meet the worshippers of the Lord face to face with triumphant heathenism, the prophets who lived there among their

* Judges vi. vii. † 2 Kings xix. xx. Observe xix. 19.
‡ 1 Kings xiii. § 1 Kings xviii.

fellow-countrymen—like their predecessors—did no miracle; but there were pious Jews whose home was in the heathen court, and one who occupied a most exalted position, and retained it through changes of dynasty. On behalf of these, great signs and wonders were wrought, so that both Nebuchadnezzar and Darius were convinced that the God of Daniel was "the King of heaven," "the living God," and they declared it in formal decrees.* But the Jews were restored to their land; they set their faces sternly against idolatry, though such resistance brought terrible persecutions upon them. For four centuries there arose no prophet, and the pious leaders made no pretentions to miraculous power.

Then there was the dawn of a brighter day. John the Baptist called the people to repentance, and pointed to "the Lamb of God," but it was not to himself that the new revelation was entrusted, and "John did no miracle." But Jesus, to whom he pointed, is described in all the extant biographies, as living a life superhuman from its commencement to its close upon this earth, ever surrounded with marvellous events, saying marvellous words, and doing marvellous deeds. Winds and water obey Him, substances change their nature or their quantity at His command, and innumerable forms of human suffering—leprosy and fever, paralysis and atrophy, lunacy and demoniacal possession, blindness and dumbness, even death itself—are vanquished by His word.† This, we are told, attracts the attention of the populace to the great Teacher, and his claims to the Messiahship are freely recognized by the brave Galileans who flock round Him from the cities of the lake. Yet we must not imagine that this was the sole purpose of His miracles;

* Dan. iv., vi. † The four Gospels throughout.

many of them were acted parables; and the example of His benevolence, caught up by the Christian Church, has laid the foundation of every hospital, and started almost every deed of self-denying charity in later ages. In Jerusalem we read of His miracles riveting attention, and exciting controversy. A ruler of the Jews says to Him in early days, "Rabbi, we know that Thou art a Teacher come from God; for no man can do these miracles that Thou doest, except God be with him;" and afterwards a man born blind, but restored to sight, uses the same argument, though he puts it more bluntly. We find Jesus frequently appealing to these mighty works as bearing witness that the Father has sent Him: and after the raising of Lazarus from the dead had convinced very many, the chief priests call together the Sanhedrim to discuss the serious question, "What do we? for this man doeth many miracles. If we let Him thus alone, all men will believe on Him."* And this was the cause of His judicial murder.

A few days after His ascension, we meet with His apostles preaching in this strain : "Ye men of Israel, hear these words; Jesus of Nazareth, a man approved of God among you by miracles, and wonders, and signs, which God did by Him in the midst of you, as ye yourselves also know." But the Master had previously conferred on His disciples the power of working miracles, and when His personal presence was taken away, they continue to challenge attention to their statements by doing wonderful works.† Thus, to single out Paul, we read of

* Compare John iii. 2; v. 36; vii. 31; ix. 16, 30, 33; x. 37, 38; xi. 47, 48; xii. 10, 11, 18, 19; xv. 24.
† Compare Acts ii. 6-11, 43; iii.; v. 12-16; vi. 8; Heb. ii. 4; 1 Cor. xii. 10, 28, 29.

him performing miracles at Cyprus, Iconium, Lystra, Philippi, Ephesus, Troas, and Melita, and he appeals to his possession of this power in his letters to the Corinthians, the Galatians, and the Romans,* and that with express reference to the later developments of Christian doctrine.

I am not assuming the reality of these miracles, but merely inquiring what was taught and believed. The records may in some cases have been written long after the events they profess to describe, but in regard to Christ there can be no doubt whatever that His personal friends attributed this superhuman character and power to Him; the superhuman element is no late addition to the gospel story, it is the very substratum, the very texture of the story itself, an essential part of the original tradition,† for maintaining which they suffered the greatest opprobrium and the severest persecutions.

From the sketch we have just made it will be seen that the miracles of the Bible group themselves principally round three great personages, Moses, Elijah, Jesus, and that in each of the three cases the wonder-working power is continued for awhile to their followers. There is a great difference certainly between the three: for Moses and Elijah are represented as performing their miracles as servants of the Most High, Jesus Christ as a son; *they* give their commands to nature in the name of the Lord, *He* in His own name. We are led to understand that each of these men was in very special communion with God; they were large-souled men, in whom dwelt so much of the Spirit of God that His power was at their disposal in a way far above that

---
* 2 Cor. xii. 12; Gal. iii. 5; Rom. xv. 18, 19.
† See St. Luke's preface to his Gospel.

granted to their fellows. The great mission of Moses was to proclaim the Law, and to form the nation that was to be the guardian of the Law; the great mission of Elijah was to bring back the kingdom of Israel to its allegiance to Jehovah; the greater mission of Jesus was to reveal the Father, to found the kingdom of heaven, and to make that great sacrifice which should reconcile man to God. We have seen that each of these, as well as their followers, appealed to their mighty works as seals of God's approval. Were not the objects worthy of the attestation?

My own deduction, from the study of the Bible and from other things, is this: Many imperfect and erroneous answers have been given to the cry of sinful, suffering humanity; but God, in love to man, has gradually made known His true answer. The way which He has chosen for doing this is to fill certain men more or less with His own Spirit,* and then to send them as ambassadors to their fellow-men; and just as ambassadors from an earthly potentate are accredited by some seal or signature from the royal hand, so do these representatives of Heaven (especially where their mission was contested) bring with them signs of superhuman power. These are not their only, perhaps not their best, credentials; but some credentials are absolutely necessary, if our faith is to be grounded on reason. This removes from my mind all *à priori* difficulty about miracles, and my scientific training leads me to place the highest value on any well authenticated departures from the ordinary course of nature, in fact a higher value than could have been assigned to them in former days.

* Of Christ it is written, "God giveth not the Spirit by measure unto Him."

But my conclusion will be challenged, and that from different quarters.

It will probably be contended that many of the miracles recorded in the Bible are trivial, and unworthy of so high a purpose. Yes, some are trivial, if we take them by themselves; but not so if we take them as parts of a whole system. We must not, in fact, look upon every miracle as a separate credential, but rather as an outcome of that superhuman power with which the prophet was invested; often rather as a part of the revelation itself, a lesson in the care of God for man.

It may also be affirmed that some of the miracles are grotesque, even absurd. Yes, there are miracles which appear so, but only, I think, to those who have never taken the trouble to transport themselves in imagination to the distant period and different state of civilization, and to make themselves familiar with all the circumstances of the case.

I shall be asked too, If a man does a miracle, are we bound to believe everything he says? To this I answer, If a man brings the signature of a foreign prince, are we to believe everything he says? We are to accept as authentic what his credentials are designed to attest, but not necessarily anything more. Yet in the case of God's ambassadors, we may also regard their credentials as high certificates of character. Still I shall be asked, Are there not such things as false miracles? Assuredly there are. Let me give one instance from the history of the Magi, when their power was slipping away. A priest of the name of Adurabad Mabrasphant, in the year 241, offered to submit to the fiery ordeal; he proposed that eighteen pounds of melted copper glowing from the furnace should be poured upon his body, on condition that if he were

Miracles as Credentials of a Revelation.

unhurt the unbelievers should yield to so great a miracle. The trial was attended with such complete success, that it is said his opponents were all brought back to the faith of their ancestors. Now there was really nothing miraculous in this. Molten metal, if sufficiently hot, does not come into contact with a moist body; and it was once part of the secret knowledge of the masonic guilds of the middle ages that the hand might be dipped with impunity into melted lead. I myself have often passed my fingers through it, and even through melted iron and gold. The feats of honest jugglery or the newest discoveries of science, may of course at any time be pressed into the wretched service of religious, or rather irreligious imposture; and this shows that miracles, to be of value as credentials, must be unmistakably beyond the sphere of man's unaided power at the time, and that their value is greatly enhanced if they are of various kinds grouped together, as in each of the three great epochs of miracles mentioned above. But the question will still be pushed, If an act is clearly superhuman, is it necessarily divine? There are passages of Scripture which at first sight suggest the idea of real miracles in support of falsehood; and there are said to be some fairly authenticated stories of miracles in attestation of Roman Catholic doctrines or Mormon tenets; but in my opinion these passages of Scripture refer always to false miracles, forged credentials, like that of Adurabad Mabrasphant, and those miraculous narratives have never come before me with anything approaching the weight of testimony possessed by the gospel narratives, or that which is perhaps the best authenticated of all events in past history, the resurrection of Christ. I am fully aware that in this view of the authority of miracles I differ from some of the most thoughtful of my Christian brethren; still my faith in the uniformity of natural laws, and in God, render it almost inconceivable to me that He should ever turn aside from the ordinary course of His procedure at the dictation of falsehood.*

I wish it, however, to be distinctly understood that I do not exalt the testimony of miracles above that of other evidences of Christianity. The relative value of different kinds of evidence will change in process of time, and will certainly be very differently estimated by different minds. I have considered it my special duty as a scientific man, to point out how the recent progress of the physical sciences, by completely overthrowing the rule of chance or caprice, has shown that the origin of miracles must be sought in the will of God, and that they may take their place in the fore-determined order of the universe, but only on condition of an adequate motive being assigned. Such a motive the Christian religion does assign.

Many will seek the confirmation of their faith rather in the fulfilment of prophecy, the victories of Christ in the individual soul or in the world at large, the wonderful  adaptation of His religion to produce a noble and holy life, or the self-evidencing power of truth. Probably if our minds and consciences were stainless, truth, when once presented to us, would, like the Light of the world, need no credentials; but we may well be thankful that God has attested His revelation by proofs adapted to the various minds of men.

* For an elaborate examination of this question see Dr. Wardlaw's work "On Miracles;" for the opposite view see Archbishop Trench's "Notes on the Miracles of our Lord."

THE HISTORICAL EVIDENCE OF THE RESURRECTION OF JESUS CHRIST.

BY THE

REV. C. A. ROW, M.A.,

AUTHOR OF "THE NATURE AND EXTENT OF DIVINE INSPIRATION,' THE JESUS OF THE EVANGELISTS," "THE MORAL TEACHING OF THE NEW TESTAMENT," ETC.

The Historical Evidence of the Resurrection of Jesus Christ.

THE writers of the New Testament have directly staked the truth of Christianity on the actual performance of a single miracle, the Resurrection of Jesus Christ. If this cannot be established as an historical fact, it is a mere useless waste of time and trouble to attack any other of the miracles of the Bible, or to attempt to prove their truth. If Jesus Christ did not rise from the dead, all the other miracles in the New Testament would not avail to prove that Christianity is a Divine revelation. If He did, this one alone would prove it, and support the weight of all the rest. As, then, this miracle forms the very key of the Christian position, I challenge unbelievers to join issue on its truth or falsehood.

I shall treat this subject precisely as I would any point of secular history. I shall not ask you to believe that the New Testament is inspired. I shall make use of the Gospels as I would any other memoirs. I shall claim no other authority for the letters of St. Paul than I would for the letters of Cicero. You on your part must not object that miracles are impossible; for, whether they are, or are not, is a philosophical question which lies beyond the regions of historical enquiry. In this lecture I can only deal with historical evidence.

I am now going to prove that the truth of the Resurrection of Jesus Christ rests on the highest form of historical evidence. In doing so I shall take for granted that no one who reads this lecture will deny the truth of certain *facts*, which all the learned unbelievers of Europe who have studied this question admit to be *facts*. To attempt to prove what they allow to be true would be pure waste of time. I shall take it for granted that what such men as Strauss, Renan, Baur and the whole Tubingen School admit, they will not deny. I shall assume therefore,

1st. That Jesus Christ existed; that He collected round Him a body of followers, who believed in Him as the Messiah; and that He was crucified by the authority of the Roman government.

2nd. That the first three Gospels were published, in the form in which we now read them, not later than A.D. 110; and that one of them was composed at least ten years earlier.

3rd. That the four most important letters of St. Paul, viz., that to the Romans, the two to the Corinthians, and that to the Galations, were unquestionably written by St. Paul himself; and that the latest of them cannot have been written at a later date than twenty-eight years after the crucifixion.

4th. That before the end of the first century, or less than seventy years after the crucifixion, Christian churches were to be found in all the great cities of the Roman Empire.

If any unbeliever refuses to concede these points,

I appeal from his judgment to that of all the eminent unbelievers of modern Europe, and say, Do not ignorantly deny as historical facts what all your own great men affirm to have been so.

The first point in my proof is, that the Christian Church has existed as a visible institution, without a single break in its continuity, for a period of more than eighteen centuries, and that it can be traced up to the date which is assigned to its origin, by the most unquestionable historical evidence. The Christian Church asserts, and ever has asserted, that the cause of its renewed existence, after the death of its founder, was not the belief in a dogma or a doctrine, but in a fact, that Jesus Christ rose again from the dead.

Now, observe the importance of the fact that the Christian Church is, and ever has been, a visible community. All communities must have had an origin of some kind. The supposed designs of its founder were cut short by His being executed by the authority of the Roman Government. Yet it is certain that the institution was set agoing again after His death. The belief in the resurrection formed the ground of the renewed life of the community. The Christian Church asserts in all its documents, that the sole cause of its renewed life was not that *His followers found a new leader;* but that *they believed that Jesus Christ rose from the dead.*

But observe further; if Jesus Christ rose from the dead, or his followers were firmly persuaded that he did so, this forms a rational account of the origin of this great institution. If the fact is denied, unbelievers are bound to give a rational account of its origin. We affirm that no other theory can account for it.

Let me illustrate the importance of the calling into

existence of a great historical institution, and its continuous life, as a proof of a fact. Take the instance of Mahomedanism. Like the Christian Church, the Church of Mahomet has existed as a visible community since the seventh century. It claims to owe its origin to the peaceful preaching of Mahomet at Mecca, followed by his being acknowledged as prophet and sovereign at Medina. The facts as reported by his followers are adequate accounts of its origin, and the continuous existence of the Mahomedan Church, from the time of its foundation to the present day, affords the strongest possible corroboration to the truth of the fact, as handed down by its first historians, that its institution was due to Mahomet, and that certain events in his life were the causes of its existence. These events are adequate and philosophical accounts of it.

Unbelievers have adopted a summary way of disposing of the entire question of the historical character of Christianity. They tell us that the three first Gospels consist of a bundle of myths and legends, united with a few grains of historic truth, which were slowly and gradually elaborated between A.D. 30 and A.D. 100. About that period three unknown persons reduced them into their present form. These accounts gradually superseded all the other stories, and became accepted by the Church as the only true account of the actions and teaching of Jesus. All the miraculous stories in the Gospels gradually grew up in the form of myths and legends in the course of the seventy years which followed the crucifixion. They are, in fact, a growth formed by the imagination of the early Church. The fourth they assert to be a late forgery.

My answer involves a distinct issue. Let it be fairly met. There is *one of the miraculous narratives in the*

Gospels, which certainly did not originate in this manner. This is the miracle of the Resurrection of Jesus Christ, which, whether it occurred as a fact, or was invented as a fiction, was believed in by the Church shortly after the death of its founder. This belief was the foundation on which the Christian society was erected, and the cause of its renewed vitality.

As it is allowed to be an historical fact by all the distinguished unbelievers of Europe, that an eminent Jew, named Jesus, collected a number of followers, who believed in Him as the Messiah of Jewish expectations, I shall not waste your time in proving it. It is evident that His public execution must have extinguished their hopes that He could ever fulfil the expectations which they had formed. Such being the case, the community which He sought to found must have gone to pieces, unless a new leader could be discovered who was capable of occupying His place. But as its existence to the present hour proves that it did not perish, it is certain that it must have made a fresh start of some kind; something must have happened, which was not only capable of holding it together, but which imparted to it a new vitality. It is no less clear that this was not due to a new leader, who stepped into the place of its original founder, but to a new use made of the old one. Our histories tell us that this new impulse was imparted by a belief that Jesus had risen from the dead. Whether this belief was founded on a fact or a fiction, it is evident that it is one which could not have occupied many years in growing; for while this was taking place, the original community founded by Jesus must have perished from the want of anything to sustain it in being.

This being clear, I now draw your attention to the

fact that we have the most unimpeachable historical evidence that this renewed life of the Church rested on the belief that its founder, after He had been crucified, rose again from the dead. The evidence of this will be derived from the four letters of the apostle Paul, which all the eminent unbelievers of modern Europe admit to be His genuine productions. As these letters form historical evidence of the highest class, I must draw attention to their importance.

It is often urged by unbelievers, that we have no contemporaneous historical documents. The first three Gospels, they say, are by nameless authors, which cannot be proved to have been in existence until seventy or eighty years after the events narrated in them, and the fourth is a forgery. I reply, that if for the sake of argument I suppose this to be a true statement of facts, which it is not; yet we are in possession of letters written by one who was a contemporary, and such contemporary letters are the most valuable of all historical documents. We have an example in those of the great Roman statesman and orator, Cicero, which were collected and published after his death, somewhat about a century before St. Paul wrote his. They still exist; and it is not too much to say that they form the most important documents we possess, for giving us an insight into the history of Rome between B.C. 100 and B.C 50. They contain a continued reference to current events, in which the great statesman and orator was himself personally engaged, and to the times during which he lived; and enable us to estimate the secret springs of the events of the time, and the agencies which brought them about, in a manner which we should fail to do if we had nothing to trust to but the ordinary histories of the period. It is true that we could not compose a perfect history from them alone. Their allusions to current events are incidental; but the general facts of the history being known from other sources, they form the most important means of enabling us to estimate its true character. Cicero's letters form the most important historical document handed down to us by the ancient world.

A similar historical value attaches to all collections of contemporaneous letters. The modern historian is continually hunting them up, as the best means of throwing a clear light on the history of the past. They are far more valuable as a means of discriminating truth from falsehood, than even formal histories which have been composed by writers contemporaneous, or nearly so, with the events. Such are frequently written under a bias, as, for example, Lord Clarendon's history of the Rebellion. But the incidental allusions in letters frequently put us in possession of facts and motives which have been carefully concealed from the world, especially when they are the confidential communications between friends. They form the highest description of historical evidence.

It is imposible to over-estimate the importance of the concession made to us by learned unbelievers, that we are in possession of four documents of this description, carrying us up to the earliest days of Christianity. The latest date which can be assigned them is *twenty-eight years after the crucifixion*. They put us into direct communication with the mind of the most active missionary of the infant Church. Their character is such that they depict the whole man before us; what he did, what he thought, what he believed, with a freshness and vigour which is scarcely to be found in any other letters in existence. By means of them we can hold direct communion with the man himself. There are hardly any letters in existence which bear on them so distinct an impression of the individuality of the author. It is of no little consequence that these four letters, thus admitted to be genuine, are the most important of those which have been attributed to the apostle.

I shall rest my argument on these four letters only. At the same time let me draw your attention to the fact that Renan, who is one of the most eminent unbelievers of modern Europe, admits the genuineness of four more,* and has very little doubt about that of two others.† By their aid he has written a Life of the Apostle, so vivid in details as to vie with that which has been pronounced to be the first of biographies—Boswell's Life of Johnson. For some reason our English unbelievers, while they could not make too great haste in translating into English this writer's Life of Jesus in a cheap form, have not yet seen good to exhibit his Life of St. Paul in an English dress. Why do they not publish it?

Having pointed out the value of contemporary letters as witnesses to historical events, I now draw your attention to the fact that these four letters of St. Paul were written within that interval of time from the date of the crucifixion, which the most rigid canons of criticism lay down as within the most perfect period of historical recollection. There is no possibility of dating them eighty or ninety years after that event, as unbelievers for their own convenience date the first three Gospels, in order that they may get time during which it might have been possible

---

* The two to the Thessalonians, that to Philemon, and the Philippians.

† Those to the Ephesians and Colossians.

for a number of fictions to have grown up in the bosom of the Christian Church. Not only was the latest of them written within *twenty-eight years* of the crucifixion, by a man whose activity as a missionary of Christianity had extended over the preceding *twenty years*, but who was of such an age that his historical recollections were good for at least fifteen years earlier. Although he had not seen Jesus Christ before His crucifixion, he must have conversed with multitudes who had done so. In reading these letters, therefore, we are in possession of a contemporaneous record of the highest order, according to the strictest rules laid down by Sir George Cornwell Lewis, in his great work on the credibility of early Roman history. In this work Sir George has rigidly analysed the value of historical evidence. As it is on a subject purely secular, and is considered to be very rigid in its demands for historical evidence, I appeal to it with confidence.

Let us now test, by our own experience, the value of historical recollections which are only twenty-eight years old. The repeal of the corn laws took place at exactly this interval of time from the present year. Those who are forty-five years old must have a clear recollection of the events by which it was brought about; and while they continue alive, it will be impossible to encircle the chief agents in it with a mass of fable, so as to hide the real character of the events. Two years later occurred the revolution in France, which expelled Louis Philippe. Our recollections of that event are so fresh as to render it impossible that we could become the prey of a number of legendary stories respecting it. Such stories can only grow up after the lapse of considerable intervals of time, when the recollection of events has lost its freshness, and the generation which witnessed them has died out.

Observe, then, that St. Paul was separated from the crucifixion when he wrote these letters by the same interval of time which lies between us and the two events in question.

Having pointed out the value of these letters as historical evidence, I now state the chief facts which can be distinctly proved by them, and the nature of the evidence which they afford of the historical truth of the Resurrection.

1. It is clear that not only did St. Paul believe in the resurrection of Jesus Christ as an historical fact; but that he considered it as the foundation on which the revived Christian community was erected. He received it as the one only ground of the existence of the Church. Whatever may be said of his references to other miracles, his references to this one are of the most unimpeachable character. They are too numerous to be quoted in proof of this in a lecture of the length of the present one. One will be sufficient. In the fifteenth of the first letter to the Corinthians he expressly asserts that if the resurrection of Jesus Christ is not a fact, Christianity is a delusion.*

2. His mode of reference to this event proves that he not only himself believed in it as a fact, but that he had not the smallest doubt that those to whom he wrote believed in it as firmly as he did. He refers to it in the most direct terms; he refers to it also in the most incidental manner, as the foundation of the common faith both of himself and of those to whom he wrote. He evidently calculates that they would accept his statements without the smallest hesitation. Now nothing is more valuable than a set of incidental references to an event. They prove that both the writer and those to whom he writes know all about them, and have a common belief in them. Now observe how

* See Appendix.

this is exemplified in the ordinary letters which we write. When we are of opinion that our correspondent is fully acquainted with an event, we simply allude to it, without entering on a formal description of it. We feel sure that our view of the fact will be accepted by him. Such is the manner in which St. Paul refers to the resurrection of Jesus Christ, throughout these letters,* with the exception of 1 Cor. xv. and 1st and 2nd of Galatians, where his reference is for purposes directly historical and controversial.

3. There are circumstances in these allusions which render this testimony stronger than any other in history. Party spirit raged fiercely in two of these churches, to whom these letters were written. In the Corinthian Church there were several parties who were more or less adverse to St. Paul. He names three of them; an Apollos party; another which designated themselves by the name of Peter; and a third which used the name of Christ as their special designation. Besides these, he specifies a party which was especially attached to himself. One of these parties went the extreme length of denying *his right to the apostolical office, on the ground that he had not been one of the original companions of Jesus*. No small portion of the second Epistle is occupied with dealing with this party, and defending his own position against them.†

Such being the state of affairs in this Church, it is obvious that if the party in opposition to his apostleship had held any different views respecting the reality of the resurrection of Jesus Christ from himself, the demolition of the entire defence which he puts in for it was certain. He puts the question, "*Have I not seen*

* See Appendix. † See Appendix.

Jesus Christ our Lord?" I do not quote these words as evidence that he had really seen Jesus Christ, but as a proof that if his opponents had not been firmly persuaded that the resurrection was a fact, the moment this letter was read, they would have instantly denounced him as a falsifier of the Gospel; and declared that his claim to apostolical authority, based on his having seen the risen Jesus, was worthless, because he had not risen. It is evident, therefore, that as far as the fact of the resurrection was concerned, St. Paul and his bitterest opponents were agreed as to its truth.

4. The evidence furnished by the Epistle to the Galatians is yet more conclusive. Here was a strong party, who not only denied St. Paul's apostleship, but who had so far departed from his teaching, that he designates their doctrines by the name of *another gospel*. This party had been so successful, that they had drawn away a large number of St. Paul's own converts. No one can read this letter without seeing that the state of things in this Church touched him to the quick. It is full of the deepest bursts of feeling. Yet the whole letter is written throughout with the most entire confidence, that however great were the differences between himself and his opponents, there was no diversity of view between them and him, that the belief in the resurrection of Jesus was the foundation stone of their common Christianity. Hear his words at the beginning of this letter. "Paul, an *apostle* (not *of man*, neither *by man*, but by Jesus Christ, and God the Father, *who raised him from the dead*,) and all the brethren who are with me, to the churches of Galatia. . . I marvel that ye are so soon removed from him that called you into the grace of Christ *unto another gospel*: which is not another;

but there are some which trouble you, and would subvert the gospel of God." If St. Paul's belief, and that of his opponents on this point, had not been at entire agreement, no man in his senses would have thrown them down such a challenge as is contained in these words, and is continued in the strongest terms throughout the entire letter.

5. But the evidence furnished by this letter goes far beyond the mere belief of the Galatian churches at the time it was sent to them. It involves the testimony of two other churches, viz., that of the great Church at Antioch, which was the metropolis of Gentile Christianity, and that of the mother Church of Jerusalem, and carries it up to a much earlier date. St. Paul's opponents were Judaizing Christians, who professed themselves to be the followers of St. Peter and St. James. St. Paul, in the second chapter, asserts that his teaching was in substantial harmony with that of these two great chiefs of the Jewish Church. St. Paul's opponents were Christians who belonged to the most extreme Juadizing party in the Church, and who maintained that the observation of the law of Moses, with all its rites and ceremonies, was an integral portion of Christianity. Yet this party was at one with Paul in believing that the resurrection of Jesus was a fact. If so, the whole Jewish Church, even its most extreme members, concurred in that belief. The second chapter makes it plain that the whole Church at Antioch did the same at the period when St. Peter and St. Paul jointly visited it, and involves the fact of St. Peter's direct testimony to the truth of the resurrection. This alone is sufficient to prove that the belief, that Jesus Christ rose from the dead, was no after-growth, but was coincident

with the renewed life of the Christian Church immediately after the crucifixion.

6. Let us now look into the evidence supplied by the Epistle to the Romans. If it be urged that St. Paul had founded some of the other churches, and that even his opponents some way or other had adopted his views on this point, this was a Church which he had neither founded nor visited. It had evidently been in existence years before he wrote his letter to them. This Church was so large and important, that he felt that he was not in danger of being misapprehended, when he stated *that their faith was a subject of conversation throughout the whole world*. It contained a large Jewish element; and from the number of strangers who visited that city, there can be no doubt that among its members were representatives of every variety of Christian thought. Yet he addressed this Church with the full confidence that its members held the same views respecting the resurrection as he did himself. Not only is all his teaching based on the supposition of its truth, and the fact again and again reiterated; but the opening of the letter declares that Jesus Christ was marked out as the Son of God *by the resurrection from the dead*, and that on it was founded his claims to be an apostle.

We have thus firmly established the fact that within a period of less than twenty-eight years after the crucifixion three large Christian Churches, who were separated from each other by hundreds of miles of space, were all of the same mind in believing that Jesus Christ had risen from the dead, and that this belief was the sole ground of the existence of the Christian community. Consider how long it would have taken for such a belief to have grown up in Churches thus widely separated. We have found that similar was the belief of the Jewish Church, and of that at Antioch, and proved that it was believed in by those churches from their first origin We may therefore safely infer that it was the belief of the entire Christian body wherever situated. It is useless therefore to assert that the belief in the miraculous stories of the Gospels grew up very gradually during the first century, and for the purpose of enabling them to have done so, to put off the publication of the first three Gospels to its close or the first ten years of the second. On the contrary, we have indisputable evidence that the greatest of these miracles was implicitly believed in within much less than twenty-eight years after the crucifixion.

6. This belief was evidently not one of recent growth. The mode in which allusion is made to it proves that it was contemporaneous with the first belief in Christianity on the part of those to whom St. Paul wrote. As we have seen, many of them were Jewish Christians, who must have been very early converts themselves, or who must have derived their faith from those who were. The allusions in the letter to the Galatians plainly include the testimony of St. Peter and St. James. We also find, by a most incidental allusion in the letter to the Romans, that there were two members of that Church who had embraced Christianity before St. Paul. The allusion is so incidental, that it is worth quoting. It occurs in the midst of a large number of salutations, "Salute Andronicus and Junia, my kinsmen, and my fellow-prisoners, who are of note among the apostles, who also were in Christ before me." Yet they were all agreed on this point. St. Paul had believed it from his conversion, *i.e.*, within less than than ten years after the crucifixion. Andronicus

and Junia believed it still earlier. Peter, James, and John also believed it from the first; for St. Paul states that he communicated to them the gospel which he preached among the Gentiles; and that they generally approved of it; and in the fifteenth to the Corinthians he expressly affirms that Peter and James had seen Jesus Christ after He was risen from the dead. Let it be observed than in the Epistle to the Galatians he informs us that he paid Peter a visit of fifteen days, three years after his own conversion; and that during this visit, he had an interview with James. We cannot err, therefore, in asserting that we have here the direct testimony of these two men, that they had seen the risen Jesus. It follows, therefore, that the belief in the Resurrection was that on which the Church was reconstructed immediately after the crucifixion.

7. St. Paul makes, in the fifteenth to the Corinthians, a very definite statement as to a numher of persons who had actually seen Jesus Christ after He had risen from the dead. He tell us that on one occasion He was seen by more than five hundred persons at once, of whom the greater part, *i.e.*, more than two hundred and fifty, were still living when he wrote. Now consider how St. Paul, in making this assertion, put himself in the hands of those opponents who denied his apostleship. If the resurrection was not generally believed to be true, the discussion between them might have been put an end to then and there, by a simple exposure of the falsehood of such a statement. But if these five hundred persons really thought that they had seen Jesus Christ alive after He was crucified, how is it possible to account for so singular a fact, otherwise than on the supposition of its truth?

8. But further: in the Corinthian Church there were persons who denied the possibility of a resurrection, after the body had been dissolved into its various elements (1 Cor. xv. 14, 25), and who affirmed that all that was meant by the future resurrection was a great spiritual change. Yet, with defective logic, they admitted that the resurrection of Christ had been a bodily one (see 1 Cor. xv. 12—17). The apostle presses them with the following reasoning, How can you deny the possibility of a bodily resurrection hereafter, when you admit that Christ actually rose from the dead? If this latter point had not been the foundation of the faith of the Church, they might have made short work of the apostle and his logic by simply denying the truth of the bodily resurrection of Jesus Christ. This circumstance also proves that there were persons in the Church to whom this letter was written who were far from being disposed readily to believe in a story of a resurrection from the dead. In one word, they were not over-credulous.

We are now in a position most positively to affirm that the story of the resurrection of Jesus Christ was no fiction which slowly grew up during the latter half of the first century, but that it was a fact, fully believed in by those who gave the new impulse to the Christian Church after the crucifixion of its Founder. I have not quoted the testimony of the Gospels to prove this, because my opponents deny its validity. I have simply deduced it from historical documents, which they allow to be genuine. It is evident, therefore, that one miracle narrated in these Gospels is not a late-invented myth. It remains for me to inquire whether this belief could have rested on a delusion. But before doing so, I will sum up briefly the points I have proved on the highest historical evidence.

1. That within twenty-eight years after the crucifixion, the Christian Church, without distinction of party, believed that the one ground of its existence was that Jesus Christ had risen from the dead.

2. That at that period there were more than two hundred and fifty persons living who believed that they had seen Him alive after His crucifixion.

3. That it is an unquestionable fact that the whole Christian Church believed in the resurrection of its Founder as the sole ground of its existence, within less than ten years from the date of the crucifixion.

4. That the belief in the fact of the resurrection was equally held by St. Paul and his most violent opponents.

5. That at least three of the original apostles asserted that they had seen Jesus Christ alive after His death.

6. That a belief that He had risen from the dead was the cause which imparted its renewed vitality to the Church.

Such having been proved on unquestionable evidence to have been historical facts, it remains for me to examine whether they are consistent with any other assumption, than that the belief in them was founded on a reality.

There are three, and only three possible alternatives :—

1. The resurrection of Jesus Christ was a fact; or,

2. The belief of the Church in it was the result of a fraud, deliberately and consciously concocted; or,

3. The original followers of Jesus were the victims of a delusion.

I shall deem myself exonerated from the necessity of examining the second of these alternatives, because it has been abandoned as untenable by all eminent modern unbelievers.

Two alternatives have been suggested to account for the belief in the resurrection, on the ground that it originated in a delusion, of which the followers of Jesus Christ were the prey. The first of these is, that they were intensely enthusiastic and credulous; that some one or more of them fancied that they saw Jesus alive after His death, and succeeded in persuading the others that it was a fact. Of these theories, that of Rénan is a fair representation, that Mary Magdalene, in the midst of her grief and emotion, mistook the gardener for Jesus; thought that He had risen from the dead, and communicated her enthusiasm to the rest.

The second is, that Jesus did not really die, but was taken down from the cross in a swoon, from which He awoke in the sepulchre; that He managed to creep out in an exhausted state, lived in retirement, and died shortly afterwards.

To this last supposition I will reply first. I allow that it was possible for a man who had been suspended for some hours on the cross, if taken down and carefully treated, to recover. This, as we are informed by Josephus, happened to one of his friends, though it was the exception, for two out of three died under cure. But in the case of Jesus, we have to meet the fact that He was in the hands of His enemies, who would have seen to His burial as a criminal who had been publicly executed; and thus have put the possibility of recovery out of the question. It is true that our Gospels assert that Pilate gave His body to His friends. But my opponents affirm that the whole account is unhistorical. If, however, they accept the statements of the Gospels on this point, they are bound also to accept their further assertion, that Pilate took care to ascertain that the body was dead before he resigned it, and that it was interred, and left in a sepulchre closed with a large stone.

But as after the crucifixion He disappears from history, except in the supposition that He rose from the dead, those who propound the theory that He was taken down alive are obliged to admit that He died from exhaustion shortly afterwards. Now it is certain that if He left the grave alive, He must have been kept in concealment out of the way of His enemies; for those who had succeeded in crucifying Him would not have allowed Him to remain undisturbed. It is also evident, that if He lived in concealment, His followers had access to Him, or they had not; if the former was the case, it would have been impossible to have mistaken a wounded man, dying from exhaustion, for the Messiah of Jewish expectation, or to have magnified this into a resurrection from the dead. But if they never saw Him, then the belief in His resurrection resolves itself into the case of simple credulity and fanaticism.

But a Messiah who crept out of His grave, and died from exhaustion shortly afterwards, was not one who could have satisfied the exigencies of the community which had been crushed by His crucifixion. They had expected Him to reign as the Messiah; and, lo, a cross was the only throne allowed Him. Yet it is the most certain of historical facts, that the Christian community commenced a new life immediately after its original foundation had been subverted by His execution. Nothing but a resurrection, or one which was mistaken for a reality, could have served the purpose. Something had to be done, and that quickly. Without it the Church must have perished in the grave of its founder.

As there is not a single trace in history that the place of Jesus was taken by a new leader, who assumed the position of the Messiah, which had been rendered vacant by the crucifixion of Jesus, or even by His retirement, it is evident that some event must have taken place, which enabled Him to occupy the place which He originally assumed in the opinion of His followers. It is certain that if He was supposed to be alive, living in retirement, this would have never succeeded in revivifying the Church. The Church had before it the alternative of finding a Messiah or perishing. If it be urged, that if Jesus succeeded in creeping out of His grave, and living in retirement, after an interval of time this might have grown up into the idea of His resurrection, the requisite time is not to be had; for while the idea was growing, the Church would have become extinct, and I have proved that the belief in the resurrection can be traced up to a very short interval after the crucifixion, so that the requisite time cannot possibly be found.

I now proceed to examine the question, whether it was possible that the original followers of Jesus could have been deceived into a belief of His resurrection by means of their enthusiasm and credulity. Nothing is easier than to assert that some one of them fancied that he had seen Him alive, and communicated his enthusiasm to the rest; and that others got into their heads similar fancies, and mistook them for realities. But in practical life such things are not easy nor possible; for they contradict all the facts of human nature.

I will, however, assume, for the sake of argument, that the original followers of Jesus were men of the mose unbounded credulity and enthusiasm; only observing that we have not one atom of evidence for the assumption.

Let it be observed, however, that the profoundest credulity has certain limits, which it has never yet been known to overstep. A belief in a certain round of supernaturalism is one which has been widely diffused among mankind; and a large number of marvellous stories are readily accepted by them, on little or no evidence. It is comparatively easy to get men to believe that they have seen ghosts, still easier that others have seen them. But there is one marvel which human credulity has not been induced to accept, that a man who has actually died, has been seen and conversed with in bodily reality. I believe that no case can be found in history in which a man has asserted that he has seen with his own eyes a human body revivified after it was actually dead. The old Pagans, who accepted supernaturalism enough, would have scoffed at such a belief as lying beyond the bounds of the possible. I am aware that a few old Pagan stories exist about men who were brought back from the other world; but they belong to poetry, and were wisely placed by the poets in the remotest ages of the past. Evidence that a man ever existed, who really believed that he had seen and conversed with one who had been raised from the dead, wholly fails. Celsus scoffs at the idea.

If, then, it is a most difficult thing to get a single person who is in possession of his reason, to believe that he has seen and held communications with one who has been actually revivified, what shall we say as to getting a considerable number, not to speak of the five hundred persons mentioned by St. Paul, to believe in such a fact. Yet considerable numbers must have believed this fact before the Church could have commenced its renewed life. Such beliefs are only possible when they have become reports at second hand, or after a long interval of time. This latter condition is absolutely necessary. But as I have proved that the belief in the resurrection of Jesus must have originated within a very brief interval after his crucifixion, it is useless to discuss any supposition which renders it necessary to invoke the aid of a long interval of time to bring it about. There is no such interval at our command in the present case. The historical evidence is overwhelming, that the belief in the resurrection of Jesus was the starting-point of the renewed life of the Church.

It is evident, therefore, that, under any conceivable view of the case, a belief in a resurrection, if entertained by any considerable number of people, must have taken years to grow. No amount of credulity can account for its rapid dissemination. How long would it take to persuade one hundred of the most credulous persons in London that a man who had been executed at Newgate, and buried in the custody of the authorities, had not only appeared alive again, but had actually conversed with some of them, and to unite them into a community on the basis of this belief? It is obvious that such a belief, if possible at all, could only grow up after a considerable number of years; and only then among persons who did not profess to have seen the dead man actually revived. Before it could have been possible, memories must have faded, and events must have been removed into the obscurity of the past. I put it to my opponents to say how many years they think that it would require to render such an operation possible. Would ten, fifteen, or twenty suffice? Until this had taken place no development of the Church was possible. Yet the Church spread immediately. But with respect to the resurrectio of Jesus Christ, I have proved, on the most indisputable historical evidence, that it was believed by the entire Church, as the foundation on which its existence rested, within a brief interval after the crucifixion.

But observe further : the belief in the resurrection was no idle belief, like that in a common ghost story, or an ordinary marvel. Such beliefs begin and end in nothing. But this had an energy and power sufficient to reconstruct the Church. It was not the mere belief entertained by individuals, but one which sustained the weight of an institution. This belief went on spreading itself until within less than seventy years it had firmly established itself in all the great cities of the Roman Empire, and had long before shown itself capable of standing the test of martyrdom. It must, therefore, have been a profound conviction, and not a sentimental dream. Where in history will you find a rapidly progressing community, or any institution at all, which has been founded on the belief that a man, who had been dead, rose again from the dead? Let us consider the state of things during the days, or weeks, or even months, which must have followed the crucifixion. The devoted followers of Jesus had brought themselves into a belief that a new kingdom of God was about to be established in His person. His public execution must have extinguished the hope that it would be established by Him. Could all the enthusiasm and credulity in the world have thought otherwise? Suppose, even, that a fanatic woman had reported that she had seen Him alive some hours, days, or months afterwards : would His depressed followers have been satisfied if He did not appear to them? Would such a report set them to reconstruct a blasted institution, which had no ground of existence except in its Founder's life?

But further: the followers of Jesus must have immediately resolved on a change of tactics. A visible Messiah was the one which they wanted, not an invisible one after the old type. It must have been evident that Jesus would be a visible one no longer. He appeared no more in public, either as a teacher or worker of miracles. An entire change of front was therefore necessary, before it was possible to reconstitute the Church. Was the mere report of a credulous enthusiast, that He was risen from the dead, likely, under these circumstances, to have been accepted, while He withheld His presence from His own personal friends?

One solution, and one only, is adequate to account for the renewed life of the Church, that Jesus verily appeared alive to those persons who asserted that they had seen Him, and that He afforded them such evidence of the truth of His resurrection as is recorded in our Gospels. If this event is an historical fact; if Jesus gave His followers evidence of His resurrection, by allowing them to see Him with their eyes, and to touch Him with their hands, this gives a rational account of all the phenomena. No other supposition will. That the faith of His followers was revived in Him as the Messiah within a short interval after His death, is a fact for which I have adduced the strongest historical testimony. His resurrection was believed in by multitudes, while historical recollections continued of the freshest character. His appearance would have imparted to His followers a faith which gives a rational account of their subsequent conduct. Nothing else can explain it on rational principles. It was a moral power adequate to effect the great change.

I have hitherto withheld from quoting the narratives

of the Evangelists as a portion of the evidence of the resurrection. My reason for having done so is, that those with whom I am reasoning assert that they are unhistorical. I have therefore only employed data which they concede to me; from these data I have shown that the resurrection of Jesus Christ has the highest evidence as an historical fact. No event in past history has a stronger attestation. It was believed in by the whole Church as the ground of its existence. The Church was torn by parties. The most adverse parties in the Church believed it. It was believed in by churches widely separated from one another; it imparted to them all their vitality. It was believed in by the original Jewish Church; it formed the sole ground of its renewed existence. If a fact, it fully accounts for it. Peter asserted that he had seen Jesus Christ after He had risen from the dead; so did James, so did all the apostles, so did more than five hundred others. Paul believed that he had seen Him also; and this belief of his changed him from a persecutor into a preacher of Christianity, and caused him to devote the whole of his life to the most self-denying labours in its service.

Such being the case, I am now in a position to restore the Gospels to their proper place as historical documents. With these facts proved, it is useless for unbelievers to affirm, as far as the resurrection is concerned, that they were written by nameless authors long after the events which they profess to record. The truth of the resurrection of Christ can be proved independently of their testimony; but their statements respecting that event are strictly in conformity with the facts which I have proved to be historical. They fully corroborate them, and offer a rational explanation of them. The fourth Evangelist asserts that on three occasions he saw the risen Jesus, in such a manner as to leave no doubt of the truth of His actual appearance. The accounts of the three others are fragmentary, but afford substantial narratives of facts. They describe several appearances of Jesus Christ after He was risen from the dead, at which He afforded to His disciples the means of testing the reality of His resurrection by their bodily senses.

It will be asserted that their accounts contain narrations which are difficult to reconcile with one another in their minute details. I admit that such is the fact, and that it results from the peculiar form of writings to which the Gospels belong. They are not regular histories, but religious memoirs; as such, they do not profess to furnish us with a complete and continuous narrative. But they agree in all their great features according to the conditions of the case. The events of the day of the resurrection must have thrown the followers of Jesus into the greatest excitement. The accounts, as we read them in the first three Gospels, are exactly such as we should expect from men and women under similar circumstances. They are broken, disjointed, without any attempt being made to weave them into a complete whole; yet, in all the main facts, their testimony agrees. This is what they should be, if they contain the reports, not of forgers, not of myths or legends, but of genuine witnesses. We may not be able to reconcile the various details; of this difficulty unbelievers have made the most they can. Let them hear and attend to one of their greatest authorities. The *Westminster Review* tells them that the habit of carping at small minor details is useless. All histories contain variations, or, if you like to call them, contradictions, on minor points. This, says the *Review*, has been the case with every history which has ever been written from Herodotus to Mr. Froude.* Let unbelievers therefore join issue in the main facts of the gospel history, just as they would with any secular history, and we will meet them. Above all, let them not carp at minor details about miracles; but join issue in the truth or falsehood of the resurrection of Jesus Christ; with the truth of which miracle the writers of the New Testament affirm that Christianity stands or falls.

* See the number for January, 1873

EXPLANATORY NOTE.

The reader should observe that this Lecture was composed from the point of view of the unbelievers of London, with reference to the special difficulties raised at the discussions at the Hall of Science. I am aware that it might have been somewhat simplified if I had added a fifth to the four simple assumptions on which the Lecture is based, which are conceded by an overwhelming majority of the most eminent modern unbelievers, viz., that many of them readily concede that the original disciples of Jesus fully believed that they had seen their Master alive after His crucifixion, but that in entertaining this belief they were the victims of a delusion. If, however, I had based my reasoning on this assumption, I should have failed to meet the difficulties of those for whose benefit the Lecture was specially composed; and I should have greatly weakened the cogency of the proof of the resurrection as a well-attested fact of history. It will be seen by a reference to p. 245, that I distinctly recognise the fact that many eminent modern unbelievers do not dispute that the original followers of Jesus really believed in the truth of His resurrection. Those, however, for whom I was writing, are under the impression that no contemporaneous evidence of a really historical character can be adduced in proof of it. My object has been to dissipate this delusion, and to show that we have as strong an historical attestation for the truth of the resurrection of Jesus Christ, as we possess for any fact which we have not seen with our eyes. I therefore confined myself to the four simple assumptions with which the Lecture opens, as being historical facts too evident to be disputed, except by persons who are incapable of appreciating historical evidence at all; and from them I have proved the truth of this central position of the Christian faith.

APPENDIX.

I SUBJOIN the most important passages in these Epistles, in which reference is made to the Resurrection, with such observations as are necessary for pointing out their historical value.

Rom. i. 3-5 :—"Concerning His Son, who was made of the seed of David according to the flesh, and declared to be the Son of God with power, according to the Spirit of holiness, *by the resurrection from the dead.*"

Here the reference, occurring as it does at the opening of the epistle, proves that the writer was firmly persuaded that those to whom he wrote were equally persuaded of the fact of the resurrection as he was.

St. Paul concludes a long argument with these words :—

Rom ii. 16 :—"In the day when God shall judge the secrets of men *by Jesus Christ,* according to my gospel."

The reference here is inferential and indirect, and therefore most valuable. The position assigned to Christ as future Judge, shows that the whole Church accepted the fact of His resurrection as one beyond all question.

Rom. iv. 24, 25 :—"To whom also it shall be imputed, if we believe on Him *who raised up Jesus our Lord from the dead,* who was delivered for our offences, and was *raised again* for our justification."

Such a doctrinal use of the resurrection proves that the fact had long been accepted by the Church, as it would have been impossible to have used it in this way if it had been a recent invention. Let it be remembered that this Church contained a Jewish and Gentile element, and had been planted quite independently of the apostle. It follows, therefore, that the resurrection must have been accepted as the foundation of Christianity by the founders of this Church.

Rom. v. 10:—" For if when we were enemies, we were reconciled to God by the death of His Son, much more being reconciled, we shall be saved *by his life.*"

The reference here is incidental, and therefore a strong evidence of the universal acceptance of the fact.

Rom. vi. 3-11 :—Know ye not, that as many of us as were baptised into Jesus Christ were baptised into his death? Therefore we are buried with him by baptism into death, that, like as Christ *was raised from the dead* by the glory of the Father, even so we also should walk in newness of life. For if we have been planted together in the likeness of His death, we shall be also in the likeness of His *resurrection.* Knowing this, that our old man is crucified with him, that the body of sin might be destroyed, that henceforth we should not serve sin. For he who is dead is freed from sin. Now if we be dead with Christ, we believe that we shall also *live with Him.* Knowing that Christ *being raised from the dead* dieth no more ; *death hath no more dominion over Him.* For in that He died, He died unto sin once ; but in that *He liveth, He liveth* unto God. Likewise reckon ye also yourselves to be dead indeed unto sin, but alive unto God, through Jesus Christ our Lord."

This passage is one of great importance. It refers to the fact of the resurrection both directly, incidentally, and inferentially. The parallel between Christ's death and resurrection as exhibited in baptism, the reference to its moral power as a resurrection to holiness in those who cordially accept the fact, and its pledge of future life hereafter, all imply that the belief in it, was the very foundation of that Christianity which had been accepted by the Roman Church, and was a part of the original Christian teaching from which they had derived their faith.

Rom. vii. 4 :—" Wherefore, my brethren, ye also are become dead to the law by the body of Christ, that ye should be married to another, *even to Him who is raised from the dead,* that we should bring forth fruit unto God"

The apostle's argument is here very peculiar, as any one will see who reads the entire context. The allusion to the resurrection shows that that fact was never absent from the writer's thoughts, and proves that he was of opinion that it was little less so from those to whom he wrote.

Rom. viii. 10, 11 :—" And f Christ be in you, the body is dead because of sin, but the spirit is life because of righteousness ; for if

Appendix. 257

the spirit of Him *that raised up Jesus from the dead* dwell in you, *He that raised up Christ from the dead* shall also quicken your mortal bodies by His Spirit that dwelleth in you."

Rom. viii. 17 :—"And if children, then heirs, heirs of God, and joint heirs with Christ, if so be that we suffer with Him, that we *may also be glorified together.*"

Rom. viii. 33, 34 :—"Who shall lay anything to the charge of God's elect? It is God that justifieth. Who is he that condemneth? It is Christ that died, yea rather, *that is risen again*, who is even at the right hand of God, who also maketh intercession for us."

These three references are entirely incidental. Nothing was further from the writer's thoughts than the intention to make direct assertions about the resurrection of Christ. He is treating throughout the chapter on some of the deepest subjects of Christian thought. Yet his references to the resurrection are at once distinct and natural, and prove that the belief in it was interwoven into the very texture of his own thoughts, and, as he considered, into those to whom he wrote.

Rom. x. 6-9 :—"But the righteousness which is of faith speaketh on this wise, Say not in thine heart, Who shall ascend into heaven? (*i.e.*, to bring down Christ from above:) or, Who shall descend into the deep? (*i.e.*, to bring up *Christ again from the dead.*) But what saith it? The word is nigh thee, even in thy mouth, and in thine heart, (*i.e.*, the word of faith which we preach). For if thou shalt confess with thy mouth the Lord Jesus, and shalt believe in thine heart that God hath *raised Him from the dead*, thou shalt be saved."

The reasoning in this passage is difficult, owing to the fact that it contains allusions to passages in the Old Testament, which none but those who were familiar with them would catch the meaning of. It proves that the writer calculated that those to whom he wrote were very familiar with them. Of a precisely similar character are the two references to the resurrection, and they would have been without meaning, except to persons who admitted their doctrinal value.

Rom. xiv. 7-9 :—"For none of us liveth unto himself, and no man dieth unto himself; for whether we live, we live unto the Lord; and whether we die, we die unto the Lord: for to this end Christ both died *and rose*, that He might be Lord both of the dead and living."

In the context the apostle was speaking of the observance of particular days, and similar subjects which deeply interested the minds of the Christians of that time. For all questions of difficulty and duty, he had one solution, and only one, the relation in which the Christian stood to his risen Lord. *He died and rose*, that those who believed on Him might live and die to Him. This was the solution of every duty to the believer. It is impossible to conceive of any allusion to the resurrection, which would more plainly show its all-commanding influence on the Christian conscience, or its more universal reception as a fact.

The earlier references in the First Epistle to the Corinthians are all incidental or inferential. The later ones are of the most direct character.

1 Cor. i. 7, 8 :—" So that ye come behind in no gift ; waiting *for the coming of our Lord Jesus Christ :* who shall also confirm you to the end, that ye may be blameless *in the day of our Lord Jesus Christ.*

These references to His future coming, imply the prior acceptance of the fact of His resurrection. The reasoning of the remainder of this chapter presupposes the same fact. Similar remarks apply to the two following passages.

1 Cor. iv. 5 :—" Therefore judge nothing before the time, *until the Lord come*, who will bring to light the hidden things of darkness, and make manifest the counsels of the hearts."

1 Cor. v. 4, 5 :—" In the name of our Lord Jesus Christ, when ye are gathered together, and my spirit, *with the power of our Lord Jesus Christ*, to deliver such an one unto Satan for the destruction of the flesh that the spirit may be saved *in the day of the Lord Jesus.*

1 Cor. ix. 1, 2 :—" Am not I an apostle ? am I not free ? *have I not seen Jesus Christ our Lord ?* are ye not my work in the Lord ? If I am not an apostle to others, yet doubtless I am to you," etc.

The whole of this chapter is addressed to the party in this church which denied Paul's right to be an apostle. It is obvious that this party must have fully believed in the resurrection of Christ, as the ground of their Christianity. Had it been otherwise, nothing short of madness could have induced the writer to write as he has done throughout the entire chapter.

1 Cor. xi. 23-26 :—" For I received of the Lord that which I also delivered unto you, how that the Lord Jesus, the same night in which He was betrayed, took bread," etc. " For as often as ye eat

this bread, and drink this cup, ye do shew forth the Lord's death *til He come.*"

Here we have a direct account of the institution of the great rite of the Christian Church, which was to be celebrated in perpetual memory of Christ's death. The constant celebration of it in the Church of Christ, by a succession of continuously repeated acts, carries us up to the very period of the crucifixion by one of the highest forms of historical testimony. Yet the whole passage proves that while this institution was designed to preserve a perpetual memory of the death of Christ, it was indissolubly united with a belief in His resurrection, thus carrying up the historical testimony of that event to the period directly following the crucifixion.

1 Cor. xv. 3-20 :—"For I delivered unto you first of all that which I also received, how that Christ died for our sins according to the Scriptures ; and that He was buried, and that *He rose again* the the third day according to the Scriptures ; and that *He was seen* of Cephas ; then of the twelve; after that, *He was seen* of above five hundred brethren at once ; of whom the greater part remain unto this present, but some are fallen asleep. After that, *He was seen* of James ; then of all the apostles ; and last of all, *He was seen* of me, as of one born out of due time. For I am the least of the apostles, that am not meet to be called an apostle, because I persecuted the church of God. Now if Christ be preached unto you that *he rose from the dead*, how say some among you that there is no resurrection of the dead ? But if there is no resurrection of the dead, then *is not Christ risen*. And *if Christ be not risen*, then is our preaching vain, and your faith is also vain. Yea, and we are found false witnesses of God ; because we have testified of God, that *He raised up Christ*, whom *He raised not up*, if so be that the dead rise not. For if the dead rise not, then *is not Christ raised*. And if *Christ be not raised*, your faith is vain ; ye are yet in your sins. Then they also who are fallen asleep in Christ are perished. If in this life only we have hope in Christ, we are of all men most miserable. But now is *Christ risen from the dead*, and become the first fruits of them that slept."

I have already remarked in the body of the lecture on the high historical value of this passage. I need not repeat what I have there said. I shall only add, that it seems to me impossible to read it, and to entertain a doubt that the fact of the resurrection was not only accepted by all the parties into which this Church was divided; but that it was the foundation on which the Church was reconstructed immediately after the crucifixion.

2 Cor. i. 2:—"Grace be to you, and peace from God the Father, and *from the Lord Jesus Christ.*"

2 Cor. ii. 10:—"To whom ye forgive anything, I forgive also; for if I forgave anything to whom I forgave it, for your sakes forgave I it *in the person of Christ.*"

2 Cor. iv. 10, 14:—Always bearing about in the body the dying of the Lord Jesus, that *the life also of Jesus* might be made manifest in our body. Knowing that He that *raised up the Lord Jesus* shall raise us *up also by Jesus*, and shall present us with you."

Here we have a mixture of direct and indirect references, all proving that the fact of the resurrection was the foundation which underlay all Christian thought.

2 Cor. v. 13-15:—"For whether we be beside ourselves, it is to God; or whether we be sober, it is for your cause. For the love of Christ constraineth us; because we thus judge, that if one died for all, then were all dead; and that He died for all, that they which live should not henceforth live unto themselves, but *unto Him that died for them, and rose again,*" etc., etc.

In this passage the resurrection of Christ is set before us as the foundation on which Christian self-sacrifice rests, and as the new great spiritual power which has been created by Christianity.

2 Cor. xi. 3-5:—"But I fear, lest by any means, as the serpent beguiled Eve through his subtilty, so your minds should be corrupted from the simplicity that is in Christ. For if he that cometh *preacheth another Jesus, whom we have not preached;* or if ye receive another spirit, which ye have not received, or *another gospel, which ye have not accepted*, ye might well bear with him. For I suppose that I was not a whit behind the very chiefest apostles," etc., etc.

This passage is a very remarkable one, and the argument is carried on throughout the remainder of the epistle. In it the apostle comes face to face with the party in this Church in opposition to himself. The careful reader will see that he very often uses the strongest irony in dealing with them. Yet, in the passage I have cited, he distinctly avers that the Jesus whom they preached differed in no substantial point of historical outline from his own. The reader should observe that by the expression "He that cometh," the apostle evidently means his Jewish opponents, who professed to represent the views of

Appendix.

the apostles of the circumcision. We have here a distinct testimony that they must have believed from the first in the resurrection. If it had not been so, St. Paul would have placed himself in the power of his opponents, when this letter was read to the Church.

2 Cor. xii. 8, 9 :—"For this thing I besought the Lord thrice, that it might depart from me. And *He said unto me, My grace is sufficient for thee: for my strength is made perfect in weakness.* Most gladly therefore will I rather glory in my infirmities, that the power of Christ may rest upon me.

2 Cor. xiii. 3, 4 :—Since ye seek a proof of Christ speaking in me which toward you is not weak, but is mighty in you. For though He was crucified through weakness, yet *He liveth by the power of God.* For we also are weak in Him, but *we shall live with Him* by the power of God toward you."

Nothing can be more incidental than such allusions.

The first and second chapters of the Epistle to the Galatians contain the strongest historical proof that the belief in the resurrection of Jesus Christ constituted the one sole and only ground of the renewed life of the Church. To quote them partially would weaken the force of the historical evidence which they supply. You must carefully read them for yourselves. I will, however, enunciate in as many distinct propositions the facts which they assert, and the inferences following from them.

1. St. Paul begins by distinctly affirming that the fact of the resurrection was the ground of his claim to the apostleship.

2. A party existed in the Galatian Churches who were most adverse to his claims.

3. This party did not dispute the fact of our Lord's resurrection.

4. They professed to represent the views of the Churches in Judæa, and those of their chief men.

5. St. Paul professed to have derived his gospel, not from human teaching, but by express revelation from Jesus Christ.

6. His belief in the resurrection as a fact, converted him from a persecutor of the Church into a preacher of the gospel.

7. Three years after his conversion he visited Peter and James at Jerusalem for a period of fifteen days, but saw none of the other apostles. These two apostles must therefore have agreed with Paul in believing in the resurrection as a fact.

8. Fifteen years after he visited the Church at Jerusalem, and explained to its chiefs the gospel which he preached among the

Gentiles; and received the approbation of James, Peter, and John, the three most important members of that Church.

9. The Church at Jerusalem must therefore have believed in the fact of the resurrection immediately after the crucifixion.

10. The fundamental facts of Christianity were accepted alike by the different parties in this Church. The ground of their disagreement respected not the facts themselves, but the doctrinal inferences to be drawn from them.

11. The differences which arose in the Church at Antioch were respecting the obligations of Gentile Christians to observe the Jewish rites, and had nothing to do with fundamental facts.

12. The words which St. Paul addressed to St. Peter prove that both apostles were at agreement as to the fact of the resurrection, and the Churches of Antioch and Galatia with them. The conclusion of them is very remarkable, "I am crucified with Christ: nevertheless I live, yet not I, but Christ liveth in me; and the life which I now live in the flesh I live by the faith of the Son of God, who loved me, and gave Himself for me."

Each of the subsequent chapters contains incidental and inferential references to the resurrection as the common belief of St. Paul, and of those to whom he wrote, of the same nature as those which I have already deduced from the Romans and Corinthians.

THE MORAL TEACHING OF THE NEW TESTAMENT.

BY THE
REV. HENRY ALLON, D.D.

The Moral Teaching of the New Testament.

CHRISTIANITY is distinctively a system of religious faith and life. It therefore differs from mere systems of philosophy, which give a scientific account of the mental and moral faculties, and of such obligations as may be deduced from them. It differs also from mere ethical systems, which define right and wrong, demonstrate their principles and sanctions, and formulate them in precepts. It differs also from systems of social economy, political, municipal, or domestic, which deal with the relationships, duties, and interests of social life.

It is not easy to express the difference in exact definition; inasmuch as Christianity not only covers and controls all these, as parts of universal life,—but these are elements of Christianity—they intersect and pervade each other. Religion claims to be the supreme philosophy of man's moral nature, the supreme law of his moral obligation, and the supreme good of his social life. But the converse is not always true : while philosophy, morality, and social economy must always enter as constituent elements into a true religion, religion does not always enter into them. A man may be an acute philosopher, a pure moralist, and a benevolent political economist, and yet both practically and formally reject not only Christianity, but every form of the theism which is the essence of all religion. Systems of philosophy, of ethics, and of social economy are propounded, from which religion is formally excluded. The philosopher, moreover, finds his end in the determination of scientific truth; the moralist in the determination of ethical virtue; the social economist in the well-being of the commonweal. Each avowedly stops short of the end of the religious apostle. We think, that without religion neither can attain to supreme truth and excellency, even in his own recognised sphere; but the ends contemplated are formally different, and as a matter of fact men eminent in each disavow and reject the truth and influence of religion.

We have, therefore, to find some definition of religion which will distinguish it from both philosophy, morality, and social economy. Will it suffice for our present popular and practical purpose if we designate religion as being, in its fundamental principles, recognised relations between the human soul and God, and in its practical workings the effort of the soul to realize its true relations to God?

A religious man recognises God as the author, the ruler, and the supreme good of his life, and he adjusts all the principles, activities, and affections of his life to this recognised relationship. Neither the philosopher, the moralist, nor the social economist necessarily recognises God at all. Even the moralist, whose science and aim the most nearly approach those of the religious man, is ruled by mere moral distinctions, the consciousness of right and wrong.

The distinction comes out more clearly when we speak of the pure science of each domain. The science of the religious life is theology, a doctrine concerning the supreme God, His nature, relations, and claims; which determines all the religious man's notions of the universe, enters vitally into his conceptions of right and wrong, and practically controls all the personal and social actions and affections of his life. The science of the moralist is ethics, intrinsic right and wrong, the nature and practical methods of virtue.

Religion, therefore, necessarily includes philosophy, morality, and social economy, although these do not necessarily include religion. Starting from the fundamental assumption of a personal God, religion affirms, first, that that there can be no adequate philosophy of human nature that does not take into account the relations between the personal soul and the personal God;— next, that the ultimate root and supreme inspiration of all true morality is to be found in these relations of the soul to God;—and next, that in the manifold social relations of life there is no influence so purifying, so elevating, so benevolent, and so potent as the influence of the religious sentiment.

Christianity therefore is bound to give an account of itself. First, as a theology. Can it, to scientific and religious questioners, justify its doctrine of the personal God, and its asserted revelation of His character and will through the Lord Jesus Christ, as described in the New Testament? Next, as a moral philosophy. Can it justify its teachings and its influence by the actual phenomena of human nature; and can it establish its claim to be the supreme exponent of the moral life of men? Next, as an ethical system. Can it make it clear that its distinctive principles and dogmas, precepts and influences, are in harmony with the highest morality, and conducive to the purest and noblest moral virtues that human nature can attain? And next, as an economy of social life. Can it prove that wherever its principles and teachings are acted upon, social evils of all kinds are ameliorated, and men in their social relations realize a purer righteousness, a nobler philanthropy, and a greater happiness than any other system produces?

We think it can; and that nothing is more easy than the historic demonstration; nay, we are constrained to say, that, if in each of these departments it could not prove itself to be the supreme truth, the supreme virtue, and the supreme social good, its entire claim would be invalidated. It is not an option, whether or not we will submit Christianity to these tests; its claim necessitates them. If there be any higher philosophy of human nature, that is the true theology; if there be any nobler ethical teaching, or any more powerful moral influence, that is the true religion; and if there be any more beneficial and constraining law of social life, that is the true order of God. Either Christianity is this, or it is not from God, the supreme wisdom, purity, and love; and if Christianity be not from God, its claim to be so is so explicit and so absolute, and its pretensions are so inordinate, that it must be denounced as the greatest imposture of history.

I have to deal now with only the moral test of Christianity; to show that, under all conditions of human life, the moral character of its dogmas and influences is supreme over every system of human thought. And I shall apply this moral test practically rather than scientifically, and ask, what are the moral character and influence of Christianity as a system of religious thought and life according to the teachings of the New Testament, and as illustrated by the effect of these teachings upon Christian nations and Christian men?

The Moral Teaching of the New Testament. 269

Whatever points of the Christian system I may touch, my only use of them will be to test their moral bearings. With their historical, scientific, or theological apologetics, I do not deal. Whether true or false, I shall, for the purposes of this lecture, assume the Christian system of the New Testament writers, and try to estimate the moral value of their idea.

First, I shall offer some remarks on the general principles and conditions of Christian ethics.

Secondly, Test the moral value of certain particular elements of Christian teaching.

I. With respect to the general principles and conditions of Christian ethics, I remark—

1. That the moral sentiment of human nature has two necessary relations to Christianity.

First. To this moral sentiment every religious system must ultimately appeal. Every spiritual or moral appeal which demands our obedience, worship, and love, must necessarily justify itself to our spiritual and moral nature. No religious system can stand on the ground of mere external authority. In the very nature of things we cannot give faith, moral obedience, and love, to any system that does not commend itself to our moral consciousness. No teaching of the Bible, no element of Christianity, can take religious hold upon me, save by securing the assent of my moral conscience. It must approve itself as true to my sense of truth, and as good to my sense of goodness. I cannot, through the intrinsic qualities of my moral nature, receive a religious system so as to become in virtue of it a religious man, on any mere external authority whatever. No mere evidence of miracle, or prophecy, or divine inspiration, or divine origin or authority, can make my religious nature accept any system of theology or morals. If God were audibly to speak to me from heaven, the utmost effect would be to convince my understanding of the truth of what was thus attested. I might submit as to an authority that could not be gainsayed, I might accept the theological teaching as true, just as a man ignorant of mathematics might, on the authority of Sir Isaac Newton, accept the Binomial theorem; but the acceptance of the former would no more make me a religious man, than the acceptance of the latter would make me a mathematician. Before a revelation can become a religion to me, its moral character must convince my religious consciousness, and engage my religious sympathy. And this applies not only to revelation as a whole, but to each separate statement of it. No fact or doctrine of the Bible can be a religious teaching to me, unless it approves itself to my religious conscience. Facts may be stated, the religious character of which may be to me obscure, or apparently contradictory, and I may accept them as true in virtue of the authority that affirms them; but they are of no religious value to me; and in accepting them I must believe that, when fully understood, they will be found in harmony with my own moral conscience. There cannot be two moralities, one in God, another in man; everything that is true must, when fully understood, approve itself to my moral conscience. This therefore is the ultimate test of Christianity. If its teachings do not justify themselves to our religious conscience—when that is, it is earnestly excited, and desirous of right—they are either misconceived or untrue. This indeed is the glory of Christianity as Christ taught it—" Every one that is of the truth heareth my words;" and as Paul preached it,—" commending ourselves to every man's conscience in the sight of God."

The *second* necessary relation of the moral sentiment of human nature to Christianity is, that the final cause of every true religious system must be righteousness—personal virtue—practical goodness. It may seek more than this, but it must include this. Christianity, for example, includes in its conception of righteousness, right conduct and feeling towards God, personal duty, worship and love, the sentiment and character that we designate piety. But this does not diminish the sentiment of personal and social virtue; rather does it increase it by additional and cogent sanctions; it makes morality an obligation of piety, right doing to man a duty to God.

It is quite true that sometimes theological notions or pietistic sentiments have been so perverted as that the sentiment of piety has been strong and fervid, while the sentiment of morality has been very feeble and loose. But abnormal developments are characteristic of every system; and in Christianity this has always been abnormal, and has been uniformly repudiated by the religious sentiment itself. Thus our Lord denounced those who said, " Lord, Lord, and did not the things that He commanded them." And the Apostle Paul vehemently protested against the immoral perversion of his doctrines of grace, represented by the phrase, " Let us do evil, that good may come;" or, " Let us sin, that grace may abound." And uniformly the mysticism that has merged morality in religion, practical duty in sentimental pietism, even when exemplified in such saintly men as Eckart and Tauler, has failed to commend its pseudo-spiritualism to the common religious sense of the community. The pestiferous monasticism which was one form of this, and which has filled so large a place in the history of the Church, so far from being a disparagement of morality, was the product of a morbid intensity of the moral sentiment. To avoid moral contamination in the lawful ways of life, men and women secluded themselves from their wholesome discipline, and soon developed evils far more erroneous—they became immoral through mistaken moral methods of their own.

The Antinonianism of modern church life, again, has been but an exceptional and transient element in it; and has nowhere excited a protest and an antipathy so great as in the Church itself. While the huge corruptions of sacerdotal hierarchies, like those of the Greek and the Roman Churches; the unfaithfulness of almost every Protestant Church; and the moral inconsistencies of individual Christian men and women, are not only admitted apostacies from the New Testament dogma and ethics, but they attest the presence and power of the moral sentiment in Christianity by the vehemence of the protest and the emphasis of the condemnation they provoke. No candid opponent of Christianity will confound palpable unfaithfulness of the professors of a religious system with the system itself.

It is the universal acknowledgment of Christian Churches, and of Christian men, that the final cause of all theological dogma, of all religious cultus, of creed, of fellowship, of ritual, is personal practical righteousness. Other things are sometimes contended for in passionate forgetfulness of this, never in denial of it.

Few persons have assailed Christian dogma with more vehemence, perhaps it might be said unfairness, than Mr. Matthew Arnold. Christian apologists have not been slow to repel his assaults, but almost uniformly they have rejoiced in his emphatic demand and intense yearning for righteousness. It is the key-note of his polemic.* He

* Literature and Dogma.

conceives that the prominence given to Christian dogma, that the notion of a personal God even, are inimical to the "tendency that makes for righteousness," and in the name of righteousness he ruthlessly discards them, and holds them up to ridicule. The Bible, he admits, is the most intensely righteous book in the world; Jesus Christ is the most perfect ideal of righteousness. "The Bible has such power for teaching righteousness, that even to those who come to it with all sorts of false notions about the God of the Bible, it yet teaches righteousness, and fills them with the love of it."

But the notion of a personal God, he says, is not verifiable. These old Hebrew writers did not mean it; they meant only in a vivid way to express "a power not ourselves which makes for righteousness." Righteousness, he says, is the most important of all things. "The object of religion is conduct," and conduct has to do with "three-fourths of human life." In this estimate of righteousness we are heartily at one with him, as also in his estimate of the Bible as teaching and promoting it above all other books in the world. From Genesis to Revelation this is its constant idea. We agree with him also when he says that "the true meaning of religion is not simple morality, but morality touched by emotion; and this new elevation and inspiration of morality is well marked by the word righteousness." Now if the recognition of the personal God of the Bible, if the fundamental dogmas of the Christian system, were not above all things the inspiration of "the sentiment that makes for righteousness," Mr. Arnold would be right. The supreme idea of religion is righteousness; nothing taught as religion can be objectively true that does not supremely make for righteousness. Mr. Arnold's mistake is in supposing that men fail of righteousness because of their belief in a personal God, and in Christian dogmas, instead of in spite of them, and because of the strength and selfishness of human passion. In order to attain to righteousness he rejects its most cogent constraints. What is there so calculated to touch morality with emotion, to give it dynamic power, as the Christian recognition of the personal God as a loving Father, and of the Lord Jesus Christ as a self-sacrificing Redeemer? Were the Apostle Paul living to characterize such speculations, he would need only to make a fresh application of his own words, "Israel, which followed after the law of righteousness, hath not attained to the law of righteousness. Wherefore? Because they sought it not by faith, but as it were by the works of the law. For they, being ignorant of God's righteousness, and going about to establish their own righteousness, have not submitted themselves unto the righteousness of God. For Christ is the end of the law for righteousness to every one that believeth."

2. The reason and root of all morality is the moral element which is an essential part of our nature. The consciousness of right and wrong is an inseparable part of our self-consciousness. We need say no more than this—perhaps we cannot. Whatever my genesis, whatever my destiny, I am consciously a moral being, and distinguish between good and evil. Hence I am consciously free to choose between good and evil. My will exercises itself in the domain of moral things. Where there is no freedom, there can be no morality. The feeling that I *ought* to do, necessarily implies that I *can* do. If, therefore, freedom of the will be denied, all possible moral conduct is denied. And it is singular how different perversions of truth concur in this. The "Fate" of the old Pagan mythologists, the predestinarianism of Calvinistic

theology, the physical necessity of modern Positivism, all concur in representing man as the creature of mere circumstances, and character as the involuntary issue of inevitable laws. All, therefore, degrade human nature from the moral dignity of its freedom; shut it up to one form or other of necessity. But against one and all of these our moral consciousness rises up in irrepressible self-assertion. I feel that I am free; and against this consciousness argument is powerless. My conscience condemns me as guilty when I do wrong, approves me as righteous when I do right; and against this consciousness all the subtle metaphysics of philosophy and theology are powerless.

3. We cannot fully appreciate the transcendent excellence and power of Christian morality without some acquaintance with the ethics of other systems.

For instance, what may be called the empirical ethics of peoples like the Chinese, whose political and social virtue is purely utilitarian, and seems to be utterly destitute of the higher ideas and inspirations of philosophy and religion,—an elaborate world-order, expressing itself in rules according to the wisdom of the ancients, without any idea of moral perfection to be striven after. Without spiritual source or goal, it is a mere social expediency; its only golden age the wisdom of the past.

Or the Pantheistic morality of Buddhism, the supreme good of which is not active benevolence, but passive surrender; not individual perfection, but universal absorption into an all-pervading essence.

Or the morality which the Persian system represents— two eternal antagonistic principles of good and evil— which, although a nobler moral conception than that of Buddhism, inasmuch as it solicits men to an active struggle with evil, is yet defective in sanctifying urgency; inasmuch as the evil against which he is called to struggle is an external evil, part of the world-order, not an inward or personal one. It is a conflict with Ahriman, not with his own heart.

Or the ethics of classical philosophy, first developed in Greece, and culminating in Plato and Aristotle; which, in diversified forms, is simply æsthetic development, not personal regeneration and perfection. It is the ideal morality of perfect knowledge, according to Socrates; the ideal morality of perfect happiness, according to the Cyreniacs and Epicureans; the ideal morality of perfect beauty, according to Plato; the ideal morality of a perfect symmetry, or the golden mean, according to Aristotle.

It is enough to name these various ancient systems in order to show their infinite inferiority in conception and dynamic force to the moral system of Christ. The highest point of pagan morality was attained by Socrates, Plato, and Aristotle. And yet who can remember their teachings concerning the relations of the sexes,—the community of wives advocated by Plato, the badinage about courtesans which abounds in the conversations of Socrates, in language often worthy of Sodom itself,—without feeling the divine purity of Him who lifted up the woman who was a sinner, insulted even by the comparison? Who can recal the cruel and oppressive social institutions advocated by Plato and Aristotle, such as infanticide and slavery,* without feeling that the very first principles of social morality were imperfectly apprehended by him? Who can think of the exaltation of suicide to the dignity of a heroic virtue by the Stoics and others, without

* The first formal philosophical theory and defence of slavery is contained in Aristotle's Politics.

The Moral Teaching of the New Testament. 277

feeling what an ignominy was put upon life as its crown? Zeno hanged himself because he had broken a finger; Cleanthes starved himself to death because his gums became tender. Suicide was the crown put upon some of the noblest virtues of Pagan life by men like Cato, Brutus, and Seneca. What a cowardly contrast to the moral heroism of Christian teaching and example!

How mournfully Pagan ethics culminated in the formal subordination, and at length the abandonment of the moral idea in Epicureanism and Skepticism, need not be told. It is enough to suggest its contrast with the Christian apotheosis.

4. Christian morals have a history of their own which must be discriminated. The moral sentiment of every class or cultus has necessarily its subjective development. It is not enough to possess an objective moral system. Actual moral result, as embodied in feeling and life, demands subjective perception and sympathy; and these are developed by education. Moral defects of Christian people are not necessarily chargeable upon their Christian teaching. The higher the moral teaching, the more incongruous shortcoming appears. And is not this the explanation, first, of the high expectation of moral excellency which is instinctively looked for in Christian people; and next, of the eager exultation with which their defects are paraded?

The moral sentiment of Christian men develops through successive ages a truer perception of the meaning and spirit of Christ's inculcations, and a more elevated and sympathetic conformity to it. By a process of action and reaction—Christian truth inciting the moral conscience, and the purified heart more clearly discerning Christian truth—communities are being transformed. It may be taken as a conclusive proof of the divine origin of New Testament truth, that it is ever impelling the moral progress of those who receive it, and that no attainable degree of moral progress exhausts it. It is as supreme over the moral sentiment of this nineteenth century as it was over that of the first. Our moral consciousness has ever to confess, " Not that I have already attained, or am already perfect, but I follow after." Both the formal knowledge and the spiritual sentiment of Christian people are ever developing. For example, the sentiments about war and slavery, about penal laws, and about the succour of the ignorant, wretched, and the oppressed, which are the accepted standards of one generation, are far below those of the next. We are ever outgrowing our own conceptions, advancing upon our attainments, developing our piety, our morality, our humaneness into more spiritual forms, broader charities, more refined sympathies. A couple of centuries ago pious men could burn their fellow-Christians at the stake for the good of their souls; a century ago it gave no compunction to English Christian ministers to be slave owners; a dozen years ago American Christian ministers could utter from the pulpit elaborate apologies for slavery; many men now living have suffered fine and imprisonment for their religious opinions. Thank God, we have changed all that. The simple development of Christian sentiment has rendered the idea of such things abhorrent.

Such development of Christian morality is simply in harmony with every other human development,—whether in politics, sciences, social life, or personal conviction and feeling. In every science, objective data are better understood, and practical applications of them are extended.

Hence, there is much in theological science yet to be attained; errors of interpretation and conception have yet to be corrected, and largely, no doubt, by means of hostile criticism; the misconceptions of selfishness or passion have to be removed; incapacities of defective moral attainment have to be remedied.

In both the individual and the community there is a continual advance from the lower to the higher, an improvement in morality, an attainment in holiness, a growth in grace, which is one of the fundamental principles of the Christian life. The moral ideal of the patriarchs was far below that of David, that of David was far below that of the apostle Paul. The religious standard of the mediæval centuries was far below that of the Reformation, and that of the Reformation far below that of our own day. Hence it follows that the only fair estimate of practical Christian morality is to test it by the conceptions of the day.

The same principle must be applied to the Bible. The biblical history of religious men is often indeed recklessly adduced as the biblical standard of moral goodness; and the wise, practical dealings of God with imperfect men, or His acceptance of their conduct, as the Divine ideal of what human goodness should be. But clearly the moral ideal of the Bible is not to be found in its historical records as such, but only in its didactic principles and precepts. Our contention is, not that in the character or the words of Abraham, or David, or John, we get the Divine ideal of goodness, but that in the divinely affirmed principles and teaching of the Bible we have the ground and standard of the loftiest morality ever propounded to men;—a morality that, if fully realized, would elevate human nature to its utmost conceivable perfectibility.

The God of the Bible, in the ethical conception of His character, and of His historical relations to men, not only surpasses all other theological conceptions, but, in its absolute perfection, is unspeakably glorious; it satisfies not only our moral sentiment, but our moral imagination —we can conceive nothing higher. The God of the Bible is not a pagan Fate, an Olympian Zeus, an arbitrary or lustful tyrant, a philosophic necessity, a physical law; He is a pitying, loving, yearning Father, with whose helping tenderness the most miserable and sinful are placed in the closest relations.

The ethical conception of holiness presented in the Bible has its root in the recognition of absolute human freedom and responsibility; its essence, in the perfect purity of the inner heart; its practical possibility in the redemptive work of Jesus Christ, and in the regenerating influences of God's Holy Spirit; and its consummation in the absolute holiness and benevolence which are idealised in the character of Christ, and in the moral perfection of God. The supreme ethical precepts of the New Testament are, "Let the mind be in you which also was in Christ Jesus;" "Be ye therefore perfect, as your Father who is in heaven is perfect." Whatever Christian men may actually realise, this is the recognised standard by which they measure themselves, the avowed ideal after which they strive.

5. It has been urged, in disparagement of Christianity, that the great ethical principles upon which it insists, and which are embodied in the teaching of Christ, are not its creation, but are derived from Jewish rabbis or pagan philosophers. Considerable interest was caused some

four or five years ago by the appearance of a remarkable article on the Talmud, which cited from it a series of maxims which had generally been supposed to be peculiar to the New Testament. The excitement might have been less, had it been remembered that the compilation of the Talmud, by Jehudah Hanassi, dates from the year 219 after Christ.

But we are not careful to reply to such objections. Christianity does not profess to propound new principles of morals; no stronger condemnation of it can be imagined. Principles of morals are immutable; they have their reason in the nature of things, in the eternal distinction between right and wrong, of which we can give no other account than that it is.

Isolated principles and maxims, moreover, are no more a moral system than separate bricks are a house, or separate columns a cathedral. The claim of Christianity is, that it is the supreme expression of moral sentiment, the flower and fruit of the world's purest feeling; it lifts moral principles to a degree of spiritual significance, elevation, and sympathy never before associated with them; it combines the manifold moral sentiments of human life into a system of moral obligation, the purity, symmetry, beauty, and penetrating thoroughness of which are without parallel in the history of human speculation, and touches it with a peculiar emotion which makes it a religion, the dynamic force of which is incalculable and all-pervading. Further, it is the claim of Christianity to have propounded a morality that is as universal as it is supreme. It is a fitting and adequate moral law for the life of humanity under all its manifold conditions and degrees of development, so marvellously generalized, that no local peculiarities disqualify it; so marvellously adjusted, that, while it transcends the highest degree of moral attainment, it is perfectly adapted to the lowest—none can escape its requirements, or evade the application of its principles; and so marvellously cogent, that every mind and heart must either submit to it, or strenuously resist it. Like great laws of nature, the moral code of Christianity is perfectly applicable, wherever men are found.

6. Another distinctive element of Christian morality is the personal relations in which it is rooted. It eminently fulfils Mr. Matthew Arnold's requirement, and creates an enthusiasm for righteousness; and it alone, among the moral systems of the world, does this. Morality cannot be practically realized through the mere sense of right and wrong. The attainment of virtue is possible only through the earnestness that strong emotion generates; and the problem of all moral systems is how to generate it. It does not suffice for the generating of this emotion that virtue tends to happiness. This Mr. Arnold imagines to have been the inspiration of the passionate religious affection of the old Hebrews.

But all human experience testifies that the mere calculation of happiness does not make a man virtuous. "Honesty is the best policy." Yes, but we instinctively feel that it is not a very elevated honesty that is produced by mere policy. "Goodness commands respect." Yes, but we all concur in designating a man a Pharisee, a Pecksniff, who is good in order to be respected. Nobler natures will rather recoil from such motives, and hate themselves for the meanness of entertaining them. It needs a deeper, more potent influence than that of mere selfish calculation, to make men love virtue with a passion that is a worship. It needs reverence, gratitude,

The Moral Teaching of the New Testament. 283

enthusiasm. We cannot feel reverence for an abstract principle—gratitude for an unrecognising law—enthusiasm for a calculated policy. When, in the history of human enthusiasm, of religion, of patriotism, of moral movements, such as the abolition of slavery, has it been generated thus? Whatever *ought* to be theoretically, practically all the noble enthusiasms of history, which have swept away wrongs, and achieved great reformations, have been inspired by personal elements.

That in Christianity which applies to virtue the touch of emotion, and elevates it to a religion, is its peculiar conception of our relations to the personal God as our tender Father, and to the Incarnate Christ as our self-sacrificing Redeemer.

Suppose the basis of moral obligation to be merely the instinctive sentiment of right,—what is to constrain the affections and passions to obey it, or to prevail against the selfishness that urges us to disregard it? Why should I not, if I choose, obey the instinct of selfishness, as well as the instinct of righteousness? The moral conscience may approve the latter, and condemn the former; and it may be true that the natural fruits of righteousness are better and more precious than any possible fruits of selfishness; but suppose that, as myriads of men do, I prefer to indulge the selfishness, and pay the price—the disapproval of conscience and the disadvantage of evil. What is there to hinder such a preference—to give a supreme sanction to the " ought "? Can any system be more palpably weak in motive than utilitarianism is?

Or, suppose the external ethical obligation to be a digest of rules, addressing themselves to the merely moral instincts—a codified system of precepts like the ten words of Sinai; or even a philosophy of the spirit, that is, of the spiritual and moral nature of man. Its rules would be merely the commands of a supreme authority, the philosophy would be simply a cold metaphysical science which only few would apprehend, and which could have no appeal to passion, or, at the utmost, could appeal only to the low passions of selfishness. The mere instinct of right, the mere demand of authority, the mere apprehension of scientific truth, are utterly inadequate as motives to control the practical lives of men. Their impotence is attested by universal experience. Take the conception of the Greek $\eta\theta os$—custom—rite—institution—behaviour—character; or the analogous conception of the Latin *mores*, or manners. How entirely external to the living spirit they are, and therefore how impotent as its law.

Take the Positivist conception of moral education, which, according to Comte, is the mere knowledge of facts;—"of causes of phenomena, whether first or final, we know nothing;" according to Mr. Herbert Spencer, that children be made to experience the true consequences of their conduct; to Mr. Mill, the inculcation of what experience informs us "of direct power over my volitions, I am conscious of none;" to Mr. Bain, a deliverance from "the whole series of phrases connected with the will, freedom, choice, deliberations, self-determination, power to act if we will;" as being "contrived to foster in us a feeling of artificial importance and dignity." That is, you are to educate a child morally by telling him that moral freedom is a delusion, and responsibility a superstition; that the highest good of life is happiness, and the supreme motive of conduct that which promotes it.

Even Cicero felt that the only possible ground of

moral obligation was the recognition of a personal God; that without a Divine Being there can be neither laws nor duties.

"Moral philosophy leans on the aid of religion for accomplishing its mission of human reformation. It piles up the wood for the sacrifice, and slays the victims, and scatters the incense; but it expects the fire to descend from heaven, and kindle the offering into flames. Its system is perfect and beautiful, but its working cannot be ensured."*

The power of Christian sanction and constraint is unique. Christianity makes every moral obligation a personal feeling. It is not a righteous law that I have to keep—it is a personal and loving Father whom I have to please. It is not a mere observance of a Christian code which will make me happy, to which I am urged—it is the crucifixion of the evil within me, which rendered it necessary that the self-sacrificing Redeemer should be crucified for me. I am urged by simple gratitude to crucify the lusts which crucified Him. Because in unspeakable love He died for my sin, through His cross "the world is crucified unto me, and I unto the world."

No matter, so far as the present argument is concerned, whether this conception historically and morally is true or false. It is Christianity, and Christian men believe it. The Christian writings are full of its urgency as the supreme motive for a holy life, and Christian men admit their constraint, and practically submit their actions and their affections to it. It is impossible to exaggerate the moral power of this personal element in Christianity, and we cannot exaggerate this emphasis. All its ideas have

* Hampden's "Moral Philosophy," Lect. iii., p. 100.

their origin, all its affections their object, all its activities their law, in our personal relation to Christ as the Incarnate Son of God, and our Redeemer from sin. Christian dogma is "truth in Jesus," Christian discipleship is "learning Christ," Christian virtue is "putting on the Lord Jesus Christ." The Christian life is "being quickened with Him." We pursue our Christian path "walking in His steps;" we run our Christian race, "looking to Jesus;" we endure our trials, " considering Him." So far did the early Christians carry this personal reference, that the apostle Paul speaks of his proper individual life as lost in that of Christ : " Christ who is our life;" " I knew a man in Christ ;" " that I may be found in Christ ;" " I live, yet not I, but Christ liveth in me."

The influence of all this upon our emotions, our enthusiasm, is incalculable ; the world has known no "tendency to righteousness" that can be compared with it. It is not a mere teacher who comes to me with a moral message, it is the Divine Son of God who comes to me with a moral salvation, to deliver me from the moral power of evil by His death on the cross as an atonement for my sin. And by this He appeals to our grateful affection and obedience. " How shall we that are dead to sin live any longer therein ?"

Imagine that Christian morality were merely a written code, presented to us in a book. Its power of appeal would be nothing compared to that of its embodiment in Jesus Christ. It is not merely that Christian doctrine is more truthful, that its morality is more pure, than those of other systems; it is that these are embodied in a personal life. It is not that Christianity brings more light; the moving power of the world is heat, not light. It is because the religion of Christ supplies the greatest heat, that its dynamic power is the greatest that men know. Instead of a creed to be subscribed, or a code to be obeyed, we have a personal life to love and to imitate; and this makes Christian motive so cogent, Christian obedience so holy, Christian worship so loving. Had Christ been a mere lawgiver, like Moses, His teaching could not so have constrained us. Moses was not an embodiment of the law that he gave, Moses did not lay down his life to redeem us from sin. The distinctive power of Chistianity is the power of Christ's person. He stands before His maxims; we love Him first, then listen to His teaching. He is the personal centre around whom our affections gather, our life revolves. All our religious thought and obedience and love enshrine themselves in Him. His peerless perfection is ever before us—individual, vivid, divine, all that we can reverence in Deity, all that we can love in humanity—a presence that we cannot banish, a power that we cannot resist, a beautiful incarnation of purity and love that we can neither gainsay nor corrupt. The most perfect moral system can excite no enthusiasm compared with such a life. "What the law could not do, in that it was weak through the flesh, God sending His own Son in the likeness of sinful flesh condemned sin in the flesh." To learn virtue we go not to a book of dogmas, but to the life of a man; it is a discipleship of personal imitation; we are thrown upon a living human heart; we learn duty from His obedience, love from His tenderness; "we learn Christ," His fidelity to principle, His fearlessness in duty, His self-sacrifice in helping; we clasp His hand, we walk by His side, we witness His life, the beautiful and perfect exemplification in Him of all human virtues and graces, the moral possibilities of a sanctified manhood.

In our conception of it, His life has a purity and a pathos, His image a beauty and a power, that rebuke sin wherever we see it, and kindle enthusiasm and desire whenever we remember it. And when we do sin, it is our first and bitterest penitence that we have sinned against His holy love.

In our practical struggle with evil, the New Testament image of the man Jesus Christ is unspeakably precious to us. We attain familiarity with the holiest conception of character that the world has known; we come to feel as if we had lived with Him as a friend, and communed with Him as a brother; we carry His image in our heart, we think His thoughts, we imbibe His spirit; we find Him everywhere present with us, the model and inspiration of our life—perfect law in a perfect example. We learn from the study of the personal Christ more than from all other studies beside: we are constrained by His unspeakable love to an enthusiasm of grateful adoration that nothing else can kindle. Mere law could give us only maxims, the personal Christ gives us an example, and love to Him gives, as love always does, divinations. It is a combination of holy law and worshipping love that is unique.

This, then, is the moral supremacy that we claim for Christianity, that it is not only ethically superior to all other moral systems, but that its personal relationships with Christ give it a dynamic power of which other systems know nothing.

This might be abundantly justified by an appeal to history and to experience. Other systems have failed as signally as Christianity has succeeded. Where can successful moral effort on any large scale be adduced apart from the gospel of Jesus Christ? What pagan philosophy ever renewed a nation? Wha uttilitarian morality ever sanctified a community? What positivist mission is effecting moral reformations among heathen peoples, or the ignorant and criminal classes of our own cities? Where in the world's experience has atheism or infidelity ever been a moral and beneficent power? Which of the great moral ameliorations of social life can it claim? Did it reform prisons, or abolish slavery, or make oppressive laws humane? Does it build hospitals, or teach ragged schools, or visit dying men? It has no inspiration that prompts it to do such things; it has no gospel that could give it success, were it to attempt them. True to its instincts, it evades the obligation by denying the misery, by disallowing moral distinctions or responsibility; and it consummates its benevolence by preaching the gospel of suicide to the hopelessly wretched. It lacks the power which touches the heart of virtue, and arrays on its behalf the enthusiasm of the soul. It leaves the world to the barren coldness of passionless understanding and the stern judgments of the conscience.

On the other hand, the gospel of the Incarnate Christ takes its place, not among the barren speculations of a mere theosophy, but among the powers of the world's moral life, the most practical, the most potent moral force that has ever inspired men. It has subdued the most savage moral natures, and overpowered the fiercest evil passions; made the lawless obedient, the dishonest upright, the drunkard sober, the unchaste pure, the fiend a saint. Our churches are full of such instances; there is scarcely a minister who could not adduce numbers of such, as the direct results of his religious teaching, his preaching of Christ. Evangelising and benelovent agencies for helping and blessing men in every conceivable way, at home and abroad, religiously and socially, are devised and carried out at a great cost of money and of life; the more distant, savage, and degraded, the stronger the claim. Robert Moffat and Bishop Mackenzie consecrate genius and learning that might have adorned any country to the savages of central Africa. Mrs. Fry consecrates her noble womanhood to prison visiting, Florence Nightingale to hospital nursing. There is no form of ministry to human misery and sin, however self-sacrificing, that Christian men and women are not ingenious in devising, eager in undertaking, unwearied in prosecuting. We can more than justify all that we have said about Christian morality by its realized achievements; first, by its noble inspirations of philanthropy in its disciples, and next by its almost miraculous moral transformations in those to whom they minister. Like their Master, His disciples " go about doing good."

For the first time in the world's history Christianity has solved the great problem how virtue may become the object of passion; how it may excite the enthusiasm of the heart, as well as the approbation of the conscience. Its secret is the personal Christ, and the love that He inspires. Christ has won for Himself, in the hearts of men, a religious reverence and a fervent devotedness to which there is no parallel. Nothing among men is so sacred as the name of Christ, no reverence so great as that which hallows it, no rapture so great as the love which gathers round it, no blasphemy so great as that which profanes it. Myriads of the noblest minds and hearts of men do Him homage. They who scoff are, in both number and intellectual greatness, insignificant in comparison with those who believe. It is a name as potent in the secret soul as in the open life, in the closet as in the street. The devoutest invoke it when they offer their worship, the holiest adore it when they pour forth their love. "It is a name that is above every name."

II. For an examination of the moral character and influence of separate elements of the Christian system, such as I contemplated at the outset, there is scarcely any necessity. Principles stand in the stead of instances; and general characteristics, such as have been specified, may well dispense with detailed particulars. From the indubitable moral aspect and influence of the whole we may fairly infer the character of its parts. "By their fruits ye shall know them." Conscience, the moral affections, experience, history, all attest the transcendent moral excellence of the Christian system. Two or three indications must suffice—

1. We affirm the moral excellence, both in principle and influence, of distinctive Christian dogmas.

Christian dogmata have too often been exalted to absolute supremacy in the Christian system. Right notions, which relatively and practically are only ministers to right life, have been regarded as of independent sufficiency and supremacy. It has been deemed more important to subscribe a true creed, than to live a holy life. More and fiercer conflicts have been waged about creeds than, about practical holiness. If we may judge from our Lord's attitude and words, the reverse would be nearer the truth. A man's notions are surely of less importance than his moral and religious character. A right heart and a noble life are surely the supreme end of religion.

But while admitting this, it is surely a blind and suicidal petulancy to disparage and denounce dogma altogether, and to correct the perversion by denying the use.

Dogma is the affirmation of the reality of things, and no system can be satisfactory or permanent that has not an intelligent and a true scientific basis. Even for its own sake truth is an intellectual necessity for us; and it would be an anomaly indeed if, while in every other science true dogma is passionately sought, it should be deemed unimportant in theology.

Dogma, again, is the parent of feeling and conduct; dogma is right knowing, morality is right willing. We cannot will rightly if we do not know rightly. Our notions nurture our purposes and affections, and determine our actions. The moral instincts and sympathies of a man may keep him right religiously, in spite of wrong theological notions, but it is surely a perilous position for the conscience and the life, when neither is sustained, when both perhaps are contradicted, by the intellectual apprehensions.

Both as a true conception of the highest things, and as a ministry to the moral life, therefore, dogma is of momentous importance; so that if it could be shown that Christian dogmas were imcompatible with the highest moral truth, it would be a fatal invalidation of Christianity itself.

(1.) The Christian dogma of the Incarnation does not directly involve moral principles, or directly affect moral conduct. Its chief aspects are metaphysical and benevolent; and it affects moral conduct only through the great stimulus supplied to weak and desponding men, by the helping grace of a "strong Son of God."

(2.) The moral elevation and influence of the doctrine of Christ's human sinlessness is self-evident. But,

(3.) The dogma of sacrificial atonement touches very vital moral principles, and exerts a most potent moral influence. I assume the teaching of the New Testament to be that the sufferings of Christ were not merely submissive and holy—the sufferings of a faithful servant and martyr of God in a world that was evil—but that they were vicarious and piacular, a substitutionary atonement for human sin, and this in virtue of His incarnate character, and as the provision of God's infinite love.

We vindicate the inherent and relative morality of this conception on grounds such as these. (*a.*) The very idea of such an atonement has its root in an intense realization of righteousness : lax moral feeling could not generate it. (*b.*) The representation is of perfect voluntariness on the part of the substitute, and of concurrent pity and love in Him who gave and Him who was given. (*c.*) There is in it no violation of the righteousness of law, inasmuch as it is appointed and accepted by the lawgiver. (*d.*) If it be unjust, *per se*, that the perfectly holy Christ should die for the guilty as an expiatory sacrifice, it is, in principle, equally unjust that He should suffer in the slightest degree as an example. (*e.*) The avowed moral end of substitution is not to appease personal feeling in God, but to vindicate righteousness in the inviolable maintenance of law. Christ obeys the law perfectly to vindicate its reasonableness, and then bears its penalty to vindicate its inviolableness ; not indeed the penalty which its transgressors would have borne, which in the nature of things is impossible, but a penalty which, borne by the holy Son of God, was adequate for the vindication and the impression necessary. Now whether this conception of Christ's atonement be the true one or not, it is clearly based upon the very highest moral conception of righteousness—a much higher conception than that of the mere exercise of a pitiful feeling; to me it is the only conception of the forgiveness of sins that is in all its aspects and principles moral—the only conception that perfectly satisfies my conscience. That its practical influence should be to deepen our sense of the evil of sin, and to fill us with grateful and adoring love to Him, who at such a personal cost has redeemed us from it, is inevitable. "We look upon Him whom we have pierced, and mourn." "The love of Christ constraineth us." "The blood of Jesus Christ cleanseth us from all sin." And the experience of all who receive this construction of Christ's death is, that its constraining moral influence, arising from its combination of peculiar elements, is greater than that of all other Christian ideas combined. In the consciousness of Christian men there is no constraint to daily watchful inward purity so potent as the death of Christ for sin. It would be difficult even to imagine an influence of it inimical to holiness. He who can deduce from it the slightest encouragement to sin, not only belies the testimony of all its disciples, but proves himself the most superficial of all theorists, not only destitute of its personal experience, but incapable of apprehending either its true philosophy or the most potent motives of man's moral nature.

4. The dogma of spiritual regeneration, viz., that in our moral helplessness, our practical inability to attain to the perfect holiness to which we are summoned, we are helped by the gracious Spirit of God—helped by a divine co-operative energy, whereby our holy affections are quickened and strengthened—is essentially moral in both its principles and influences. It would, I think, be contrary to moral principles, and destructive of holy influences, if in His divine helping God were represented as superseding personal moral responsibility, or as producing

upon us an involuntary or a mechanical transformation. But this is not the conception of the New Testament, which in manifold figurative expression represents God as helping us in our struggle after a better life. We "work out our own salvation with fear and trembling, because it is God who worketh in us." The moral responsibility which would be traversed by divine substitution is not traversed by divine help; while the fact that God does thus give grace as well as injunction, inspires the strong encouragement and the strenuous endeavour after holiness which are most manifest in those who the most devoutly believe in the "renewal of the Holy Ghost."

5. It is impossible to characterise the doctrine of election, the metaphysical conception of the divine side of salvation, in a sentence. Few conceptions have been represented in a more unscriptural and immoral way. No teaching of the New Testament is more explicit than that of personal responsibility, and none is more emphatic than that of God's universal love. Complete and congruous expressions of such metaphysical conceptions probably surpass the capabilities of human thought. This is exemplified every whit as much in philosophy—where the analogous question of liberty and necessity has been fruitlessly debated for generations, and has led to quite as extravagant theories—as in the theological doctrines of predestination and freewill. It is enough for the vindication of the New Testament morality that nothing can be more unequivocal than its affirmation of man's freedom and responsibility, and of God's yearning and universal love.

6. It is enough to say here, concerning the New Testament dogma of the final destiny of the wicked, that

whatever be the exact import of its teaching, it certainly does not err on the side of lax morality; while the vindication of the Divine character is, that its severest expressions fell from the lips of Him with whose infinite love our poor compassions can bear no comparison. Whatever perplexity our thought may feel about the possible meaning of New Testament threatenings, we may surely trust His love, that it will do nothing from which our human love would shrink.

7. Need I speak of the moral sentiments and precepts of our Lord's teaching? How profound the principles, and how wise the discriminations of His discoursings about life and its uses!

He denounces the strong tendency of men to trust in riches, He points out the deteriorating character of such trust, but He never disparages wealth itself. He denounces the over-anxious, fretful care of struggling poverty, as a disabling weakness, and as an irreligious distrust of God's fatherly care, but He never disparages patient industry or prudent foresight.

In the beatitudes of the Sermon on the Mount He lays down a moral basis of life, so profoundly true and wise, that all the noblest consciousness of men endorses it. How searching and spiritual, again, His tests of pretended goodness, of almsgiving, fasting, and prayer; and His tests of subtle sin, of murder in an angry feeling, of adultery in a lustful look! How elevated His doctrine of marriage! How wonderful His blending of purity and pity in His treatment of sin! How perfect His theory of human brotherhood, and true neighbourliness, and forgiveness, and unselfishness! far transcending the most chivalrous and sentimental schemes of modern communism. Who can doubt that if the great teachings of Christ were realized, social sin and wrong would disappear?

8. I cannot speak of the moral teaching of Paul's Epistles, and of their startling contrast to the ethics of Gentile life. They develop into greater precision and fulness the moral inculcations of Christ, and enforce them with the great sanctions of His love and death. How they vindicate individual right, while they preserve social order! How they make every man a law unto himself, by insisting upon perfect love and purity of heart, and by placing him under law to Christ! Where in the literature of the world can a more elevated and yet simple directory of social morality be found, than the twelfth chapter of the Epistle to the Romans, or the fourth, fifth, and sixth chapters of the Epistle to the Ephesians?

But I must forbear: it were easy to develop each separate point into a treatise.

It is enough to say that, tested by any other theory of morals that has been propounded to men, by the consentaneous verdicts which the moral consciousness of men have pronounced upon it, by the conscious influence of it upon individual hearts and lives, by the involuntary testimony which is furnished by the judgments of its adversaries upon its disciples, and by the entire scope of its history and results both in communities and individual lives, Christianity not only transcends all the philosophical and moral systems of the world, it so transcends them as to be virtually unique, and as to leave nothing for even imagination to add. From its ideal of life now, it rises to the prophecy of its own grand consummation hereafter, when "the people shall be all righteous, every one;" and from its perfection on earth it soars in its holy rapture to the kingdom of God in heaven, into which "there shall in no wise enter anything that defileth, neither whatsoever worketh abomination, or maketh a lie; but they who are written in the Lamb's book of life."

THE GRADUAL UNFOLDING OF REVELATION.

BY THE

REV. GORDON CALTHROP, M.A.

The Gradual Unfolding of Revelation.

ONE of the best commentaries on Holy Scripture that I am acquainted with, is the daily newspaper. What the Bible tells me, I find frequently backed up, of course without deliberate intention, by the Press. I read painful things in the one, about the sinfulness and selfishness of the human heart; but there is a very distinct echo of these statements in the continuous record of vice, and crime, and wrong-doing, supplied by the other. The Bible, again, talks about a judgment to come. Men ridicule the idea; but when I turn to my newspaper, I find a curious kind of process going on in the world, which seems to correspond, very closely, with the scriptural assertion. Every now and then a great exposure takes place. Perhaps it is a bubble-company that has exploded; perhaps it is a religious hypocrite that has been unmasked; perhaps it is some long-successful fraud that has been brought to light and punished; perhaps it is some gigantic system of usurpation, founded upon an iniquitous disregard of the rights and liberties of men, and maintained by a more iniquitous appeal to their passions, which has come crashing to the ground in masses of frightful ruin. Whatever it is, it looks uncommonly like the interference of a power that is on the side of the right, and is opposed to the wrong; that will allow what is false and unreal to stand for a time, but only for a time; that comes in at last to make a separation, and to show up things and men as they really are. I say, "It looks like it." I do not venture to appeal to the fact, as if it were a proof of any kind, but I claim that thus much be admitted, that there is something in human history which harmonizes with, and which points in the direction of, a great final interference in the affairs of men. The newspapers record a number of *little judgment days*, which are possibly anticipations and foretastes of the great judgment day, of which we believe Scripture to speak.

Now may I be permitted to say that we, who are friends and advocates of revealed religion, fancy that we have an ally of the most useful kind in the correspondence which exists between what we read in the Bible, and what we see going on continually in the world round us? The commentary upon the Bible, which the world at large supplies, is to us invaluable. It throws light on many a dark passage. Frequently, if it does not solve a problem for us, it serves to reconcile us to the existence of the problem; for we see that it is not created by Scripture, nor to be found there alone; but that it is part of the conditions under which we are actually living. Is it hard, for instance, to understand what the Bible tells us about the Divine dealings with nations? Well, it is no less hard to understand much that we see actually taking place, and much that we have heard of as actually having taken place, on the stage of a national history. Or, are there difficulties in the scriptural statements about the transmission of hereditary taint; about

The Gradual Unfolding of Revelation. 303

the suffering of the innocent for the guilty? There are. But, whatever the difficulties may be, we do not get rid of them when we turn from the printed page to the outer world. They haunt us still, and in the misery and the loss which a man has power to inflict upon others,—those others not consciously, or not intentionally, participating in his evil,—we may find distinct corroboration of some of those very doctrines of Scripture which are represented as being totally unworthy of the character of God. I say then that this correspondence between the world in the Book, and the world outside the Book, is of essential service to us, when we have a painful problem to solve. We expect to discover traces of the same mind, and traces of the same mode of operation, in the two things; and we do discover what we look for, and we do not allow ourselves to be too much disturbed at our inability to solve a scriptural difficulty, when we detect precisely the same difficulty intertwined and interwoven with the fabric of our ordinary existence.

Now it has occurred to me, Gentlemen, that the plan of glancing from the Book of God to the Book of Nature, and back from the Book of Nature to the Book of God—which many of those whom I represent here have found to bring much comfort and strength to their own minds—may be very serviceable to me, in my present undertaking. And my object will be to show, as well as I can, why, to my mind, no real objection lies against revelation, on the ground that the process by which God has made Himself, His person and character, known to man, has been a slow one, requiring long ages to bring it to a satisfactory and successful issue.

Now, if there be a God and a Creator (as we believe), two things seem to follow from the fact: first, that it must be very important for any intelligent and accountable creatures that may be made, to understand something about this Divine Person, as much, at least, as shall keep them from coming into collision with Him. Next, that it must be impossible for the created being to understand the Creator perfectly, because that which is finite can hardly be expected to comprehend that which is infinite. But, besides this, I think we may say—on the supposition still that there is a Creator—that, inasmuch as the artificer is superior to his work : the poet being greater than the poem ; the painter being greater than his picture ; the man, out of whose fertile and inventive brain a piece of mechanism proceeds, being himself something better, nobler, higher, than his own handiwork ; inasmuch as this is the case, it will be more elevating to the character of the created to contemplate the Being Who makes, than to contemplate the thing that is made ; and that, therefore, an essential part of the educational process through which a progressive race like that of man is to be made to pass, may be expected to consist in a communication to them, by some means or other, of the knowledge of God. But, if this be conceded, it seems inevitable that the communication must be made in the way of a gradual unfolding. It were no proof of wisdom or of love to pour in light upon the eye, in so full a stream that the organ was tortured and blasted by the excessive effulgence. Such an attempt would be nothing better than a wanton exercise of arbitrary power. Granted such a Being as we suppose God to be; granted that He wishes to make Himself known to certain creatures of His hand, who are fashioned with faculties for comprehending and appreciating Him—but those faculties of necessity inferior to

The Gradual Unfolding of Revelation. 305

His own,—it seems to follow, that He will put forth His wisdom in adapting the faculty to the revelation; in fitting the one to the requirements of the other; in expanding the receptive power in proportion as He increases the amount to be received; in carefully providing that no single step be taken before the strength has been acquired for taking it, and that no communication be made until there is room and place for its entertainment in the capabilities of the mind that is dealt with. Surely it is difficult, gentlemen, to discover in such a procedure as this any inconsistency with the idea of a creating God! Indeed, it would seem an indispensable part of the relation between Creator and created (supposing such a relation to exist), that all unveiling of the one to the other must be gradual in its character. Put out of the question, if you like, what you consider the fiction of the Fall. Imagine the creature to be perfect and flawless; complete in all its parts and faculties. Still, being a creature, it must be subject to the condition of development, at least, with respect to knowledge; and it is only step by step that it can climb up to more accurate acquaintance with the illimitable Mind, which still rises and towers above it. But this argument, gentlemen, if it be a sound one, will be enhanced by the supposition that there is some difficulty in the way; something which renders the created mind inaccessible, to a certain extent, to the knowledge which it is so important that it should receive. And it will be enhanced again by the further supposition that the Divine intelligence is not dealing with an individual merely, but with men in masses, who act and react upon each other; and that the Divine plans for human education embrace a long succession of generations and ages. Again, let me say that I am not intending to import into this argument the question of the Fall. All I ask is, that you will allow me to assume that, if there be a God, He does not find it altogether an easy task to convince some of His creatures of His own existence; and that even, where His existence is admitted, He does not find it an altogether easy task to convey to His creatures a correct and distinct and accurate acquaintance with Himself. The very room in which we are now met justifies the assumption. And if so, if there be special difficulties, from whatever cause arising, in the way of communicating to the human race the knowledge of God, we may reasonably expect that the communication should be a work of time; that there should be something of the character of a deliberate march about it; that it should be, in fact, a gradual unfolding to an intellect and heart prepared to receive it.

And certainly, gentlemen, the analogy of nature seems to be in favour of this view. The geologists tell us that a procession of mighty periods rolled along, each with its own peculiar work to do, and each contributing a fresh stage of advancement to the total scheme, before the globe on which we live was fitted to be the home and habitation of man. This task, we think, might have been accomplished in a moment. But it was not accomplished in a moment. Nor was it accomplished in so short a time as the ancient defenders of Revelation seem to have imagined. It took millenniums to achieve. So the scientific men tell us; and to their decision we bow. But when we accept this dogma at their hands, we think that it does at least remove the charge of unreasonableness and absurdity from our belief in the gradual preparation of the human race for the mighty purposes of the Being Who created it. If the one was a work of time, the other may well be a work of time; if the one was a gradual unfolding, the other may well be a gradual unfolding. And it is not altogether inconceivable—on the hypothesis, of course, that there is a Creator, and that He had a purpose in making man—that there is some great result in the future, towards which all that is taking place now in the world of matter, and in the world of mind, is really converging; and of which, the strife and the struggle that we see going on around us, the faith and the doubt, the incessant intellectual and spiritual movement, the collisions of thought, the growth and decay of ideas, the rise and the fall of systems, are constituting, at least in part, the predetermined and prearranged preparation. You say that you do not see it. Probably not. We are not exactly in the right position at present for seeing it. When an intricate and complicated scaffolding is surrounding an unfinished building, and the hodmen are ascending and descending the ladders, and the busy click of the trowel is heard in every direction,—that is not the best moment, is it, for judging of the conception which lies in the architect's mind? If you stand watching a piece of tapestry as it issues forth, breadth after breadth, from the loom under the cunning fingers of the skilful weaver, do you pass your comments upon the pattern, then? do you criticise the conception, the execution, the colouring, the shading, then? or do you postpone your criticism until the whole work is finished, and is placed before you? Or, again—you that understand music—will you consent to form your opinion of a noble composition by going into an orchestra and examining the "scores" provided for each individual instrument? There is the score for the first fiddle, and the score for the second fiddle, and the tinkling score for the triangle, and the score with the huge gaps in it for the big-voiced drum ; there is the score for the trombone, and for the hautboy, and for the ophicleide and for all the rest of them : will you dip into this and that, and flutter about, and take a cursory survey, and then pass your judgment, and express your opinion? Not you! You have too much sense, and too much of that modesty which is closely allied with sense, to do such a thing. You just wait ; for you know that it is not until each little rill of sound pours in to swell the full tide of harmony, it is not until each musical thought moves forward into its place in the grand array, and marches on, that you can feel yourself capable of grasping and appreciating the idea that is hidden in the master's mind. In these things, and in such things as these, we are all of us contented to wait. Ready enough to judge results, we are slow about criticising processes. Why should it not be so when we come to the larger scale and the grander platform of the destinies of the human race, and the purposes of the Most High?

But now, gentlemen, as I am not arguing with you in a controversial spirit, but speaking—in a brotherly way, as I hope—about matters in which we are all interested, permit me to tell you in what way the question of the unfolding of revelation presents itself to my mind, when I look into that volume which we commonly call the Bible.

We might expect, I think, before coming to examine the subject, that there would be an analogy, a correspondence more or less close, between the development of the human individual and the development of the human race. Now we find in childhood a sense of right and wrong, but that not very keen or discriminating. A boy, for instance, will do deeds of cruelty, perhaps with respect to his companions, perhaps with respect to dumb animals, which would be simply atrocious and unpardonable in a man. We do not, of course, excuse the child. We feel that his conduct is guilty, and we punish him. And he feels, too, that he has done wrong. But after all, he is not so guilty, his conscience is not so defiled, his character is not so impaired, nor do we think so badly of him, as we should it he did precisely the same thing, neither more nor less, after arriving at the clearer understanding and fuller moral perceptions of manhood. And here it is, I think, that we may discover a hint as to the right way of dealing with the so-called moral difficulties of the Old Testament. We *make the difficulties ourselves*, by importing into those earlier and ruder times the pure and noble and kindly feelings which we ourselves have been educated up to in the lapse of centuries; by setting up, in fact, for the childhood of the race, a standard that is applicable only to its maturity. Well, to put my notion into few words, (but those, words which will seem to you, I fear, to be tinged with too distinct a theological colouring,) the child has an idea of being "naughty," of having done wrong, but he has not any deep sense of *sin*. And I hold that teachers or systems that endeavour to bring out that sense, in anything like intensity, in a child, are forcing on the processes of nature, and doing incalculable mischief to a human soul. Afterwards, as time passes on, and the mind expands, and the relations of things to each other are more distinctly seen, a deeper and more serious perception of the evil, and of the evil consequences of wrong-doing, takes possession of us, and very considerably modifies our view of the world around us. We come to understand and to f el the nature of what we call "Sin." Now I turn to my Bible, and I think I detect there something corresponding to this process in the Divine method of dealing with mankind. In Genesis, in the Patriarchal times—of which Genesis tells the tale—I find the record of enough sin. (Yes, and I should not believe in my Bible if I did not, any more than I should believe in a medical book which professed to give an account of the human body, but omitted all mention of disease.) I find, I say, the record of enough sin : but very seldom, if ever, do I find the expression of deep distress and self-abasement on account of it.

Adam, for instance, sins : but he does not appear to feel very much sorrow for the offence. Why not? Because Adam, instead of being the full-orbed wonder that some imaginative people have represented him to be, was, morally, spiritually, and I suppose also intellectually, a child. He had no intense perception of the nature of moral evil, and indeed I do not think it was to be expected that he should have.

But now, contrast Adam's comparative indifference—his coolness, if I may so call it—with the anguish expressed by another man, a man who has furnished more occasion for objections to Scripture than almost all other Scripture characters put together—I mean King David. Look at some of his Psalms. They are simply miserable in their expressions of mental distress, although I grant you, through all the gloom and the misery, the Psalmist clings hard to his belief in the mercy of the God whom he has so grievously offended. Do you remember what Thomas Carlyle says about David? And Thomas Carlyle is none of your narrow-minded, small-brained, prejudiced religious bigots. Permit me to quote his words to you : "Who is called the man after God's own heart ? David, the Hebrew King, had fallen into sins enough : blackest crimes—there was no want of sin. And therefore the unbelievers sneer, and ask, Is *this* your man according to God's heart ? The sneer, I must say, seems to me but a shallow one. What are faults, what are the outward details of a life, if the inner secret of it—the remorse, temptations, the often-baffled, never-ended struggle of it—be forgotten ? David's life and history, as written for us in those Psalms of his, I consider to be the truest emblem ever given us of a man's moral progress and warfare here below. All earnest souls will ever discern in it the faithful struggle of an earnest human soul towards what is good and best. Struggle often baffled, sore baffled—driven as into entire wreck—yet a struggle never ended ; ever with tears, repentance, true unconquerable purpose, begun anew." This is what Thomas Carlyle says about David. Or turn to the Apostle Paul, and remember what sorrowful expressions that sincere and true-hearted man employs, when he speaks of his past life in its unhappy opposition to the will and the kingdom of God. What, then, is it that makes the difference between the coolness of Adam and the deep distress of David and of Paul? Just that, gentlemen, which makes the difference between the feeling of the child and the feeling of the man, with respect to wrong-doing. There has been, in the one case, what there has not been in the other—an education and training of that part of our being through which we come to the perception of moral evil. The patriarchal times, then, (as I understand it,) were the childish, or rather the childlike, times of the human race. There was no deep understanding then of the problems of life, and no very anxious enquiry into the relations existing between God and man. But this period of simplicity could not, of course, be expected to last for ever. The mind of the race was advancing. Men were beginning to feel more distinctly the awfulness of being placed in this mysterious universe, and made part and parcel of it: and questions were rapidly arising on every side which demanded an answer. Consequently, another stage in human education was called for: and that other stage was entered upon when the Jewish nation was called into existence.

Now this remarkable people was to be, we think, the central point in the Divine dealing with mankind. They are the teachers of the world, consciously or unconsciously, in things which concern religion. Whether we like to acknowledge it or not, the Jewish influence radiates throughout civilized humanity. You cannot get rid of the Jew, do what you will. He constitutes the most unmanageable argument with which doubt and unbelief have to deal. A sceptical prince (I believe it was Frederick the Great) once asked his court chaplain to give him some clear evidence of the truth of Christianity, but to do so in very few words, because a king had not much time to spare for such matters. And the chaplain replied—"The Jews, your Majesty." That chaplain was a sensible man, and knew what he was about. Get rid, gentlemen, of the Jews, and of that strange Jewish history, and you may soon dispose of other evidences. But, believe me, until you succeed in clearing those troublesome Jews out of the way, you will make marvellously little real progress in the work of

The Gradual Unfolding of Revelation. 313

demolishing Christianity. Well, then, according to our view, God began to teach these Jews, intending, through them, to teach the whole world, deeper views of moral evil, deeper views of man's position in the universe, and his personal relation to the Divine. And how did God do it? By the instrumentality of that much-derided Levitical system, with its distinction of clean and unclean animals, of clean and unclean food; with its sacrifices and offerings; with its multitudinous laws about leprosy, and dress, and agriculture, and fasts, and feasts, and many other things; with its whole apparatus, in fact, of what may seem to us to be petty prohibitions and insignificant details. People laugh at the Levitical system. But why? You go into an infant school to see the skilful master teaching and training the little ones. And how does he do it? By appeals to the eye, by simple models, by roughly-sketched diagrams, by things which he sends round from form to form for the children to touch and handle for themselves. You don't laugh at *his* symbolism, gentlemen. You don't ridicule *his* "object-lessons." You know that the method which he is employing is the best way, if indeed it is not the only way, in which he can communicate truth to the feeble, undeveloped, inexperienced minds of his pupils. And why, I ask you, why should men allow themselves to ridicule God, when He condescends, out of the infinite tenderness of His love, to be the infant-school teacher of the human race? In this school the Jews learnt the nature of moral evil. They learnt to understand what a conscience is, when it has been awakened to susceptibility, and called into vitality of action. They learnt the meaning of that word "sin." And they learnt, too, though indistinctly at first, but afterwards with ever-increasing clearness, by what means God proposed to meet and counteract the widespread disease of human nature. Thus they were prepared for that higher stage of education in which they could realize the Fatherhood of the unseen God. It was only after Jesus Christ appeared that men could intelligently and unfalteringly speak of God as their Father. "Our Father" is the keynote of the Christian dispensation, and it could only have been struck after Christ came, and lived, and died. To this point of spiritual development it was, we believe, the Divine intention to lead up the human race. And I think you may easily trace a gradual process, by which the ideas of greatness, and power, and protection, and self-existence, and holiness, and justice, passing each in well-considered and well-ordered succession before the mind, merge themselves at last in that to which they have all been the preliminaries, in the gracious and loving image of One Who is a God and Father in Jesus Christ.

Well, gentlemen, you will excuse my talking in this way instead of arguing. And perhaps the simple laying of my own course of thought before you may do better than argument. At all events, I trust I may have succeeded so far as to convince you that it is not altogether foolish of us to expect that there would be a gradual unfolding of the Divine character and will to our race, when we observe the gradual moral and spiritual development of the individual. Three stages seem to be indicated by the language of Scripture; for one of the New Testament writers speaks of the child, the young man, the father, in reference to this subject of spiritual unfolding. "'The child, the young man, the father." The period of unquestioning thought, of undeveloped perceptions. The period of enquiry and conflict. The period of assured position, of calm rest, of broadening knowledge. "First the blade, then the ear, after that the full corn in the ear." The third period is that at which we are now placed. And what more is wanted? Only this, that the recognition and acceptance of our position should become universal.

And suffer me to say, before I bring my address to a close, that the considerations just adduced may possibly serve to reconcile us to the slow progress which Christianity, after all, has made and is making in the world. Nearly two thousand years have passed away since the Prophet of Galilee, the Man who "went about doing good," hung, the rejected of His people, upon the cross of Calvary. It is true that in that time untold millions, seeing in Him something more than human, have given Him their hearts' best affections, have lived in the faith of His name, and found their dying pillow smoothed and softened by the recollection of His love. True also it is that the faith which this teacher inculcated has become an undeniable influence and power in the world. Just as in cathedrals the form of the Cross may frequently be detected in the mode of their construction, so the doctrines of the Cross have somehow worked their way into the very fabric and texture of our modern civilization; and now the most enlightened and powerful nations of the earth are just those nations who call themselves Christian. But it is also true that we seem very far from an universal acceptance by mankind of this religion, which claims to be *the* religion for every man. To say nothing of what is going on at home, there are vast populations on our globe who are almost as much untouched by the influences of Christianity as if Jesus of Nazareth had never existed. Is this slow, gradual unfolding an objection to Christianity? Well, if it is, it is an objection which lies against all the other works of God. If you maintain that the process of Christianising mankind should have been a sudden one, an instantaneous burst of enlightenment and conviction, sweeping all at once irresistibly before it, you must maintain also that, in this special instance, the Deity departed from His usual method of procedure. According to your hypothesis, He acts in matters of religion as He acts in no other matter. Now, is this at all likely? I venture to think that it is not. At all events, even if it is more in accordance with your ideas of what should be, that the spread of Christianity should not be a gradual work, you cannot say that the fact of its being gradual is fatal to the theory of its emanation from a Divine source. If God works by slowly evolving processes in one department of the universe, it is certainly conceivable that He may see fit to work in the same way in another. If it be true that He occupied centuries upon centuries in building up the fabric of the earth on which we dwell, it is surely not incredible that He may take a long time in bringing about an universal adoption of Christianity by the men He has put on that earth. The Most High need not be in a hurry. He is not like the creature of a day. He has plenty of time to work in. And who shall undertake to deny that He is slowly preparing the intellectual and moral world for the reception of His Truth? And who shall undertake to affirm that in working slowly He is not working for the best? We see but an infinitesimal portion of the manifold scheme. We stand in a little corner of the vast battle-field. Is it well, then, to come to a conclusion upon such very imperfect and very scanty data as we have before us?

The Gradual Unfolding of Revelation.

And yet, again, gentlemen, it seems to me well to remember that the Creator does not treat men as machines, does not take us by storm. He does not compel us to believe. Nay, I may say (and without irreverence) that He cannot compel us to believe. "Cannot;" because He has made us on conditions which do not admit of compulsion; and from these conditions He will not, of course, depart. "He cannot deny Himself." So He influences us really by persuasion. And persuasion is oftentimes very slow work. Men have, ere now, changed sides in matters of opinion; having been Christians, they have become unbelievers; or having been unbelievers, they have become Christians. The change itself was the thing of a moment. It was done instantaneously. But what a long series of ponderings and meditations, of mental conflicts and strifes, preceded it and prepared the way for it! You heap weights in one of the scales of a balance. The conditions are such that you cannot put in many at a time. Your task is one of gradual accumulation. And so you go on adding first one weight, then another, then a third, and many others, without producing any appreciable effect upon the condition of your balance. Presently, however, you cast in one, only a little one, and the scale is turned. But the last weight would have done nothing without all the previous elaborate preparation. Now, the conditions in the case of the human spirit are these: that God will not and cannot force the reception of Himself upon us; that He leaves us the awful power of resisting and rejecting Him. And therefore in the individual He works by the slow and gradual process of moral suasion. And why not so also on the larger scale of the national life? We cannot see why not. Unless God works on the human spirit by compulsion, offering no choice, and permitting no power of disbelief,—a supposition impossible by the very terms of creation,—we must surely expect to find the Christianization of the world a gradual process; and we must surely feel that it is not for us to decide by what gradations, whether slower or more rapid, the work shall proceed.

Gentlemen, I have done. How far I have really met your difficulties on this subject, I cannot tell. I shall be glad if anything I have said should obtain your approval. I hope I have not been betrayed into any theological bitterness. If I have been, or if you should think I have been, pray forgive me. Of course, I should like to find that my arguments are better than your arguments; but, above all things, I wish to be brotherly. And now that the discussion is about to begin, let me say that we do think it a little hard that Christianity is so often endangered by the very blessings which we believe her to have conferred upon mankind. The poet speaks of the eagle stretched upon the plain, and feeling the bitterness of the death-pang increased at the sight of his *own feathers* on the arrow that is drinking his life-blood. Well, that is poetry, of course. But the idea conveyed in the verses may illustrate the feeling of some amongst us, when we see the intellect to which Christianity has given its acuteness, brandished against her life; when we find the nobler, purer, kindlier sentiments which she has herself inspired and fostered, turned into arguments against her character, into instruments for her destruction and overthrow.

THE PERFECTION OF THE HUMAN CHARACTER OF JESUS CHRIST.

BY THE

REV. CANON BARRY, D.D.,

PRINCIPAL OF KING'S COLLEGE, LONDON.

The Perfection of the Human Character of Jesus Christ.

I AM to speak to-night on a very old subject—the Perfection of the Human Character of Jesus Christ. You probably know—for certainly this present age realizes it in an especial degree—what a wonderful power there is in the character of a living man, whether you learn it through your own personal experience, or read it in the pages which reproduce it as a living thing, when he himself has long passed away. If, in some noble picture gallery, such as that which is open to us at Bethnal Green at this moment, you even look upon the face of one who lived in the past, you know how you seem to understand his history and the history of his time better. What otherwise would seem to you cold and distant starts into warmth and life. But a true biography, especially if it is practically written by the man himself, in his words as well as his deeds, is a picture of his real self, not as it comes out obscurely in his outward form, but as it exists within, at least so far as other eyes than his own can see it. And you will always find that it is through such a picture of a human life that you can understand best the great Laws of Humanity and therefore of the Power—whatever it is—that rules Humanity. Partly because, instead of floating vaguely as it were on the clouds above us, they are brought down and visibly embodied in a man like ourselves. Partly because, after all, a man has in him something deeper and greater than even the principles which he holds, and by which he lives; and therefore, much as we think of him and know of him, we always feel that there is in him an inner fulness of being, which it is beyond us to comprehend and to analyse.

It must be therefore at all times and to all men, whatever they think or believe, a work of surpassing interest—and, I think I may add, of a reverent and wondering interest—to contemplate the Life which beyond all contradiction has produced consequences infinitely beyond those which have flowed from all other lives put together. And to those who study it rightly as a life, the true interest lies in its exhibition of His character. For this is always the kernel of the interest in all stories of great and noble lives. He is but a poor dramatist, who, even in fiction, makes all interest turn on plot, costume, situation, and dwells not chiefly on the characters of his play. He is but a shallow writer or reader of a biography, who tries not chiefly to understand, not merely what the man did, but what he himself was. My subject therefore to-night —the character of Jesus Christ—must always be a subject of the very deepest interest to all who really care to know humanity.

But, of course, I need not say that it is not for that reason that I speak of it to-night. A busy man myself, and speaking to those whose lives are busy, I should not have time or inclination for a subject of a leisurely and speculative interest. These Lectures have one object, and one only. They are given by men who profoundly believe that in Christianity and Christ there is a real Divine Power, which can and which does transform the individual, and pervade the whole mass of society, to make it truer, better, happier than it could otherwise be, in this life and on the other side of the grave; and who, profoundly believing this, seek to bring before your minds and consciences what is to them the life of their life, with no purpose whatever, except what they hold to be the good of man and the glory of God. Now it is because the Perfection of the character of Jesus Christ is one of the various forces which have drawn men to Him, that it has been resolved to include it among the subjects of these Lectures, and that I am to try to put it before you to-night

It seems to me that we may put the general case of Christian evidence thus. As you look on human society at the present day, you find Christianity to be a great fact, which, whether you like it or not, is full of a far-spreading and deep-reaching power over men's thoughts and lives. It has so entwined itself with all the civilization of the present, that when—as lately at Paris—men sought to alter the whole form and basis of that civilization, they attacked Christianity with a vehement and almost frantic determination. You find, again, a Society called after the name of Christ, existing under different forms in every race and climate—through every age and under every circumstance of life. It has expressed itself in visible fabrics and institutions; it is a society really and absolutely "International," only including, not one class, but many. Now, these two great facts—Christianity and the Church of Christ—have to be accounted for: and, if you ask Christianity itself what it is based upon, and whereby it exists, the answer will come at once—that it is based on the Life of Christ. Its creed,* so far as it is distinctively Christian, is not one of doctrines—if by doctrines you mean theories and speculations,—but of facts of that life, which claim to be true, and to be of infinite consequence because they are true. Now what are these things which call themselves facts?

It is clear, that when we speak of the facts of any man's life, there are two kinds of facts, which I may call visible and invisible. There is, for instance, with regard to yourselves, a certain series of facts about you happening every day, which any one who is near you, if he will, can see; and about which there is only one question, whether they are false, or whether they are true. You did something, or you did not do it; you suffered something, or you did not suffer it; you lived through such and such a time, or you died; and the like. But there are invisible facts about you, which no one but yourself knows perfectly, and which others, we say, can see "only so far as they have eyes to see." You did such and such a thing with this or that motive. The existence of the motive is just as much a fact as the doing of the thing; but those who look on can see it only in various degrees, according to their intelligence, or still more according to their sympathy; you, and you only, actually know it. Or, again, such and such effects followed on your act; and their following was as much a fact as the act itself. But here it is only in varying degrees, and in all cases with imperfection, that you or any one else can trace these effects. Just in proportion as any man enters into what we call the "laws" of the world and humanity, and has time to look for forward and backward over the stream

---

* I refer, of course, to the Apostles' Creed—the only one which the Church of England makes the test of simple membership.

of events, he will see them, more or less. But the only Eye, which can see them universally and unmistakeably, is clearly an eye placed above them all, and therefore able to pierce into every nook and every depth of history.

Now the life of Jesus Christ is full of both these visible and invisible facts. I must digress for a moment to explain how I know anything of that life. We have it recorded to us, as you know, in certain books which we call the Gospels; these profess to be directly or indirectly the work of eye-witnesses; and they undoubtedly represent it with a vividness and minuteness, of which only simple eye-witness, or a power of fiction of almost superhuman genius, is capable. But we ought to understand and remember that these Gospels are only the representatives of a great number of traditions as to the life of Jesus Christ, which were held by hundreds and thousands in the time immediately following that life, and held with such extraordinary certainty and vividness, that men gave up all and faced death on the strength of their belief in them, and—what is perhaps stranger still—found in them (so they said) the reason and the power of a complete change of heart and life. They come to us, then, not merely on their own intrinsic evidence as ancient books,—although, even in this, I am bold to say they would be absolutely unquestioned, if it were not that they dealt with the supernatural—but also with the reflected light of an ancient and universal Christian belief in the first ages, which indeed was the power which gave birth to the Church itself. I allude only to these things; for it is not my business to-night to enter into any critical questions about them. When I speak of the life of Christ, I speak of it as it is recorded to us in the Gospels, and as it actually passed into the belief, and moulded the whole character of Christianity.

I return from this digression to the Life itself. It has in it certain visible and certain invisible facts; so far it is like other lives. But if it be what it is on all hands allowed to be, it is likely that while the visible facts remain a fixed quantity, the invisible facts will extend almost infinitely. How little can an ignorant peasant see of the life of a great poet or a great philosopher! How infinitely less could any human eye see of a life which undoubtedly rises, by common consent, far above the level of ordinary humanity!

There are, first, certain visible facts—such as His birth at Bethlehem, His actual ministry in Galilee and Jerusalem, His death upon the cross, which were open to the observation of all. They correspond to that public commonplace part of our own life, which everybody knows. There were (so say the Gospels) certain other visible facts, seen only by the Apostles, especially the great fact that He rose on the third day from the grave, and that He ascended into heaven; which I may remark, in passing, was just the one fact on which all the earliest preaching of Christianity turned. These correspond to that deeper and more sacred private life, which only those near and dear to us know, and which the world, if it receives it at all, has to receive on their testimony.

But beyond these there are what claim to be invisible facts connected with that life, on which indeed the meaning of the visible facts depends, and which can be learnt only from the words of Jesus Christ Himself, or those whom He expressly taught. The birth (so says Christian belief) was an Incarnation of the Deity; the death upon the cross was an Atonement for sin; the rising from the grave, and the ascending up on high, were the manifestation and beginning of a new spiritual life, conquering sin and death for all humanity. Who can assure us that they were? The answer ultimately is "Jesus Christ Himself." "Why should we believe Him?" is the next question. And the answer brings out the various signs of truth, which led men to Him, and which, as usual in all cases of faith in men, induced men to believe from Him what He alone could know, and what those who received it could at best verify by their experience of its effects.

Now the perfection of the character of Jesus Christ bears upon both these classes of facts. In itself it is simply a deduction from the records of the visible facts—the actual deeds, words, and events which the Gospels record to us. Those who have read the well-known book called "Ecce Homo," will remember that it is brought out there in that way, by a thoughtful man following Jesus of Nazareth, from the moment of His baptism to the end of His earthly life, looking at the story with the eyes of clear modern insight, and drawing out from it the features of the character. But it also finds its place among the signs which bid us place faith in all that He Himself tells us of what I call the invisible facts of life. No one doubts for a moment the importance of a knowledge of character n producing such faith. Few of us, perhaps, know more than two or three men, in whose account, even of external facts, much more of their own feelings and motives, we can place an implicit confidence. Why? Because, intellectually or morally, their characters are too imperfect. But if we knew a man who, even comparatively to ourselves, was perfect in wisdom and knowledge, perfectly truthful and pure and loving, we should place a confidence in him, practically almost unbounded, even in regions beyond our own knowledge; unless, indeed, he contradicted the sacred laws of morality or the unchangeable laws of truth.

Hence it is that the perfect character of the Christ has always been so important a ground of faith in Him. His own challenge has remained: "Which of you convicts me of sin? And if I say the truth, why do ye not believe me?" It does not indeed stand alone. There are other signs. There are the signs of miracle, culminating in the Resurrection, which—let men refine as they will,—are signs as far as they go, and would be felt as signs to-day, just as truly as eighteen hundred years ago. There are the intrinsic beauty and power of the teaching itself, unlocking to men so many of the problems of life, and producing in their souls such wonderful spiritual changes. But the perfection of character is one of the signs; perhaps it is the one which most drew men to Him at first, and which has most drawn men ever since.

Now it is clear that the term perfection is a relative term:* its absolute meaning depends upon the nature to which it is attributed. It is as a well-rounded circle, the size of which must depend, not on the accuracy of the circumference, but on the radius with which it is described. The perfection of a brute creature is different from the perfection of a man; and the perfection

---

* This was the only part of the lecture which was really criticised in the ensuing discussion—a discussion otherwise touching on detached points, and not attempting to deal with the main principle of the life of Christ. But the criticism decidedly mistook its meaning, and seemed to take the term "relative," as though it meant deficient in perfection.

of man, in various narrower spheres of his life, will be different from the perfection which includes it all. Thus, a perfect workman is perfect relatively to the work which he has to do ; and the value of his perfection varies with the value and dignity of his work. Again, he may be absolutely perfect as a workman, and yet, if he limits himself only to his work, most imperfect as a man. Moreover, I would notice particularly that a man is seldom perfect in any sphere, unless he can go beyond that sphere. No man, for example, can teach perfectly all that he knows ; he wants a store of knowledge beyond his teaching, in order to make that teaching masterly and simple. Few men, if any, are perfect in technical education, who have no general culture beyond it. Few are perfect as fathers or husbands, who have no thoughts beyond their families; few are much more than hack-politicians, if their minds are quite absorbed in the circle of politics.

If, therefore, we speak of the perfection of the human character of Jesus Christ, we must, of course, consider that perfection as relating to human nature, as such, and covering all the aspects of His life as man ; we may next be prepared to infer it to be at least probable that, if He was perfect in the whole sphere of human nature and life, this was because He could in some way go beyond it.

The only difficulty before us is, that—human nature being what it is—the perfection, which implies balance and harmony, often strikes us less than the imperfection, great in one direction, and little in another, out of which arise vehemence and discord. What we call a marked character is one which is strikingly, sometimes almost amusingly, out of proportion. We are apt to mistake force in repose for weakness, and balance of various energies for languidness and tameness in all. The pure white light, in which all colours are blended, is more difficult to describe, and perhaps less striking in its beauty to a casual observer, than the brilliant red or blue, which tells of the excess of one colour and the absorption of another. Still, in spite of this difficulty, let us endeavour to consider the character in two or three of the aspects in which it presents itself to us.

There are, perhaps, three chief ways of looking at a character. The first is to estimate its general tone and impress; the second is to examine it in its component parts and its various relations; the third (which, however, leads to another subject) to consider its view of the great aim of life, and the degree of its devotion to it.

Of these I will dwell for a time on the first and second. I will content myself with a glance at the third.

Let us consider the character of Christ first in relation to its general tone and impress. If you consider any human being, you have always to look at him first in his own individual peculiarity of stamp, which makes him his true self—like others, but not absolutely identical with any other. Then you have next, perhaps, to consider him as he is affected by race, age, circumstances, in what we call national character, or even class character; for that these characters are marked and real, although they may be difficult rigidly to define, no observer of human life can doubt. But, underneath both these, there is always the basis of true humanity, like the great principles of construction of a building, which are seen through the various forms of original design and architectural style. In this humanity his character is in full harmony with the characters of his fellow-men, open for them to appreciate, open to sympathise with them. Just as it is with the human face, so with the human nature. No two faces in this room are alike; each is perfectly individual. Yet, through all, in various degrees, there is traceable the English cast of countenance; we could not be mistaken for an assembly of any other nation. And all the faces are accordant to the general human type, one in its structure and essential characteristics, which is to be seen in all races, from the highest to the lowest. So it is with the human nature; and that human nature is perfect, in which individuality and universal humanity always, and the intermediate national characteristics sometimes, are truly harmonized. We all desire to be our true selves, and to be true men; we may, or may not, desire in any particular matter to be true Englishmen; in most things we rejoice to feel our nationality; but there are some purposes for which we desire to sink it.

Now the character of Jesus Christ is certainly most marvellously harmonized in its individual and its universal humanity. No character certainly is more eminently individual, and therefore more entirely self-consistent under all circumstances, and at all periods of life. I have often thought it a very striking illustration of this, that in all pictures, from the greatest masterpiece to the merest daub, with many varieties of tone, one characteristic type is preserved. It is not a matter of tradition. In early days men shrank from any attempt at portraiture; if He was pictured at all, it was in symbol, as the Good Samaritan, for example, or, oftener still, the Good Shepherd. And it is a curious fact, that in those days there was a discussion as to his actual likeness, one party contending for His personal beauty and dignity, and another asserting (by a literal interpretation of Scripture prophecy) that His form was uncomely and His face contemptible. The representatiou of Him, which exists now, is, I cannot doubt, ideal—that is, it is an outward representation of what is gathered to be His inward character; and, I repeat, its strong individuality and unity of type is just a visible expression of the individuality and unity of His character. It is a character certainly unlike all others. Compare with it the characters of the founders of other religions, so far as we know them, a Mohammed or a Buddha; or compare with it even the characters of the Bible Revelation—Prophet, Lawgiver, Apostle. You cannot for one moment confuse it with them. It stands out quite unique and individual. And as you trace it on through the Gospel, from the early childhood through every event of the ministry to the condemnation and the cross, it never varies, although it grows and develops. Everywhere He is His true self. In each contingency we can, faintly, but not incorrectly, surmise what He will do or say; and after the event, we find that the reality has infinitely transcended, but has not contradicted, our expectations. I may remark in passing, that this is one thing which convinces a reader of the Gospels that he is there tracing the history of a real living Man. But at present I am only concerned with the point, that in this strong deep individuality we have one side of Perfection.

Nor is the other less marked. I mean the true universal humanity in it, through which there come out those great principles, moral and intellectual—those aspirations, conceptions, beliefs — with which all human nature everywhere sympathises. It has become a commonplace, that every one traces in the Christ something of the character and principles which he loves best.* You may think this natural in us who worship Him as our Master, and desire absolutely to follow Him. But it is not confined to us. I notice that those who stand quite aloof from Christianity, nevertheless claim to understand and to sympathise with the Christ. I notice that those who revolt against existing types of Christianity, always appeal to Him against them. There is a book now lying on every table, the very title of which is a kind of parody on His name, and which has for its object to make Him the impersonation, not of religion in any ordinary sense, but of universal communism and socialistic fraternity. Now this universality is a wonderful element of perfection. You know how all but impossible it is to have perfect sympathy with the character of any living man whom we know in the flesh, or even of any writer whom we know in the spirit. There is always something that jars, something which disappoints or repels. Nor is this simply from our own fault or imperfection. We never, indeed, even approach to perfect sympathy, except with a character which can enfold ours, because it is larger and deeper than ours; but that we do not attain it arises, at least in part, from the imperfection of others, which limits the scope, which impairs the right harmony, of character. Where there is perfect sympathy, where we recognise in any nature what we call the Ideal Humanity, *i.e.*,

---

* I leave this as it stood, although I observed by the discussion that it was somewhat misconceived, as though I said that each man made his own Christ. What is the truth, and what I have tried to express, is, that each man sees in Him the aspect of humanity which he understands, but always sees much more, and, according to his temper, either rejects that additional element as unhistorical or a sign of imperfection, or learns by it that there is something in Jesus of Nazareth "not dreamt of in his philosophy."

what we all can conceive more or less perfectly, and see truly but imperfectly realized—there is perfection. He of whom we speak, said once, "When I am lifted up,"—and that was when His manifestation was brought to its final perfection,—"I will draw all men unto Me;" and, putting aside such deeper meaning as we Christians recognise in His words, all must acknowledge that, in respect of sympathy and knowledge of Him, that declaration has been fulfilled, and that its fulfilment is a sign of the perfection of His human character. Greek, Roman, Jew—each represented a different type of human civilization, and each a type different from that of our modern life. All claimed Him as theirs, and yet none could claim Him as exclusively their own. The simplest child or childlike soul, the largest philosophic insight, the highest philanthropic aspirations, have found their ideal in Him; and yet again none could ever say 'He is mine wholly; He is none of yours."

Perhaps it may strike us that in Him the tone of national and local character was less strikingly marked than might be expected from perfection. I am not sure how far this idea rests on a false conception of what the Jewish character in its noblest form really was.* But so far as it is true, we can see the reason of it: partly in the

---

* There were in the Jewish faith, and therefore reflected in the Jewish character, two different elements; the one exclusive, resting on the covenant of God with Israel, and considering all without as aliens; the other comprehensive, recognising God as the Father of all men, and knowing that Israel was a representative of, and not a substitute for, humanity. The true Israelite embodied both, and the higher and deeper his character, the more he grasped the larger truth.

circumstances of His life, partly in the nature of His work. Partly in the circumstances of His life,—for He lived at a time when, under the universal sway of the Roman Empire, there were no such things as real nations, and even the types of race and their characteristics were somewhat faintly marked. The one true nationality that remained was certainly the Jewish; but this had so stiffened into formal and intolerant exclusiveness, that it presented nationality under a false type, which was soon to pass away. When He dwelt upon it with a loving and ardent patriotism, it was in the tears that He shed, and the remonstrance that He uttered, over Jerusalem. But far more we trace the reason in the nature of His work. That work was to be a strictly universal one, not only in space, but in time; and it is clear that the national characteristics, which some miss in Him, and the merely political and social works, which some reproach Him for not attempting, must have hindered this universality; and purchased immediate vividness of effect, at the price of universal scope and permanence of result. It was the glory of the Gospel that under it there was "neither Greek nor Jew, Barbarian, Scythian, bond nor free." That glory could hardly have been achieved if the character of the Christ had been deeply Jewish and oriental, out of sympathy with the present and future character and civilization of the West. All movements which aim at touching all humanity, even French Revolutions, Positive philosophies, International societies, and the like, must in great degree sink nationality. Nations pass away; and, while they last, are, and must be, exclusive. What never dies is the individual and the race. A character which is perfect may or may not clothe itself in the colouring of nationality. But it must be living in its individuality; it must be universal in its humanity. Who can doubt that the character of the Christ is both?

But pass from this, which we may call the tone and outward form of character, to the character itself in its component parts, and their harmony with each other. A character is perfect which meets all the conditions, and fulfils all the relations of humanity. Of course, it is clear that these relations are three—to self, to men, and to something above mankind, whether you call it Nature, or Law, or God. Mostly, as we see men's characters, we find that one or other of these relations predominates. There are men only fit to live alone, and mix but in slight degree with their fellow-men. There are those whose very nature is social, to whom solitude is hateful, and destructive to their best energies. There are lives so absolutely absorbed in the higher communion, that they lose the consciousness of themselves, and flee from the society of their fellow-men. But the perfect human character is that which is able to fulfil all, and which finds its real growth in the harmonious succession or coincidence of all.

What are the qualities which belong to a man, so far as he is alone? I should answer: Three—the love of truth, the spirit of purity, and the spirit of manliness.

In the study and conception of truth, man always is and must be alone, although he use the thoughts and teaching, and agree in the conclusions of others; he must grasp truth, ponder it, make it (we say) his own. Need I remind you that the whole life of Jesus Christ was (so He said), to " bear witness to truth,"—to see deep into nature and man,—to know what is the revelation of God? You know how He put aside all the traditions and teaching of His age; you know how sternly He trampled even on time-honoured prejudices. No doubt the truth which He cared for was not the truth of outward nature; but that which is nearer to us, the truth of humanity and the truth of God. But it is clear that this intense pondering and love of truth, as truth, which we rightly regard as one great glory of our time, was one element, though perhaps at times we forget it, in the character of Jesus Christ.

Because we do forget it, I have dwelt on it for a moment, but there can be no need to do more than glance at His spotless purity. Purity of soul is, as it seems to me, the love of all that is good, in itself and for its own sake, utterly irrespective of what its results may be, not even consciously regarding its relation to the good of man or the glory of God. And in that purity of soul the perfect control of appetite and passion—the perfect submission, that is, of the flesh to the spirit—is a lower subsidiary element, so much a matter of course that one hardly dreams of insisting on it. Who can doubt, who ever has doubted, the purity of Jesus Christ? that white unsullied soul, which passed through the sin of the world, and even through the company of the grossest sinners, uncontaminated as the very sunlight itself?

But it may seem otherwise as to "manliness," which I take to be a right self-assertion—first, the consideration what our work is, what our rights are, what our duty is, and then, the concentration of all our energies on this one single thing. No doubt it is true, that, living at a time of excessive self-assertion, which ran through all the noblest heathen morality, and even travestied itself in the religious pride of the Jew, He rather took such manliness for granted (as He did the love of self in His golden rule), in order to manifest and to teach the nobler, the more unselfish, the more self-forgetful, elements of humility, love, sacrifice. But yet who, while he watches Him in all the humility and gentleness of His life, will fail to see the dignity, the calmness, the impressiveness, which encircled His life, and which asserted itself without the trouble of conscious self-assertion, which could stoop to suffer and to die, but could not stoop to flatter, to palter, or to coax? "Thou regardest not the person of men," was the very language of His enemies. I know not how anything could better express the spirit of true manliness; although the words which follow ("but teachest us the way of God in truth") show how it was overshadowed and transfigured by a higher principle.*

But, if we pass from the spirit of man in solitude to the spirit of man in his relation to his fellows, what find we there as our ruling principles? So far as I can see, they are two—the spirit of righteousness and the spirit of love. Righteousness is that which recognises each man as being in some sense alone, although in contact with others. It was defined long ago (by Plato) as the "doing by each of that which it is his to do." Clearly it is the spirit which lays on ourselves and on others the burden of the inalienable responsibility of each individual soul, which refuses to bear it for others,

* It is on this side that some attack has been made on Christian Morality, which professes to be the "Imitation of Christ." It is asserted to be too feminine in type, and to disregard the masculine virtues, especially that which is called "manliness." The truth as to its method of teaching is, I believe, indicated in the text. The result of that teaching may be seen in the peculiar forms of courage or heroism which Christianity has fostered, in the fortitude of martyrdom, in the self-conquest of asceticism, in the self-forgetful heroism of charity.

and asks no others to bear it for us; which insists, if it be our part to insist, that well-doing shall meet reward and blessing, that ill-doing shall meet with punishment and a curse; which is impatient of all laziness and indolence, all sham and pretence, which stand in the way of this doing of duty by each man. A stern, cold grandeur encircles it; and, as we look on the world as it is, with all the falsehoods and pretences which poison it, we feel at times as if righteousness and it alone would be sufficient to save.

But there is another spirit tempering and balancing this—the spirit of love, which recognises the unity of all mankind, compacted by a thousand ties; so as to sink and deny self, so as to look upon the burden of humanity as one, and to struggle, as for a privilege, for the opportunity to bear as much of it as may be. Such love is, you know, our first instinct, so strong that it may overbear all righteousness, and may even become unjust and cruel to those beyond its pale. And when such love has been (so to speak) impregnated by reason and tempered by conscience, it becomes the deepest and most powerful of all principles, which has done, and is doing every day a hundred times more than all the powers of selfishness, ten times more than even the sense of right and duty. Righteousness in Love, and Love in Righteousness—these are the two great perfections of humanity, when we have to deal with our fellow-men.

What shall we say of these in Jesus Christ? Again perhaps we may allow that He brought out, taught, manifested especially, the power of love—partly because it was so forgotten that no Greek or Roman word is ound for it which does not speak either of individual preference or of sensual passion—partly because its uniting and harmonizing power was most appropriate to the work of salvation, which He declared to be the object of His whole life. And it may be true—I think it is true—that we have sometimes so proclaimed love as Christ-like, that we have forgotten the sterner element of righteousness; just as in that typical face of which I have spoken, all but the greatest painters have been tempted to make all too soft, gentle, almost feminine, and to obscure the sterner and more massive expression of Righteousness.*

But who that reads His burning words of indignation against scribe and Pharisee—His " Get thee behind me, Satan!" even to the loving weakness of an Apostle—His deep, solemn, sorrowful warning of the wrath to come—His pictures of a judgment, always going on now, but to be complete hereafter, as an unalterable law dependent on human freedom and responsibility—who, I say, will doubt that it is our own error, and not the true record of His life, which has led us to forget the harmony of this harder and sterner righteousness with the glow and the softness of love?

But there is a third relation of the human nature to that which is neither within it nor around it, but above it. It seems to me that almost all modern thought recognises the need of something, which it calls "religion;" that is, so far as I can understand it, an enthusiastic devotion to some power above. That power may be (as one teaches) the power of the universe; it may be (as another

---

* I observed, with some surprise, that these sterner elements were supposed to be inconsistent with charity and unworthy of the Christ; as if the same spirit which is fervent in love to man and God, must not, even for love's sake, be stern and indignant against all oppression, falsehood, and hypocrisy.

teaches) the culture or worship of humanity; but in any case it seems allowed that the human nature is not perfect, if it does not hold the conviction that there is something more than the human soul itself, and the society of human souls in which it shares. Now what we Christians mean, what Christ Himself meant by the word, was not a vague idea like these, but the belief in a Divine, living, personal God, the Father of men, on whom the soul could rest in trust, even in what passed its power of knowledge, because His will ruled all the events and acts of the world, and because His Spirit moved over all the spirits of men. And this conviction, I may remark in passing, is the only form of a belief in a higher power, which has lived with a vital and energetic force through all ages, which can come home alike to the simplest and wisest soul, which can embody itself in the noblest and the homeliest life.

What is the perfection of humanity in this last great relation? Surely just the spirit which we call that of sonship—the mixture of an intense and adoring reverence with a sense of freedom and, if I may dare so to say, of familiarity. It is a spirit which can manifest itself perfectly only in the conviction of this as a directly personal relation; but still it has its counterparts, though they be somewhat shadowy and vague, in those other paler conceptions of religion, which modern thought would substitute for it. Need I say to you how entirely perfect that relation was in the life of Jesus Christ? It was a relation in which He moved—free, glad, confident, and yet so absorbed into the greatness and solemnity of the presence of God, that all human companionship, all self-consciousness, vanished in it. "Alone, (He said) He was not alone, because God was with Him." In that communion He declared that He found the secret and safeguard of all other perfection. The true Son of man, He said, was the true Son of God.

I have tried to set before you in this way some aspects of His perfect human character, and yet all the while I shrink from the task. It seems like dissecting a living body, or analysing into prose the grand music of a poem. But, even so, we may see something of the great structure of its perfection, and see how it underlies the living beauty and majesty, before which millions of souls have bowed.

There is much that might still be said, as, for example, of the perfection of the aim of His ministry in life and death, uniting the culture and regeneration of the individual with the renewal of the social life of humanity; and so bringing together the two objects, which bare individualism and bare socialism pursue singly, with the certain result, through their exclusiveness and narrowness, of failure and disaster. The one deals with the undoubted fact that all men are unequal and unlike—each a whole in himself—each needing freedom to grow separately—each needing to be treated in his own peculiar way. The other deals with the equally natural fact of equality of rights and unity of mankind, in virtue of which no man lives or dies to himself; so that the individual ought to sacrifice himself, though not to be sacrificed, on the altar of society. His aim in life brought out both these together, because it viewed them both as parts of a greater aim—the manifestation of the glory of God, who is the God at once of individual and of race. But this line of thought I can but indicate; others I may not even touch.

For, before I conclude, I must urge upon you one more thought, at which I have already glanced. It is this, that as we trace the full-orbed circle of this human perfection, there is something always crossing us, which passes out beyond it, and shoots across its brightness with a still brighter trail of light. I have reminded you of what seems to be a law of humanity, that no one can fill a sphere perfectly, who never goes beyond it. And certainly, in studying the character of Jesus Christ, we are struck with a wonderful exhibition of this law. It is perfectly clear that while He is perfect as man, He obviously claims to be something more—with a claim which, if untrue, would certainly mar that perfection. I care not which Gospel you take—the simplest narrative of St. Matthew, or the profoundest discourse of St. John: such a claim is perfectly obvious.

To some degree, however reluctantly, all great men have to assert themselves, slightly in teaching, more fully in guiding and ruling. There is a kingship of men, which is a burden, but which must be borne. It is characteristic, again, of any who claim to be spokesmen of a religion, that they must speak and act with an authority which brooks no interference. But you will observe that, as a rule, all merely human greatness begins with self-assertion, and ends with self-effacement. It is anxious to be forgotten, if only the truth we proclaim may be held, and the law or freedom for which we live be recognised. Most of all, perhaps those who desire to be prophets delight to call themselves only "Voices of God;" and long for the time when they may be needless, because all men shall know without their having to teach.

But in Jesus Christ, and in Him alone, it is not so. The order, so to speak, is reversed. It is in the earliest part of His teaching that He Himself is unseen; it is in the last and most perfect that His own person and office are asserted. Clearly this is a phase in which He passes beyond the perfection of humanity, either to rise above or to sink below it. Which shall it be?* The answer must depend very much on this, whether we recognise faith in a character greater than our own as a true principle of human life; so that when we are convinced of that greatness and superiority, we are ready to believe in it when it passes out beyond our knowledge. We study the works of some great man of genius, who shines in the transcendent greatness of poetry or philosophy. Up to a certain point we fully understand and delight in him; beyond this he passes out of our full comprehension. Shall we believe or laugh? Shall we sit at his feet, or look down upon him to criticise? We gaze on the life of one whom we see to be in greatness infinitely beyond and above us. Within a certain range we understand him, and rejoice in his greatness; but at one time or another he does something which we do not understand, which seems to us perhaps like a noble rashness or the madness of excess of thought. Shall we trust him or condemn him? Shall we follow him or fall away? The question, I say, is whether we shall apply this law— I grant in a transcendent degree—to the life of Jesus Christ.

If we have at all realized that perfection, which I have faintly sketched out, and if at the same time we have felt the converging power of the other signs of His authority,

* I found, as I expected, that this self-assertion and the declaration of the necessity and responsibility of faith in His word were a cause of "offence." It is no doubt here that mere "admirers" of Christ and believers in Christ part company. The question is, which course is more reasonable, and more accordant with the actual facts of the existence and power of Christianity?

—of miracle and prophecy,—of the profound wisdom and simplicity of His lower teaching, and the like—we shall be induced to say, "Lord, to whom shall we go? Thou hast the words of eternal life." We shall think that we see that He cannot lie, cannot be deceived, cannot sink below the true humanity: and then we shall infer that He rises above it; we shall be prepared to believe the deepest words of mystery which He speaks; and so not only shall we be taught of Christ, but we shall learn Christ, who He is, and what He is, and so become Christians indeed.

This is the conclusion which, thinking as much as I can on the true essence of Christianity and the true state of the present conflict of thought, I have drawn for myself. It is the conclusion which I would suggest to you to-night: at the least, I would ask you seriously to consider it, as it is in itself, not as it is clothed in thoughts or words of mine.

[I have not thought it worth while to alter or to supplement this lecture. The discussion which followed, often marked by cleverness and evident sincerity, turned almost entirely on a number of detailed objections, chiefly dealing with some of the "offences" in the life and teaching of Christ, and not at all considering the principles of His character as a whole. It showed that something was needed which the lecture did not even attempt to do. But it appeared to me that examination of separate quotations and single events in His life could be carried out *seriatim* only in discussion or commentary. It could not have been attempted within the limits of a lecture; nor can it well be made a supplement to it. Indeed, it may be seen that the argument of the lecture, whatever its value may be, occupies a wholly different ground.]

www.ingramcontent.com/pod-product-compliance
Lightning Source LLC
Chambersburg PA
CBHW032046220426
43664CB00008B/886